TRAVELS

IN AMERICA

CHATEAUBRIAND'S

TRAVELS

IN AMERICA

TRANSLATED BY

Richard Switzer

UNIVERSITY OF KENTUCKY PRESS
LEXINGTON 1969

In memory of Professor T. C. Walker,
whose appreciation of Chateaubriand
was boundless

Contents

Introduction   xi

Travels in America
    Notice [for the 1827 Edition]   3
    Introduction [to the First Edition]   5
    The Voyage   10
    The Eastern Cities   14
    Into the Wilderness   22
    Natural History   70
    Manners of the Indians   81
    Government among the Indians   155
    The United States Today   186
    The Spanish Republics   194
    The End of the Trip   205

Bibliography   209

Notes   211

Index   219

Illustrations

Chateaubriand Portrait, from *Complete Works*.
Paris: Pourrat, 1837.   *frontispiece*

Chateaubriand with the Indian Woman and Her
Cow, from *Memoirs*. Paris: Garnier, n.d.   26

Niagara Falls, from *Complete Works*. Paris:
Pourrat, 1837.   34

Chateaubriand Falling over the Cliff at Niagara,
from *Memoirs*. Paris: Garnier, n.d.   36

Virgin Forest, from *Complete Works*. Paris:
Pourrat, 1837.   60

Indian Marriage, from J. F. Bernard, *Cérémonies et coutumes religieux de tous les
peuples du monde*. Amsterdam, 1723–1743.   86

Indian Divorce, from J. F. Bernard, *Cérémonies et coutumes religieux de tous les
peuples du monde*. Amsterdam, 1723–1743.   87

Indian Hieroglyphics, from Baron de Lahontan, *Dialogues curieux entre l'auteur et
un sauvage de bon sens*. The Hague, 1703.   112

Indian Hunts, from Baron de Lahontan, *Dialogues curieux entre l'auteur et un sauvage de bon sens*. The Hague, 1703.   128

Introduction

To look upon Chateaubriand as a source for authentic information about the America of 1791 would be folly. The relatively
few authentic details of his own trip to be found in the relation
of his *Travels in America* are hidden in a mass of heteroclite
materials that are the end product of 30 years of reading about
America in works that were often far from trustworthy; moreover the exercise of the author's imagination takes us even
further from reality.

Why, then, should Chateaubriand be read today, at least
insofar as his *Travels in America* are concerned? There is a
double answer to this question: Chateaubriand is a reflection of
the attitudes of his epoch, and, at the same time, because of his
enormous literary reputation, his works have continued to be a
major source of the Frenchman's impressions about America,
in certain cases even to the present day. Chateaubriand is then
the indication of what America was in the minds of the Europeans of the nineteenth century.

Throughout the eighteenth century there had been frequent
visitors from France to America, and in harmony with the ideas
of the *philosophes*, the Noble Savage had grown to become one
of the fundamental concepts concerning the new world. The
freedom from all restraints of society, the lack of contamination
of man's innate good nature through the evils of the city,
coincided perfectly with the other theories of the new generation of thinkers. But it remained for Chateaubriand, one of the
great writers of fiction, to present primitive America in so vivid
a way that his ideas were to influence generations to come.

François-René de Chateaubriand was born in 1768 in Brittany. His early years, to judge by his many literary references
to this period, were highly romantic: he painted himself as
isolated in an old tower of the family castle at Combourg in
eastern Brittany. The storms of his youth were a reflection not

only of an uncommon temperament but also of the turbulent political and social events that dominated the end of the eighteenth century.

In an earlier period of French history, Chateaubriand would have entered the army and stayed there unless drawn out of that milieu by literary aspirations. And in fact, Chateaubriand did start out in the traditional fashion of the aristocratic younger son and became an officer in the army. But just as Julien Sorel of Stendhal's *The Red and the Black* was to find it too late in 1830 to make a career in the army of Napoleon, Chateaubriand was to find that after 1789, being an officer in a royalist regiment was not the sure road to success and glory that it had been before.

Chateaubriand was therefore searching for another route to follow. Adventuresome in spirit, he seems to have hit upon the idea of trying to discover the Northwest Passage. Such a project may seem extravagant today, but in 1791 the call of the unknown was great enough to launch many a young man on a voyage of discovery. Later critics have at times doubted this reason behind the trip to America and have suggested that Chateaubriand may have thought it up afterwards, so as to give a greater aura of importance to his trip. Recent documentation, however, has shown that Chateaubriand did announce this intention in public before undertaking the trip.

He left, then, in the spring of 1791. It seems to have been a rather hasty departure, because he crossed the sea on the *Saint-Pierre*, which was not a passenger ship at all but a codfishing vessel that had been chartered specially for a group of seminarians being taken to Baltimore.

The duration of Chateaubriand's actual trip and its probable extent have fascinated critics and historians for over 150 years. If we are to take Chateaubriand at his word (always a dangerous thing to do with an author who often lived more in his imagination than in reality), it was an enormous trip through all the parts of America east of the Mississippi. The stay ended abruptly, according to Chateaubriand: he claims that upon reading in a newspaper of the arrest of Louis XVI as he was fleeing the country, he resolved immediately to return to France, rejoin his regiment, and take up arms in defense of the king. He joined the Army of the Princes and was wounded in battle. Later he emigrated to England, where he lived a penniless exile until conditions permitted a return to France.

The revolutionary days brought many tragedies of a personal nature to Chateaubriand, including the execution of members of his close family, so there is no wonder that the republican regime became distasteful to him. Many times he was to praise the American republic in contrasting it with the French, emphasizing in particular the true freedom without violence in the former and the repression of the Reign of Terror in the latter.

Napoleon, too, was an anathema to Chateaubriand. Here the author's personal convictions concerning government came into play. Chateaubriand, indeed, always seemed a bit amazed when speaking of American democracy, considering it a kind of fluke which should not work but does. At the end of his *Travels in America* he expressed his ideas on the South American republics, where in his view democracy was impossible. The main prerequisite for stable government according to Chateaubriand was a legitimate monarch. In this view he was obviously in harmony with a great deal of the thinking of his times: only an unquestioned and hereditary monarchy can effect the transition from one executive to another without chaos.

This then was the basis on which he opposed Napoleon, together with the lack of liberty, as he saw it, under the Emperor. For Chateaubriand even as a legitimist did not believe in any restrictions of the individual's freedom. The restorations of the monarchy in 1814 and 1815 represented exactly what he sought in government: a legitimate monarch ruling under a constitution (the *Charte*, promulgated by Louis XVI before taking the throne in 1814) which guaranteed individual liberty.

When this new liberalism took a step backward under Charles X, Chateaubriand was opposed to the reactionary movement. He dissociated himself from the government entirely in 1830 when the principle of legitimacy was overthrown by the July Revolution and Louis-Philippe. This fierce defense of the legitimist idea often caused Chateaubriand considerable difficulty, as when he was nominated as ambassador to Sweden. The Swedish king, it will be remembered, was Bernadotte, Napoleon's marshal, who had been invited to accept the Swedish crown. The king was unwilling to have as ambassador to his court so staunch a defender of the idea of legitimate monarchy, since he did not himself embody that principle. Chateaubriand's nomination was never confirmed.

Under the French Restoration, Chateaubriand held several important posts: ambassador to England (1821–1822), French delegate to the Congress of Vienna (1822), and French Foreign Minister (1822–1824). He also served in Germany and Italy.

It was, however, in the domain of literature that Chateaubriand created his most durable reputation for himself. Although a few of his literary efforts antedate the nineteenth century, it is really in 1801 that his fame begins. For many years he had been elaborating a manuscript that he called *The Natchez*, in which were gathered together the various materials which were later to be published under that title as an epic tale of the Indians in America. Chateaubriand tells of having left most of this manuscript in an old trunk in London during his exile, and he claims he was never able to find again the house where he lived; thus the manuscript was lost. However, if this is true, he was able to reconstruct the manuscript, and from it he drew some of his major works. The first of these, and the most famous, was *Atala*. This short novel is bound both to *The Natchez* and to another work on which the author was working at the moment, *The Genius of Christianity*. After the turmoil of the revolutionary period and its radical rejection of religion, there was a growing movement back to the church, at first officially banned, then finally tolerated. Ultimately the situation was to be resolved at the beginning of the nineteenth century by Napoleon's *Concordat* with the Pope, which reestablished Catholicism as the official religion of France and at the same time cut the ties of the clergy in France with the émigré nobles and bishops who had remained a powerful royalist force.

Chateaubriand was to participate in this renaissance of religious fervor in a literary way. He began constructing a great treatise that would reveal the beauties of Christianity from the point of view of the picturesque, the sentimental, and the passionate. One of Chateaubriand's major premises was that classicism as a source of literary inspiration should be replaced by Christianity. According to the author, Christianity as the true religion was far more capable of moving the reader than any representation of the pagan mysteries and religions. To illustrate this thesis he planned two short novels, to be presented as a part of the text. Of these *René* did appear for the first time in 1802 when the *Genius* was published. *Atala*, however, had been detached from the main text and published separately in 1801. The reason given was that *Atala* had been read in part in various salons and risked becoming too well known long before publication. It may be true that it was merely a bit of careful preparation, a "trial balloon," so to speak, to prepare for the publication of what Chateaubriand considered the more important work.

Literary history has known few cases in which a work became so immediately famous. Chateaubriand was at once the idol of the literary salons, the leader in the new literature. *Atala* is set in the wilds of America and centers around the tragedy of two young Indian lovers. Woven into the fabric of these events, there is a constant evocation of picturesque and exotic nature, which constitutes the true beauty of the work. Created by a master stylist, Chateaubriand's primitive paintings of the American scene are unforgettable and to this day form some of the most celebrated anthology pieces.

The Genius of Christianity and *René* enjoyed only slightly less popularity than *Atala*, so that in the course of two years Chateaubriand rose from relative obscurity to one of the dominant positions on the European literary scene.

Chateaubriand continued to write, producing a long line of works avidly read by his contemporaries and, for the most part, still considered among the major works of the period. But the final work, and for most critics his masterpiece, consisted of his posthumously published memoirs, characteristically entitled by their author *Memoirs from Beyond the Grave*. Only after the author's death in 1848 were these published. They too aroused the greatest of enthusiasm, an enthusiasm that never ceased to grow from that day forward. Chateaubriand thus avoided the temporary oblivion that is the lot of so many great authors at the moment of their death.

These then are Chateaubriand's qualifications as a literary influence. It is obvious that everything he wrote had an immediate audience ready to accept his every word. So it is that America, as described in *Atala* and later in the *Travels in America*, was the true America insofar as the average reader was concerned. This attitude persisted, even to the present day.

The *Travels in America* represents then a valuable document of the nineteenth-century European concept of what America was: its physical nature, the people who inhabited it, the events that took place there.

The exact nature of Chateaubriand's trip to America has been a subject of controversy almost from the moment he returned. Even before the publishing of his *Travels* in 1827, the author had presented in his Indian novels and in fragments of his other works his impressions of various parts of America. Quite correctly, critics on both sides of the Atlantic cast doubts on many of the things narrated by the visiting Frenchman, to the point of suggesting he never set foot in America. It is Chateaubriand's nature to attract passionate supporters and violent critics. The two camps have fought for over 150 years, without an end in sight. The reasons for the criticisms are obvious. If we take into account all the works in which Chateaubriand speaks of America, the itinerary he claims to have covered is enormous.

According to this supposed itinerary Chateaubriand visited the eastern seaboard, went up the Hudson to Albany and then along the Mohawk Trail to Niagara Falls. Up to this point the itinerary is quite precise, without however any real factual detail in the matter of dates, time spent in various places, and the like. But after Niagara the itinerary becomes vague indeed. He says he went south to Pittsburgh, then along the Ohio River and down the Mississippi as far as the Natchez country. He also claims to have visited the country at the southern tip of Florida and the Carolinas. Then he supposes a return trip along the eastern seaboard, embarking at Philadelphia. Such a trip, in the time Chateaubriand had at his disposal and with the prevailing conditions of travel in 1791, was obviously impossible. Nonetheless, when certain critics were dubious, others attempted to show how such a trip was within the realm of possibility.[1]

The great amount of scholarship that has been devoted to this trip has produced a certain number of facts which cannot be disputed. These facts are of two orders: those which tend to corroborate or disprove Chateaubriand's itinerary, and those which present indisputable literary sources for much of what Chateaubriand presents as firsthand experience.

In the first category, there are several important items. Chateaubriand's arrival date in America, July 10, 1791, is confirmed by several sources, mostly having to do with the seminarians whom Chateaubriand accompanied. When the author leaves Baltimore for Philadelphia, the stagecoach itinerary and schedule are essentially as he describes them. In Philadelphia, Washington's house, as can be seen from contemporary engravings, is in the main as Chateaubriand describes it, although the celebrated interview between the author and Washington seems to be imaginary, since Washington in answering the letter of introduction presented by Chateaubriand regrets he was ill the day Chateaubriand called.

There is not a great deal to prove or disprove the rest of the trip to New York and then to Niagara, except for one outstanding fact: Chateaubriand names the commander of the British fort at Niagara; Professor Morris Bishop discovered that the commander was indeed named Gordon. It would be difficult to explain this name unless one accepts as authentic this portion of the trip.

From then onward, all becomes doubtful. Pittsburgh was under a state of siege by the Indians in mid-1791, as Chateaubriand could have read in the newspapers of the time. He could not have been ignorant of this state of affairs if he had actually been in Pittsburgh as he claims. His failure to mention anything of the sort is indeed suspicious.

It seems highly probable that Chateaubriand did in fact, as he says he did, break his arm at Niagara and that he remained a considerable time in that region while recuperating. Paddling a canoe down the Ohio and the Mississippi with a broken arm scarcely mended seems a highly unlikely activity for our author. Rather he may have taken a more or less direct route back toward the east coast. Perhaps he retraced his steps; that would have been the easiest and the safest itinerary. He might, however, have crossed the mountains on horseback or gone through the valleys of one of the river systems.

The date he gives for his return to Europe is almost certainly fictitious. There appear to have been relatively few ships sailing for France from the United States then, and none of the sailings were even close to the date Chateaubriand gives (in the *Memoirs:* December 10, 1791). He most likely returned on November 26 or 27, on board the *Molly*. He therefore spent only four and a half months in America. Baltimore to Niagara and return to Philadelphia seems then a logical trip for the time at his disposal, especially since the shipping schedules show that he could easily have had to wait as much as a month in Philadelphia before finding a ship to take him back. Regretfully, the tardy discovery of Louis XVI's arrest at Varennes and Chateaubriand's immediate return to France, as he describes the scenes at the end of his *Travels*, seem a bit dubious.

The second class of critical discoveries is even more devastating to Chateaubriand as an authority on America than were the factual discoveries. It has been shown by critics such as Bédier and Chinard that great portions of Chateaubriand's manuscript come more or less directly from eighteenth-century travelers and writers such as Lahontan, Father Charlevoix, the naturalists Bartram, Carver, and Bonnet, the traveler Le Page du Pratz, and the nineteenth-century voyager Beltrami.[2]

All this is most curious. After all, Chateaubriand did spend four and a half months in the United States. Why does his recital depend so heavily on literary sources? If we accept the story of the lost Natchez manuscript in the London trunk, we can perhaps suppose that the authentic notes from the trip were lost there. But there is probably another explanation. Chateaubriand, like any other prospective traveler, had consulted all the books then current on the subject of America before his departure. After his return, he continued to read, extract, and preserve the materials from the newer works on the New World. All these things became much more real to him than the actual trip, since some 35 years separated the actual trip and the composing of the *Travels*. Also, as will be seen in the text, America was full of disappointments for the young traveler. The cities are without interest. There are no monuments. The Quakers of Philadelphia do not correspond to the European stereotype. The Indians are cruel and dirty instead of being the Noble Savages they should be. Thus, America as Chateaubriand portrayed it, was much more a product of his reading and his imagination than of his actual visit. Nevertheless, his approach enhances the value of the *Travels* as a document. Although the Frenchman of the nineteenth century could have obtained a much truer picture of America in any number of more realistic works, he chose the poetic evocation of Chateaubriand because they shared the same temperament, the same prejudices, the same particular view of the world.

The book appears to have been written in haste. In 1826 Chateaubriand was preparing an edition of his complete works (Ladvocat edition). In the prospectus for this edition the author promised unpublished works to the subscribers. Now he had to make good. *The Natchez*, the epic of Indian life in America, was finally ready and would furnish part of the promised unpublished material, but it was not enough. By 1826 Chateaubriand had reached the point in his *Memoirs* where the visit to America should find its place. Quite naturally then he hit upon the idea of making a book of his travels. Whether he merely extracted already written materials from the *Memoirs* or whether the *Travels* version was later revised for the *Memoirs* is not entirely clear.

At any rate, Chateaubriand, a little pressed for time, gathered together all his notes on America and made of them a volume which would retrace his travels in such a manner that would show him as having visited all the places he had previously mentioned in his works. It is probably true to a degree that, as he says, his notes based on the actual visit and those coming from his readings were so intermingled that he no longer was sure which were which. We must never lose sight of the 35-year interval between the trip and the composition.

In copying his notes, he allowed many mistakes to creep in: he mistook diameters for circumferences, he misplaced towns and rivers. The text seems to have been proofread in a very perfunctory manner, and many errors were left in the text which have persisted to the present day. It seems obvious that Chateaubriand never revised the text or returned to it in a systematic way. Therefore the basis for this translation, as well as for the 1964 French edition, is the first edition of 1827

The problem of the translation is a difficult one. Chateaubriand said himself of translation:

> A translation is not the *person*, it is only a *portrait:* a great master can do an admirable portrait; so be it: but if the original were placed next to the copy, each spectator would see it in his own fashion, and all of them would differ in their judgment on the resemblance. Translating, therefore, is the most thankless and least esteemed occupation there ever was; it is fighting with words to make them render in a foreign idiom feelings or thoughts which were expressed in another way, and with sounds which they do not have in the language of the author. (*Essay on English Literature.*)

With one of Chateaubriand's strictly literary texts, the task of translation would be forbidding. Here, however, the problem is less acute because of the nature of the account.

There was apparently some kind of standing arrangement between Chateaubriand and the London publisher Colburn, whereby as each new work was published in Paris a translation was immediately afterward published in London. This was the case with the *Travels*, which appeared in 1828. However, there seems to be no evidence that Chateaubriand saw or approved of these translations before publication. It seems highly probable that a staff translator or consultant did the work. As a result the 1828 translation is highly unsatisfactory. There are a certain number of errors in translation and a curious rearrangement of the order of the text which was certainly not sanctioned by Chateaubriand. Added to these defects are a number of obscurities that justify a new and modern translation.

Geographical names, the names of animals and plants, and especially the names of the Indian tribes have been modernized. Chateaubriand's use of these terms is highly capricious and varies according to the particular source materials he was using at the moment. In a few cases where there is a particular significance to Chateaubriand's spelling or where it is unclear what his exact meaning is, the terms have been left with their original spelling.

TRAVELS

IN AMERICA

Notice

[for the 1827 Edition]

I have nothing in particular to say about the *Travels in America* which you are about to read; the manuscript is taken, as is the subject of *The Natchez*, from the original manuscript of *The Natchez* itself: these *Travels* contain their own commentary and history.

My various works offer fairly frequent reminiscences of my excursion in America. I had first thought of gathering them together and placing them with their dates in my narration, but I gave up this project to avoid repetition; I have been content to refer to these passages. I have however quoted some of them when they seemed to me necessary for the intelligence of the text and when they were not too long.

I give in the "Introduction" a fragment of the *Memoirs of my Life*, in order to familiarize the reader with the young traveler whom he is to follow across the seas. I have carefully corrected the part already written; the part that relates facts subsequent to the year 1791, and that brings us to the present day, is entirely new.

In speaking of the Spanish Republics, I have recounted (in everything that I was *permitted* to recount) what I would have liked to do in favor of these newborn states when my political position gave me some influence on the destiny of peoples.

I have not been rash enough to touch this great subject before having provided myself with the appropriate enlightenment. Many printed volumes and unpublished notes helped me to compose a dozen pages. I have consulted men who have traveled and resided in the Spanish Republics: I owe to the kindness of the Chevalier d'Esmenard[3] precious information on the American loans.

The preface that precedes the *Travels in America* is a kind of history of travels: it presents to the reader the background of the science of geography and, so to speak, the road map of man on the globe.[4]

I have added to these two volumes of *Travels* only the pieces and documents strictly necessary to justify the facts, or the arguments of the text. These two volumes with the three volumes of the *Itinerary from Paris to Jerusalem*, already reprinted in the *Complete Works*, form and complete the collection of my *Travels*.

Introduction
[to the First Edition]

In a note of the *Historical Essay,*[5] written in 1794, I told in fairly extensive detail what had been my plan in going to America. I spoke several times of this same plan in my other works, particularly in the preface to *Atala.* I presumed no less than to discover the passage to the northwest of America, thus reaching the Polar Sea, seen by Hearne in 1772, glimpsed farther west in 1789 by Mackenzie, recognized by Captain Parry, who approached it in 1819 through the strait of Lancaster and in 1821 at the extremity of the Fury and Hecla Straits;[6] finally, Captain Franklin, after having successively gone down the Hearne River in 1821 and the Mackenzie River in 1826, has just explored the shores of that ocean, which is surrounded by a belt of ice that until now has repulsed all vessels.

One thing peculiar to France must be noted: most of its travelers have been lonc men abandoned to their own devices and their own genius; rarely have they been aided or employed by the government or private companies. Therefore, more enlightened foreign peoples have accomplished by a common national will what French individuals have not been able to perform. In France there is courage; courage deserves success, but deserving it does not always ensure it.

Today as I approach the end of my career,[7] I cannot help thinking as I look back into the past how different that career would have been if I had fulfilled the purpose of my trip. Had I been lost in those wild seas, on those hyperborean strands where no man has left footprints, the years of discord which have crushed so many generations with so much clamor, would have fallen on my head in silence: the world would have evolved just the same without me. It is probable that I would never have had the misfortune to write; my name would have remained unknown, or it would have been associated with one of the peaceful reputations which excite no envy and bespeak less glory than happiness. Who knows whether I would even have come back across the Atlantic, whether I might not have fixed myself in the solitudes discovered by me, a conqueror in the midst of his conquests. It is true that I would not have played a role at the Congress of Verona and that I would not have been called Monseigneur in the Foreign Affairs Chancellery in the Rue des Capucines in Paris.

All that is very unimportant to me at the end of the road. However diverse the routes, the travelers arrive at the common destination. They all arrive there equally fatigued, for on earth, from the beginning to the end of the race, no one sits down even once to rest. Like the Jews at the feast of Passover, we partake of the banquet of life in haste, standing, loins girt with a rope, feet shod, and staff in hand.

It is therefore needless to retell what was the aim of my enterprise, since I have said it a hundred times in my other writings. It will suffice to point out to the reader that I thought this first trip could be the last, if I managed to procure immediately the resources necessary for my great discovery; but in case I were stopped by unforeseen obstacles, this first trip was to be only the prelude to a second, only a kind of reconnaissance in the wilderness.

To explain the route that I shall be seen taking, it is necessary also to remember the plan that I had developed: this plan is rapidly sketched in the note of the *Historical Essay*, indicated above. The reader will see there that instead of going north, I wanted to march to the west, to attack the western shore of America a little above the Gulf of California. From there, following the outline of the continent, and always in sight of the sea, I planned to continue north to the Bering Straits, to round the last cape of America, to go east along the shores of the Polar Sea, and to come back into the United States by Hudson Bay, Labrador, and Canada.

What determined me to travel over so long a coast of the Pacific Ocean was the little knowledge there was of that coast. There remained doubts, even after the work of Vancouver, about the existence of a passage between 40 and 60 degrees

6

north latitude: the Columbia River, the New Cornwall deposits, Shelikof's Strait, the Aleutian regions, the Gulf of Bristol or Cook, the lands of the Chugachimint Indians, none of that has yet been explored by Kotzebue and the other Russian or American navigators. Today Captain Franklin, avoiding several thousand leagues of circuit, has spared himself the trouble of seeking in the west what could only be found in the north.

Now I shall once again beg the reader to recall to his memory various passages of the general preface of my *Complete Works*, and the preface of the *Historical Essay*, where I have related several particulars of my life. Destined by my father for the Navy and by my mother for the Church, having myself chosen service with the Army, I had been presented to Louis XVI. In order to enjoy the honors of the court and *to ride in carriages*—to use the language of the time—one needed at least the rank of cavalry captain. Thus I enjoyed the privileges of a cavalry captain but was in fact an infantry second lieutenant in the Navarre regiment. The soldiers of this regiment, whose colonel was the Marquis de Mortemart, having revolted as did the others,[8] I found myself relieved of all obligation toward the end of 1790. When I left France at the beginning of 1791, the revolution was proceeding rapidly: the principles on which it was founded were mine, but I detested the violence which had already dishonored it. It was joyfully that I set out to seek an independence more in conformity with my tastes, more in sympathy with my character.

At this same time the emigration movement was growing; but as there was no fighting, no feeling of honor forced me, against the inclination of my reason, to throw myself into the folly of Coblentz.[9] A more reasonable emigration was directed toward the shores of the Ohio; a land of liberty offered its asylum to those who were fleeing from the liberty of their homeland. Nothing better proves the high value of generous institutions than this voluntary exile of the partisans of absolute power to a republican world.

In the spring of 1791, I said farewell to my respected and worthy mother and embarked at Saint-Malo; I bore to General Washington a letter of introduction from the Marquis de La Rouairie. The Marquis had taken part in the war of independence in America; he was not long in becoming famous in France through the royalist conspiracy to which he gave his name. I had for traveling companions some young seminarians from Saint-Sulpice, whom their superior, a man of worth, was taking to Baltimore. We set sail: at the end of 48 hours we lost sight of land and entered upon the Atlantic.

It is difficult for persons who have never sailed to realize the sentiments one has when he no longer sees from the ship anything but sea and sky. I have tried to retrace these feelings in the chapter of the *Genius of Christianity* called "Two Perspectives of Nature," and in *The Natchez*, where I transferred my own emotions to Chactas.[10] The *Historical Essay* and the *Itinerary*[11] are likewise filled with remembrances and scenes of what might be called the desert of the ocean. Being surrounded by the ocean did not seem to me an abandonment of the homeland; it was so to speak as if I were being carried on my first trip by my nurse, the confidante of my first joys. May I be permitted, the better to place the reader in the spirit of the narrative he is about to read, to quote a few pages of my unpublished *Memoirs:* almost always our manner of observing and feeling derives from the reminiscences of our youth.

The lines of Lucretius apply to me:

> Tum porro puer ut saevis projectus ab undis
> Navita.[12]

Heaven decided to place in my cradle an image of my destiny.

"I was raised as the companion of the winds and of the waves; these waves, these winds, this solitude, which were my first teachers, were perhaps more propitious to the nature of my mind and the independence of my character. Perhaps I owe to this unruly education some virtue I might never have known: the truth is that no system of education is in itself preferable to another. God does well what he does; it is his Providence which guides us when it calls us to play a role on the stage of the world."

After the details of childhood come those of my studies. Soon escaping from under the paternal roof, I tell of the impression that Paris, the Court, society made on me; I paint the society of the time, the men that I met, the first manifestations of the Revolution. The order of dates brings me to the period of my departure for the United States. On my way to the port I visited the land where part of my childhood was spent. I let the *Memoirs* speak:

"I have revisited Combourg only three times. At the death of my father the whole family was united at the chateau to say farewell to one another. Two years later I accompanied my mother to Combourg. She wanted to furnish the old manor; my brother was to bring my sister-in-law there. My brother never came to Brittany, and soon he mounted the scaffold with the young wife[13] for whom my mother had prepared the marriage bed. Finally I took the road to Combourg on the way to the port, after I decided to go to America.

"After sixteen years of absence, ready to leave the native land once again for the ruins of Greece, I went to embrace what family was left to me in the midst of the moors of my poor Brittany; but I did not have the courage to make the pilgrimage to the paternal fields. On the heaths of Combourg I became what little I am: there is where I saw my family united and dispersed. Of the ten children that were, we remain only three. My mother died of grief; the ashes of my father were thrown to the wind.

"If my works outlast me, if I were to leave a name, perhaps one day, guided by these *Memoirs*, the traveler might stop a moment in the places I have described. He might recognize the chateau, but he would search in vain for the grand mall or the great wood: it was chopped down; the cradle of my dreams has disappeared as have the dreams. Remaining alone, standing on its rock, the ancient keep seems to lament for the oaks which surrounded it and protected it against the storms. Just as isolated as it is, I too have seen my family fall about me, my family who made my days beautiful and offered me their protection. Thank heaven my life is not so solidly built on the earth as the towers where I spent my youth."

Now the readers know the traveler with whom they are to deal in the recital of his first wanderings.

The Voyage

So I embarked at Saint-Malo, as I said; we took to the high seas, and on May 6, 1791, about eight o'clock in the morning we sighted the peak of the island of Pico, one of the Azores. A few hours later we cast anchor in a poor roadstead on a rocky bottom before the island of Graciosa. The description of the island is to be found in the *Historical Essay*.[14] The exact date of the island's discovery is unknown.

This was the first foreign land that I approached; for this very reason I have kept memories of it which have preserved the force and the liveliness of youth. I did not fail to have Chactas go to the Azores and to have him see the famous statue that the first navigators claimed to have found on these shores.

From the Azores, blown by the winds on to the banks of Newfoundland, we were forced to make port a second time at the island of Saint Pierre. "T.[15] and I," I say then in the *Historical Essay*, "went on excursions in the mountains of this frightful island; we became lost in the fogs with which it is incessantly covered, wandering between clouds and gusts of wind, hearing the bellowing of a sea which we could not discern, wandering on a dead and mossy heath and on the edge of a reddish torrent which rushed between the rocks."[16]

The valleys are strewn in different parts with that kind of pine whose young shoots serve to make a bitter beer. The island is surrounded by several reefs, among which is noticed that of the *Dovecote*, so called because the sea birds make their nests there in the spring. I have given its description in the *Genius of Christianity*.

The island of Saint Pierre is separated from that of Newfoundland only by a fairly dangerous strait; from its desolate coasts one makes out the even more desolate shores of Newfoundland. In the summer the beaches of these islands are covered with fish drying in the sun, and in the winter by white bears which feed on the scraps forgotten by the fishermen.

When I landed at Saint Pierre, the capital of the island consisted, as best I remember, of a fairly long street built along the sea. The gracious inhabitants were quick to offer us the hospitality of their tables and homes. The governor lived at the edge of the city. I dined two or three times there. He was raising a few European vegetables in one of the moats of the fort. I remember that after dinner he would show me his garden; then we would go sit at the base of the flagpole surmounting the fortress. The French flag billowed over our heads as we watched a wild sea and the somber coasts of Newfoundland and spoke of the homeland.

After a two-week layover, we left the island of Saint Pierre, and the ship heading south reached the latitude of the coasts of Maryland and Virginia, where we were becalmed. We enjoyed the most beautiful of skies; the nights, the sunsets, and sunrises were admirable. In the chapter of *The Genius of Christianity* which I have already mentioned, called "Two Perspectives of Nature," I have recalled one of those nocturnal splendors and one of those magnificent sunsets. "The sun's globe, ready to plunge into the waves, appeared between the ship's lines, in the midst of endless space, and so on."

An accident came close to ending all my plans.

The heat was oppressive; the ship, in a dead calm, without sail, and overburdened by its masts, was rolling heavily. Burning on the deck and fatigued by the movement, I decided I wanted to swim, and although we had no longboat in the water, I threw myself from the bowsprit into the sea. First all went well, and several passengers imitated me. I was swimming without watching the ship; but when I happened to turn my head, I saw that the current had already borne it quite far away. The crew had rushed on deck and had thrown a hawser to the other swimmers. Sharks were sighted in the waters near the ship, and the crew were firing on them to drive them away. The roll was so great that it delayed my return and sapped my strength. I had an abyss beneath me, and at any moment the sharks might snap off one of my arms or legs. On the vessel,

11

they were attempting to launch a boat, but they had to set up a block and tackle, and that was taking considerable time.

By the greatest stroke of luck, a barely perceptible breeze came up; the ship obeyed the rudder to a certain extent and approached me. I was able to grab hold of the rope, but the companions of my rashness had also caught hold of this rope; and when we were drawn to the side of the vessel, I found myself at the end of the line, and they hung on me with all their combined weight. We were fished out this way one by one, which took a long time. The rolling continued. At each roll we would dive ten or twelve feet into the waves or be suspended in the air, like fish on a line. At the last immersion, I felt ready to lose consciousness; one more roll, and it would have been all over. Finally they raised me on board half dead. If I had drowned, good riddance for myself and for others!

Several days after this accident, we sighted land; it was indicated by the tops of some trees which seemed to rise from the surface of the water: the palms at the mouth of the Nile later disclosed the shore of Egypt to me in the same way. A pilot came on board. We entered Chesapeake Bay, and that very night they sent a longboat to get water and fresh food. I joined the party that was going to land, and half an hour after having left the ship I set foot on American soil.

I remained some time with my arms crossed, looking about me with a mixture of feelings and ideas, which I could not unravel then and which I could not paint today. This continent unknown to the rest of the world through all ancient times and through many centuries of modern times; the first savage destiny of this continent, and its second destiny since the arrival of Christopher Columbus; the domination of the European monarchies shattered in this New World; the old society ending up in the young America; a republic of a kind unknown then, announcing a change in the human mind and the political order; the part my homeland had in producing these events; these seas and these shores owing part of their independence to the French flag and French blood; a great man coming forth in the midst of discord and wilderness; Washington living in a flourishing city in the same place where a century earlier William Penn had bought a bit of land from some Indians; the

12

United States sending back to France across the ocean the revolution and the liberty which France had supported with its arms; finally, my own plans, the discoveries that I wanted to attempt in these native solitudes, which extended their vast kingdom behind the narrow empire of a foreign civilization— those are the things which confusedly occupied my mind.

We advanced toward a fairly distant habitation to buy there what they would be willing to sell us. We crossed some small forests of balsam and Virginia cedar which perfumed the air. I saw mockingbirds and cardinals flitting about, their colors and songs indicating a different climate. A negress 14 or 15 years old, of extraordinary beauty, came to open to us the gate of a house which resembled at the same time an English farm and a settler's cabin. Herds of cows were grazing in the makeshift pastures surrounded by palisades, on which were playing gray, black, and striped squirrels; some negroes were sawing wood, while others were at work in the tobacco fields. We bought corncakes, chickens, eggs, and milk, and we returned to the vessel moored in the bay.

We weighed anchor to reach the roadstead and then the port of Baltimore. The trip was slow as there was no wind. As we approached Baltimore the waters narrowed and were perfectly calm; we seemed to be going up a river bordered by long avenues. Baltimore offered herself to us as if on the edge of a lake. Opposite the city rose a hill shaded with trees, at the foot of which they were beginning to build a few houses. We tied up at the quay of the port. I slept on board and didn't go ashore until the next day. I went to lodge at the inn where they carried my baggage. The seminarians retired with their Superior to the establishment prepared for them and then scattered throughout America.

The Eastern Cities

Baltimore, like all the other metropolises of the United States, did not have then the extent that it does today. It was a very pretty, clean, and animated city. I paid the captain for my passage and offered him a farewell dinner in a very good tavern near the port. I reserved my seat on the stage that three times a week made the trip to Philadelphia. At four o'clock in the morning I climbed into this stage, and there I was rolling along the highways of the New World, where I knew no one, where I was known to no one at all. My traveling companions had never seen me, and I was never to see them again after our arrival in the capital of Pennsylvania.[17]

The road that we followed was rather sketchily laid out. The country was fairly bare and flat; few birds, few trees, some scattered houses, no villages—that was what the country presented to my eyes and what struck me disagreeably.

Approaching Philadelphia, we met farmers going to market, public conveyances and very elegant carriages. Philadelphia seemed to me a beautiful city with wide streets; some, lined with trees, crossed one another at right angles in regular order from north to south and east to west. The Delaware River runs parallel to the street that follows its western shore; it would be an impressive river in Europe but is not remarkable in America. Its banks are low and lacking in the picturesque.

Philadelphia, at the time of my trip (1791), did not yet extend to the Schuylkill River; but the land in the direction of this tributary was divided into lots on which were being constructed a few isolated houses.

The aspect of Philadelphia is cold and monotonous. In general the cities of the United States are lacking in monuments, especially old monuments. Protestantism, which sacrifices nothing to imagination and which is itself new, has not raised those towers and domes with which the ancient Catholic religion has crowned Europe. Almost nothing at Philadelphia, New York, Boston, rises above the mass of walls and roofs. The eye is saddened by this level appearance.

The United States gives rather the idea of a colony than of a nation; there one finds customs, not mores. One has the feeling that the inhabitants do not have their roots in the ground. This society, so fine in the present, has no past; the cities are new, the tombs date from yesterday. That is what made me say in *The Natchez:* "The Europeans had as yet no tombs in America when they already had dungeons. Those were the only monuments of the past for this society without ancestors and without memories."

There is nothing old in America save the forests, children of the earth, and liberty, mother of all human society; that is, in itself, worth many a monument and ancestor.

A man landing as I did in the United States, full of enthusiasm for the ancients, a Cato seeking everywhere for the rigidity of the early Roman manners, is necessarily shocked to find everywhere the elegance of dress, the luxury of carriages, the frivolity of conversations, the disproportion of fortunes, the immorality of banks and gaming houses, the noise of dance-halls and theaters. At Philadelphia, I could have thought myself in an English town: nothing proclaimed that I had passed from a monarchy to a republic.

As can be seen in the *Historical Essay*, at that time of my life I admired republics greatly. But I did not believe them possible at the present age of the world because I knew liberty only in the manner of the ancients, as a daughter of manners in a new-born society. I did not know that there was another liberty, daughter of the enlightenment of an old civilization, a liberty whose reality the representative republic has proved. It is no longer necessary to plow one's own little field, reject art and science, have ragged nails and a dirty beard, in order to be free.

My political disappointment no doubt gave me the ill humor that caused me to write the satirical note against the Quakers, and even somewhat against all Americans, a note that is to be found in the *Historical Essay*.[18] Moreover, the appearance of the people in the streets of the capital of Pennsylvania was agreeable; the men appeared properly dressed; the women,

15

especially the Quakeresses with their identical hats, seemed extremely pretty.

I met several settlers from Santo Domingo[19] and some French refugees. I was impatient to begin my trip to the wilderness; everyone agreed that I should go to Albany, where, closer to the frontier and the Indian nations, I would be in a position to find guides and obtain information.

When I arrived in Philadelphia, General Washington was not there.[20] I was obliged to wait for him about two weeks before he returned. I saw him pass in a carriage drawn rapidly by four frisky horses, freely driven. Washington, according to my ideas at that time, was necessarily Cincinnatus;[21] Cincinnatus riding in a carriage upset my idea of the Roman republic of the year 296. Could the dictator Washington be other than a peasant prodding his oxen and holding the handle of his plow? But when I went to deliver my letter of introduction to this great man, I found the simplicity of the old Roman.

A little house in the English style, resembling the neighboring houses, was the palace of the President of the United States: no guards, not even footmen.[22] I knocked; a young servant girl opened the door. I asked her if the General was in; she answered that he was. I replied that I had a letter to deliver to him. The servant asked me my name, difficult to pronounce in English, which she could not retain. Then she said quietly to me, "Walk in sir," and she walked before me through one of those long narrow corridors which serve as a vestibule in English houses; she showed me into a parlor, where she asked me to await the General.

I was not impressed. Greatness of soul or of fortune does not overwhelm me: I admire the first without being crushed by it; the second inspires me more with pity than with respect. A man's appearance will never bother me.

At the end of a few minutes the General entered. He was a man of tall stature, with an air that was calm and cold rather than noble; the engravings of him are faithful. I gave him my letter in silence; he opened it and glanced at the signature, which he read aloud with an exclamation, "Colonel Armand!"

16

That was what he called the Marquis de La Rouairie and how the letter was signed.

We sat down; I explained to him as best I could the motive of my trip. He answered me in French or English monosyllables and listened to me with a sort of astonishment. I noticed this and said to him in a rather lively fashion, "But it is less difficult to discover the Northwest Passage than to create a people as you have done." "Well, well, young man!" he cried, holding out his hand to me. He invited me to dinner for the following day, and we separated.

I appeared promptly for the appointment: there were only five or six guests. The conversation turned almost exlusively on the French revolution. The General showed us a key to the Bastille:[23] those keys to the Bastille were rather stupid toys which were distributed then in both worlds. If Washington had seen the conquerors of the Bastille in the gutters of Paris as I did, he would have had less faith in his relic. The seriousness and the force of the revolution were not in those bloody orgies. At the time of the revocation of the Edict of Nantes in 1685 the same populace of the Faubourg Saint-Antoine demolished the Protestant church at Charenton with just as much zeal as it laid waste to the church of Saint-Denis in 1793.[24]

I left my host at ten o'clock in the evening, and I never saw him again; he left the next morning for the country, and I continued my trip.

Such was my meeting with this man who liberated a whole world. Washington descended into the tomb before a bit of fame could be attached to my name; I passed before him as the most unknown individual; he was in all his brilliance, and I in all my obscurity. My name did not perhaps remain a whole day in his memory. Yet how happy I am that his gaze fell upon me! I have felt warmed by it for the rest of my life: there is a power in the gaze of a great man.

I have since seen Buonaparte;[25] thus Providence has shown me the two persons she was pleased to put at the head of their centuries' destinies.

If one compares Washington and Buonaparte, man to man, the genius of the first seems less soaring than that of the second. Washington does not belong as does Buonaparte to that race of Alexanders and Caesars who exceed the stature of the human species. Nothing astonishing is attached to his person; he is not placed on a vast stage; he is not confronted by the most adroit captains and most powerful monarchs of the time; he does not cross the seas; he does not rush from Memphis[26] to Venice and from Cadiz to Moscow: he defends himself with a handful of citizens on a land without memories and without fame, in the restricted circle of the domestic hearths. He fights none of those battles which renew the bloody triumphs of Arbela and Pharsalia;[27] he does not upset thrones to build others with their debris; he does not place his foot on the necks of kings;[28] he does not have them say in the vestibules of his palace: That they delay too long, and Attila is bored.[29]

Something silent envelops the actions of Washington; he acts slowly: one would say that he feels he is the envoy of future liberty and that he is afraid to compromise it. It is not his own destiny that this hero of another sort bears, it is that of his country; he does not allow himself to toy with what does not belong to him. But from this deep obscurity, what a light is to burst forth! Seek out the unknown forests where the sword of Washington shone, what will you find there? Tombs? No, a world! Washington has left the United States as his trophy on the field of battle.

Buonaparte has no trait of this grave American: he battles in an old land, surrounded with brilliance and clamor; he wishes only to create renown for himself; he holds himself responsible only for his own fate. He seems to know that his mission will be short and that the torrent which descends from such a height will quickly spend itself. He hastens to enjoy and abuse his glory as he would fleeting youth. In the manner of the gods of Homer, he wants to reach the ends of the world in four strides: he appears on every shore, he precipitously inscribes his name in the celebrations of all peoples; rushing by, he throws crowns to his family and his soldiers; he is hurried in establishing his monuments, his laws, his victories. Leaning over the world, he casts down kings with one hand, and with the other he crushes the revolutionary giant; but in crushing anarchy he stifles liberty and finally loses his own liberty on the last field of battle.

18

Each is rewarded according to his works: Washington raises a nation to independence; a retired magistrate, he peacefully falls asleep beneath his paternal roof amidst the regrets of his compatriots and the veneration of all peoples.

Buonaparte steals from a nation its independence; a fallen emperor, he is cast into exile, where the fears of the world do not yet consider him well enough imprisoned under the guard of the ocean. As long as he struggles against death, weak and chained to a rock, Europe does not dare to lay down its arms. He expires: this news, published at the gate of the palace where the conqueror had proclaimed so many funerals, does not cause the passer-by to tarry or to be astonished. What did the citizens have to mourn?

The republic of Washington still exists; the empire of Buonaparte is destroyed. It rose and fell between the first and second trip of a Frenchman who found a thankful nation where he had fought for a few oppressed settlers.[30]

Washington and Buonaparte came from the bosom of a republic: both born of liberty, the first was faithful to her, the second betrayed her. Their destinies, according to their choice, will differ in the future. The name of Washington will spread with liberty from age to age; it will mark the beginning of a new era for mankind. The name of Buonaparte will also be repeated by future generations, but it will be attached to no blessing and will often serve as authority for oppressors, great or small.

Washington was in all things representative of the needs, ideas, enlightenment, and opinions of his period; he seconded rather than opposed the movement of minds; he wanted what he should have wanted, the very thing for which he was called; that is the reason for the coherence and the perpetuity of his work. This man, scarcely striking because he is natural and of just proportions, has bound up his existence with that of his country; his glory is the common heritage of the growing civilization; his fame wells up as from one of those sanctuaries from which flows an unending spring for the people.

Buonaparte could also have enriched the public domain: he was acting on the most civilized, the most intelligent, the bravest, the most brilliant nation of the earth. What would be the rank he would occupy today in the universe if he had joined magnanimity to what he possessed of the heroic, if combining Washington and Buonaparte at the same time, he had named liberty the heir of his glory!

But this great giant did not completely bind his destiny to that of his contemporaries: his genius belonged to the modern age, his ambition was of the olden days; he did not realize that the miracles of his life went far beyond the price of a diadem and that this gothic ornament would ill become him. At one moment he would take a stride with his century; at the next he would return to the past; and whether he went counter to the current of the times or with it, by his prodigious force he drew the waves on or repulsed them. In his eyes men were but a means of power; no sympathy was established between their happiness and his. He had promised to deliver them, he enchained them; he isolated himself from them, they drew away from him. The kings of Egypt placed their funeral pyramids not in the midst of flourishing countrysides but in the sterile sands; these great tombs rise like eternity in solitude. Buonaparte built the monument of his fame in their image.

Those who have seen the conqueror of Europe and the legislator of America as I have, today avert their gaze from the stage of the world: a few actors who make one cry or laugh are not worth looking at.

A stagecoach similar to the one that had taken me from Baltimore to Philadelphia took me from Philadelphia to New York, a gay, populous, and commercial city, which was however far from being what it is today. I went on a pilgrimage to Boston to salute the first battlefield of Amercan liberty. "I have seen the fields of Lexington; I stopped in silence, like the traveler at Thermopylae, to contemplate the tomb of those warriors of the two worlds, who were the first to die in obeying the laws of the homeland. As I trod on this philosophical ground which told me in its mute eloquence how empires vanish and rise, I confessed my insignificance before the laws of Providence and lowered my forehead in the dust."[31]

After I returned to New York, I sailed on the ship that set out for Albany going up the Hudson River, otherwise known as the *River of the North*. In a note of the *Historical Essay*, I have described a part of my trip on this river, on whose shores there lurks today among the republicans of Washington, one of Buonaparte's kings, and more, one of his brothers. In this same note I spoke of Major André, that unfortunate young man about whose fate a friend, whom I have not ceased to mourn, pronounced touching and courageous words when Buonaparte was close to mounting the throne where Marie-Antoinette had sat.[32]

When I arrived at Albany, I went to seek out a Mr. Swift for whom I had been given a letter in Philadelphia. This American was engaged in the fur trade with the Indian tribes that held an enclave in the territory which England had ceded to the United States; for the civilized powers divide up among themselves lands that do not belong to them. After having heard me, Mr. Swift made some very reasonable objections. He told me that I could not undertake a trip of this importance straight off, alone, unaided, without support, without credentials for the English, Spanish, and American posts where I would have to pass; that even if I were fortunate enough to cross so much wilderness without accident, I would arrive in frozen regions where I would perish from cold or hunger. He advised me to begin by acclimating myself, by making an excursion first into the interior of America, learning Sioux, Iroquois, and Eskimo, living some time among the Canadian scouts and the agents of the Hudson's Bay Company. Once I had performed these preliminary feats, I could then with the assistance of the French government pursue my hazardous enterprise.

This advice, whose wisdom I could not help recognizing, annoyed me; if I had followed my inclination, I would have left straight for the pole, as one goes from Paris to Saint-Cloud. However I hid my displeasure from Mr. Swift. I asked him to procure me a guide and horses so I might set out for Niagara Falls and from there for Pittsburgh, from where I could descend the Ohio. I still had in mind the first route plan that I had sketched.

Into the Wilderness

Mr. Swift hired for me a Dutchman who spoke several Indian dialects. I bought two horses and hurried away from Albany.

All the country that extends today between the territory of this city and Niagara is inhabited, cultivated, and traversed by the famous New York canal;[33] but at that time a great part of the land was wilderness.

When after crossing the Mohawk I found myself in forests which had never been cut, I fell into a sort of inebriation which again I have recalled in the *Historical Essay:* "I went from tree to tree, to right and left at random, saying to myself: Here no more roads to follow, no more cities, no more narrow houses, no more presidents of republics, no more kings. . . . And to see if I was really reinvested with my original rights, I indulged in a thousand acts of will which enraged the big Dutchman who was acting as my guide, and who in his soul believed me mad."[34]

We were entering the former cantons of the six Iroquois nations.[35] The first savage we met was a young man who was walking in front of a horse on which was seated an Indian woman decked out in the manner of her tribe. My guide wished them good day as we passed.

It is already known that I was fortunate enough to be received by one of my compatriots on the frontier of solitude, M. Violet, dancing master among the savages.[36] His lessons were paid for in beaver skins and bear hams. "In the midst of a forest, there could be seen a kind of barn; I found in this barn a score of savages, men and women, daubed like sorcerers, their bodies half naked, their ears slit, ravens' feathers on their heads and rings in their noses. A little Frenchman, powdered and curled as in the old days, with an apple-green coat, brocaded jacket, muslin frill and cuffs, was scraping on a miniature violin, having these Iroquois dance Madelon Friquet.[37] M.

Violet, speaking to me of the Indians, always said, 'These gentlemen Savages and these lady Savagesses.' He congratulated himself on the lightness of foot of his students: indeed, I never saw such capers. M. Violet, holding his little violin between his chin and his chest, would tune up the fatal instrument; he would cry in Iroquois, 'Places!' and the whole troop would jump like a band of demons."[38]

It was a rather strange thing for a disciple of Rousseau to be introduced to primitive life with a ball given for Iroquois by a former kitchen boy of General Rochambeau. We continued our way. Now I shall let the manuscript speak; I present it as I find it, at times in the form of a narrative or a journal, sometimes in letters or simple annotations.

THE ONONDAGAS

We had arrived at the edge of the lake to which the Onondagas, an Iroquois people, gave their name. Our horses needed rest. I chose with my Dutchman a suitable place to pitch our camp. We found one in a valley, at the place where a river bubbles out of the lake. This river has not gone 600 feet directly north when it bends to the east and runs parallel to the lake shore outside the rocks that form a rim about the lake.

It was in the curve of the river that we set up our equipment for the night: we drove two tall stakes in the ground and laid a long pole crosswise between the forks of these stakes. By placing long strips of birchbark from the ground to the crossbeam, we had a roof worthy of our palace. The traveler's campfire was lit to cook our supper and to drive away the mosquitoes. Our saddles served as our pillows under the *ajoupa*,[39] and our coats as blankets.

We attached bells to the necks of our horses and released them in the woods. By an admirable instinct, these animals never wander so far away as to lose sight of the fire that their masters light at night to keep away the insects and to protect themselves from the snakes. From the inside of our hut we enjoyed a picturesque view: before us stretched the lake, fairly narrow and bordered by forests and rocks; around us, the river, surrounding our peninsula with its green and limpid waves, lapped at its banks impetuously.

It was scarcely four o'clock in the afternoon when our establishment was complete. I took my gun and went wandering in the surrounding area. First I followed the river; my botanical research was not successful, for the plants were ordinary. I noted numerous families of *Plantago virginica* and other beauties of the field quite as common; I left the banks of the river for the shores of the lake, and I had no better luck. With the exception of a variety of rhododendron, I found nothing worth stopping for. The flowers of this shrub, a bright pink color, created a charming effect on the blue water of the lake in which they were reflected and the brown side of the rock in which they plunged their roots.

There were few birds: I saw only a solitary pair which flitted in front of me and seemed to take pleasure in spreading movement and love through the immobility and coldness of these places. The color of the male allowed me to recognize the white bird, or the *Passer nivalis* of the ornithologists. Also I heard the voice of that species of osprey which has been very well characterized by the definition, *strix exclamator*. This bird is uneasy, as are all tyrants: I wore myself out in vain pursuing him.

The flight of the osprey had led me through the woods to a valley hemmed in by bare and rocky hills. In this very remote spot there was to be seen a miserable cabin belonging to a savage, built half-way up the hill among the rocks; a lean cow was grazing in a meadow below.

I have always liked these little shelters: a wounded animal crouches in a corner; an unfortunate man is afraid to show himself for fear of being repulsed. Tired by my chase, I sat down on top of the hill I was crossing, with the Indian hut facing me on the opposite hill. I put down my gun beside me and gave myself over to those reveries whose charm I have often enjoyed.

Scarcely had I spent a few minutes in this way when I heard voices at the bottom of the valley. I noticed three men who were leading five or six fat cows. After having put them to graze in the fields, they walked toward the lean cow, which they drove away with sticks. The appearance of these Europeans in so solitary a place was extremely disagreeable to me; their violence made them even more annoying. Bursting with laughter, they were chasing the poor animal through the rocks, making it run the risk of breaking its legs. An Indian woman, in appearance as miserable as her cow, came out of the isolated hut, advanced toward the frightened animal, called it softly, and offered it something to eat. The cow ran to her, stretching its neck with a little moo of joy. The settlers threatened the woman from a distance as she returned to the cabin. The cow followed her, stopping at the door to be petted, and gratefully licking the helping hand of her friend. The settlers had withdrawn.

I got up, went down the hill, crossed the valley, and, climbing the hill opposite, arrived at the hut, resolved to repair as much as possible the brutality of the white men. The cow saw me and started to run away; I advanced with caution and managed to reach the mistress's house without driving the cow away.

The Indian woman had gone back in. I spoke the greeting which had been taught me: "*Siegoh!*" (I have come!) The Indian woman, instead of returning my greeting with the customary response "You have come!" answered nothing. I judged that the visit of one of her tyrants was annoying to her. Then I started in turn to pet the cow. The Indian woman seemed astonished: I saw in her yellow and saddened face signs of tenderness and almost gratitude. These mysterious relations of misfortune filled my eyes with tears. There is a sweetness in crying over ills which no one else has cried over.

Still for some time my hostess looked at me with lingering doubt, as if she were afraid I was seeking to deceive her; then she took a few steps and came herself to place her hand on the forehead of her companion in misery and solitude.

Encouraged by this mark of confidence, I said in English, for I had exhausted my Indian: "She is very thin!" The Indian woman replied immediately in bad English: "She eats very little." "She was roughly treated," I continued. And the woman answered me: "We are both used to that." I continued:

25

"Then this field isn't yours?" She answered: "This field belonged to my husband, who died. I have no children, and the whites lead their cows into my field."

I had nothing to offer this indigent creature. My idea would have been to demand justice for her; but to whom would I address myself in a country where the mixture of Europeans and Indians confused authority, where the right of force took independence from the savage, and where civilized man, becoming half-savage, had shaken off the yoke of civil authority?

We separated, the Indian woman and I, after having shaken hands. My hostess said to me many things which I did not understand and which were no doubt wishes of prosperity for the foreigner. If they were not heard by heaven, it was not the fault of the person who offered them but the fault of him for whom the prayer was offered: all souls do not have an equal aptitude for happiness, as all ground does not produce equal harvests.

I returned to my *ajoupa*, where I had a rather sad supper. The evening was magnificent; the lake, in deep repose, did not have a single ripple on its surface; the murmuring river bathed our peninsula, which was decorated by false ebony trees still covered with leaves; the bird called the Carolina cuckoo repeated its monotonous call; we would hear it close at times, at others farther away, as the bird changed the place from which it uttered its love calls.

The next day I went with my guide to visit the head Sachem of the Onondagas, whose village was not far away. We arrived at this village at ten o'clock in the morning. I was immediately surrounded by a crowd of young savages who spoke to me in their language, mixing in English sentences and a few French words. They made much noise and seemed very happy. These Indian tribes, enclaved in the whites' clearings, have taken on something of our manners: they have horses and flocks, and their cabins are filled with furniture and utensils bought at Quebec, Montreal, Niagara, Detroit, or the cities of the United States.

The Sachem of the Onondagas was an old Iroquois in all the strictness of the word. His person preserved the memory of the old ways and the old times of the wilderness: big slit ears, a

27

pearl hanging from his nose, his face striped in various colors, a little tuft of hair on the top of his head, a blue tunic, a skin mantle, a leather belt with a scalping knife and a tomahawk, his arms tattooed, moccasins on his feet, a porcelain necklace in his hand.

He received me well and had me sit on his mat. The young men seized my gun; they dismantled the firing mechanism with surprising dexterity and replaced the pieces with the same skill. It was a simple double-barreled shotgun.

The Sachem spoke English and understood French; my interpreter knew Iroquois, so that conversation was easy. Among other things, the old man told me that although his nation had always been at war with mine they had always esteemed it. He assured me that the savages never stopped missing the French; he complained of the Americans, who would soon leave to the people whose ancestors had welcomed them, not even enough earth to cover their bones.

I spoke to the Sachem of the Indian widow's distress; he told me that indeed the woman was persecuted, that he had several times approached the American commissioners on her behalf, but that he had not been able to obtain justice from them; he added that once the Iroquois would have made their own justice.

The Indian women served us a dinner. Hospitality is the last primitive virtue remaining to the Indian in the midst of the vices of European civilization. The former extent of this hospitality is well known: once received in a cabin, one became inviolable: the hearth had the power of the altar; it made you sacred. The master of this hearth would have allowed himself to be killed before one hair of your head could be touched.

When a tribe, driven from its forests, or a man came to request hospitality, the stranger began what was called the dance of the suppliant. The dance was executed in this manner: the suppliant would advance a few steps, then stop, looking at the one who was the object of the supplication, and then return to his first position. Next the hosts would intone the chant of the stranger: "Here is the stranger, here is the envoy of the Great Spirit." After the chant, a child would go take the hand of the stranger to lead him to the cabin. When the child would touch the threshold of the door, he would say: "Here is the stranger!" and the chief of the cabin would answer: "Child, bring the man into my cabin." The stranger, entering then under the protection of the child, would go, as with the Greeks, to sit in the ashes of the hearth. He would be given the peace pipe; he would smoke three times, and the women would sing the chant of consolation: "The stranger has found again a mother and a wife. The sun will rise and set for him as before."

A consecrated cup would be filled with maple water; it was a gourd or a stone vase which ordinarily stood in the corner of the fireplace and on which was placed a wreath of flowers. The stranger would drink half the water and pass the cup to his host, who would empty it.

The day after my visit to the chief of the Onondagas, I continued my trip. This old chief had been at the capture of Quebec. He had been present at the death of General Wolfe. And I, leaving an Indian's hut, had newly escaped from the palace of Versailles, and I had just been sitting at the table of Washington.

As we advanced toward Niagara, the road, becoming more difficult, was barely outlined by felled trees: the trunks of these trees served as bridges over the streams or as footing in the marshes. The American population was moving then toward the Genesee concessions. The government of the United States sold these concessions more or less dearly according to the quality of the soil, trees, and water.

The clearing offered a curious mixture of the state of nature and the civilized state. In the corner of a forest which had heard only the cries of the savage and the noises of the wild animal, one would come upon a plowed field; one would see from the same spot the cabin of an Indian and the dwelling of a planter. Some of these dwellings, already finished, recalled the cleanliness of the English and Dutch farms; others were only half finished and had only the arch of the trees for a roof.

I was received in these ephemeral dwellings; often I found in them a delightful family, with all the charm and all the elegance of Europe—mahogany furniture, a piano,[40] rugs, mirrors

—all that only four paces from the hut of an Iroquois. In the evening when the servants had returned from the fields or the woods with the axe or the plow, the windows were thrown open; accompanying themselves on the piano, the daughters of my host would sing the music of Paisiello and Cimarosa in sight of the wilderness and sometimes with the sound of a cataract in the background.

On the best lands towns were being established. One cannot imagine the feeling and pleasure afforded by seeing the spire of a new steeple being thrust up in the midst of an old American forest. English manners follow the English everywhere: after I had gone through country where there was no trace of inhabitants, I saw the sign of an inn hanging on the branch of a tree by the roadside and swinging in the wind of the wilderness. Hunters, planters, Indians, met at these caravanseries; but the first time I rested at one I swore that it would indeed be the last.

One night, as I entered one of those singular hostelries, I was stupefied at the sight of an immense circular bed built around a post:[41] each traveler came to take his place in this bed, his feet at the center post, his head on the circumference of the circle, so that the sleepers were arranged symmetrically like the spokes of a wheel or the ribs of a fan. After a little hesitation, however, I placed myself in this contraption because I saw no one in it. I was beginning to fall asleep when I felt a man's leg slide along mine: it was the leg of my guide, that great devil of a Dutchman, who was stretching out next to me. I never felt greater horror in my life. I leapt from this hospitable basket, cordially cursing the manners of our good ancestors. I went out to sleep in my coat in the light of the moon; that companion of the traveler was entirely agreeable, cool, and pure.

The manuscript is missing here, or rather what it contained has been inserted in my other works. After several days' walk, I arrived at the Genesee River; on the other side of that river I saw the marvel of the rattlesnake charmed by the sound of a flute;[42] farther along I met an Indian family, and I spent the night with that family some distance from Niagara Falls. The story of this meeting and the description of that night are to be found in the *Historical Essay*[43] and in *The Genius of Christianity.*[44]

The savages of Niagara Falls, in the English territory, were charged with guarding the frontier of Upper Canada in this area. They came before us armed with bows and arrows and kept us from passing.

I was obliged to send the Dutchman to Fort Niagara to get a pass from the commander before entering the territories under British domination; that tugged at my heart because I was thinking that France had formerly commanded in these lands. My guide returned with the pass, which I still have; it is signed by a Captain Gordon. Isn't it strange that I found the same English name on the door of my cell in Jerusalem?[45]

I stayed for two days in the village of the savages. The manuscript offers here the draft of a letter I was writing to one of my friends in France. Here is that letter:

§ *Letter Written from the Land of the Savages of Niagara* §   I must tell you what happened yesterday morning with my hosts. The grass was still covered with dew; the wind was coming out of the forests heavy with perfume, the leaves of the wild mulberry were loaded with the cocoons of a kind of silkworm, and the cotton plants of the country,[46] turning back their expanded capsules, looked like white roses.

The Indian women, busy with diverse tasks, were gathered together at the foot of a big red ash. Their smallest children were hung in nets in the branches of the tree: the breeze of the woods rocked those aerial cradles with an almost imperceptible movement. The mothers got up from time to time to see if their children were sleeping and if they had not been wakened by a multitude of birds singing and flitting about. This scene was charming.

We were seated at one side, the interpreter and I, with the warriors, seven of them; we all had large pipes in our mouths; two or three of these Indians spoke English. At a distance, young boys were playing; but in the course of their games, jumping, running, throwing balls, they spoke not a word. There were not to be heard the deafening cries of European children; these young savages bounded like bucks, and they were as mute as bucks are. A big boy of seven or eight, detaching himself from the group at times, would come to his mother to suck and then would return to play with his friends.

The child is never forcibly weaned; after feeding on other foods, he drains his mother's breast, like a cup drained at the end of a banquet. When the entire nation is dying of hunger, the child still finds in the maternal breast a source of life. This custom is perhaps one of the causes which prevent the American tribes from increasing as much as the European families.

The fathers spoke to the children and the children replied to the fathers. I had my Dutchman report the conversation to me. Here is what happened:

A savage about 30 years old called his son and suggested that he moderate his jumping; the child answered, "That is reasonable." And, without doing what the father told him, he returned to the game.

The grandfather of the child called him in turn, and said to him, "Do that"; and the little boy obeyed. Thus the child disobeyed his father, who asked him, and obeyed his grandfather, who ordered him. The father is almost nothing for the child.

The child is never punished; he recognized only the authority of age and of his mother. A crime considered frightful and unheard of among the Indians is that of a son rebellious to his mother. When she grows old, he feeds her.

As for the father, as long as he is young, the child gives him no consideration; but when he advances in life, his son honors him, not as a father, but as an old man, that is, as a man of good advice and experience.

This way of raising children in their full independence should make them prey to ill humor and caprice; however the children of the savages have neither caprice nor ill humor because they want only that which they can obtain. If it happens that a child cries for something that his mother does not have, he is told to go get that thing where he saw it; now, since he is not the stronger party and since he feels his weakness, he forgets the object of his desires. If the savage child obeys no one, no one obeys him: there lies the whole secret of his joy and his reason.

The Indian children do not quarrel, do not fight. They are neither noisy, annoying, nor surly; they have in their appearance something serious, like happiness, something noble, like independence.

We could not raise our youth this way; we would have to start by relieving ourselves of our vices; now we find it easier to shut them up in the hearts of our children, being careful only to keep these vices from being seen on the outside.

When the young Indian feels growing within him the taste for fishing, hunting, war, or politics, he studies and imitates the arts that he sees his father practicing. Then he learns to sew a canoe, braid a net, use the bow, the gun, the tomahawk, cut down a tree, build a hut, explain necklaces.[47] What is an amusement for the son forms the father's authority: his right of strength and intelligence is thus recognized, and this right gradually leads him to the power of the Sachem.

The girls enjoy the same liberty as the boys: they do more or less as they wish, but they remain more with their mothers, who teach them the tasks of the home. When a young Indian girl has acted badly, her mother is content to throw some drops of water in her face and to say to her, "You dishonor me." This reproach rarely misses its effect.

Until noon we stayed at the door of the cabin; the sun had become burning hot. One of our hosts went toward the little boys and said to them, "Children, the sun will eat your heads, go and sleep." They all cried out, "That is so." And, an indication of their obedience, they continued to play after having agreed that the sun would eat their heads.

But the women got up, one showing *sagamité*[48] in a wooden bowl, another a favorite fruit, a third unrolling a sleeping mat. They called the obstinate troop, joining to each name a word of tenderness. Immediately the children flew toward their mothers like a flock of birds. The women caught hold of them, laugh-

33

ing. With a certain amount of difficulty each one of them took her son away. Clasped in the maternal arms, each child was eating what had just been given him.

Farewell: I do not know if this letter written from the depths of the woods will ever reach you.

I went from the Indian village to the cataract of Niagara. The description of this cataract, placed at the end of *Atala*, is too well known to be reproduced here; moreover, it figures in a note of the *Historical Essay;*[49] but there are some details in this same note which are so closely bound up with my trip that I think I should repeat them here.

At the cataract of Niagara, the Indian ladder that used to be there being broken, I determined, in spite of the protests of my guide, to reach the bottom of the falls down a rocky cliff about 200 feet high. I ventured down. In spite of the bellowing of the cataract and the frightful abyss that boiled below me, I kept my head and reached a place about 40 feet from the bottom. But here the smooth and vertical rock face no longer offered any roots or cracks for my feet. I hung full length by my hands, unable to go up or down, feeling my fingers opening bit by bit with the fatigue of holding up my body and seeing death as inevitable. There are few men who have spent in their lives two minutes as I counted them then, hanging over the abyss of Niagara. Finally my hands opened and I fell. By the most unbelievable luck, although I was on the bare rock, where I should have been broken to bits, I did not feel much pain; I was a half-inch from the abyss, and I had not rolled into it, but when the coldness of the water began to penetrate me, I realized that I had not come out unscathed, as I had first thought. I felt an unbearable pain in my left arm; I had broken it above the elbow.[50] I signaled my guide, who was looking at me from above, and he ran to get some savages, who with a great deal of difficulty hoisted me up with birch ropes and took me to their camp.

That was not the only risk I ran at Niagara. When I arrived, I had gone to the falls holding my horse's bridle twisted around my arm. While I leaned over to look down, a rattlesnake stirred

in the nearby bushes; the horse was frightened and reared back toward the abyss. I couldn't free my arm from the reins, and the horse, more and more frightened, dragged me after him. Already his front legs were going over the edge, and crouching on the edge of the abyss he held on only with the strength of his hind quarters. It was all over with me, when the animal, astonished by the new danger, made a new effort and by a kind of pirouette jumped back ten feet from the edge.[51]

I had but a simple fracture of the arm: two splints, a bandage, and a sling sufficed to cure me. My Dutchman did not wish to go farther; I paid him off and he returned home. I made a new bargain with some Canadians of Niagara who had part of their family at Saint Louis of the Illinois, on the Mississippi.

The manuscript now presents a general view of the lakes of Canada.

THE LAKES OF CANADA[52]

The overflow of the waters of Lake Erie is discharged into Lake Ontario after having formed the cataract of Niagara. Around Lake Ontario the Indians found white balm in the balsam, sugar in the maple, in the walnut and in the wild cherry, red dye in the bark of the perousse,[53] roofing for their huts in the bark of the white wood; they found vinegar in the red clusters of the vinegar plant, honey and cotton in the blossoms of the wild asparagus, oil for their hair in the sunflower, and a panacea for wounds in the universal plant. The Europeans have replaced these gifts of nature by the productions of art; the savages have disappeared.

Lake Erie is more than a hundred leagues in circumference.[54] The nations that peopled its shores were exterminated by the Iroquois two centuries ago; some wandering hordes then infested the places where no one dared stop.

It is a frightening thing to see the Indians venturing out in bark canoes on this lake where the storms are terrible. They hang their Manitous from the bows of the vessels and strike out in the midst of blizzards and high waves. These waves, as high as the edges of the canoes or higher, seem about to engulf them. The hunters' dogs, their paws on the edge, give out lamentable cries while their masters, keeping a deep silence, strike the waters regularly with their paddles. The canoes advance in a single line. In the prow of the first stands a chief who repeats the monosyllable OAH, the first vowel on a high and short note, the second on a low and long one; in the last canoe another chief is standing, maneuvering a large oar as a rudder. The other warriors are seated, their legs crossed, in the bottoms of the canoes. Through the fog, snow, and waves, all that can be seen are the feathers ornamenting the Indians' heads, the stretched-out necks of the howling dogs, and the shoulders of the two Sachems, pilot and seer, seemingly the gods of these waters.

Lake Erie is also famous for its snakes. At the west end of the lake, from the Viper Islands[55] to the shore of the mainland for a space of more than 20 miles, extend wide patches of water lilies. In the summer the leaves of these plants are covered with snakes interwoven with one another. When the reptiles happen to move in the rays of sunlight, one sees rolling rings of azure, red, gold, and ebony; one can make out in these horrible double and triple knots only sparkling eyes, tongues with a triple fork, maws of fire, tails armed with darts or rattles which shake in the air like whips. A continuous whistling, a noise similar to the rustling of dead leaves in a forest, comes out of this impure Cocytus.

The strait that opens the passage from Lake Huron to Lake Erie draws its fame from its shady banks and its fields. Lake Huron abounds in fish; there are to be found the artikamegue[56] and trout which weigh 200 pounds. Matimoulin[57] Island was famous; it held the remains of the nation of Ottawas, who according to the Indians descended from the Great Beaver. It has been observed that the waters of Lake Huron as well as those of Lake Michigan rise for seven months and recede in the same proportion for seven more. All these lakes have a more or less noticeable tide.

Lake Superior occupies a space of more than four degrees between the forty-sixth and fiftieth degree of north latitude, and no less than eight degrees between the eighty-seventh and ninety-fifth degree of west longitude, Paris meridian; that is to say that this interior sea is 100 leagues wide and about 200 long, giving a circumference of about 600 leagues.

Forty rivers unite their waters in this immense basin: two of them, the Nipigon and the Michipicoten, are two considerable rivers; the latter has its source in the region of Hudson Bay.

Islands ornament the lake: among others, Maurepas Island on the northern coast; Pontchartrain Island on the eastern shore; Minong Island toward the southern part; and the Island of the Great Spirit or Island of the Souls in the west. This latter could form the territory of a state in Europe; it measures 35 leagues long and 20 wide.

The capes of the lake worthy of notice are: Point Keweenaw, a kind of isthmus stretching two leagues into the water; Cape Minabeaujou, reminiscent of a lighthouse; Cape Thunder, near the inlet of the same name, and Cape Standingrock, which rises perpendicularly from the strand like a broken obelisk.

The southern shore of Lake Superior is low, sandy, sheltered; however, the northern and eastern shores are mountainous and present a series of rocks rising in cliffs. The lake itself is carved out of rock. Through its green and transparent waters the eye can make out at a depth of more than 30 and 40 feet masses of granite of different forms, some of them appearing newly cut by the hand of the workman. When the traveler, allowing his canoe to follow the current, leans over the side to look at the crests of these underwater mountains, he cannot enjoy the spectacle for long; his eyes become blurred and he feels dizzy.

Struck by the extent of this reservoir of waters, the imagination expands with the space. According to the instinct common to all men the Indians attributed the formation of this immense basin to the same power that rounded the vault of the firmament; they added to the admiration inspired by the sight of Lake Superior the solemnity of religious ideas.

These savages were led by the air of mystery which nature was pleased to attach to one of her greatest works, to make of

39

the lake the principal object of their belief. Lake Superior has an irregular ebb and flow. Half a foot below the surface its waters, in the great heat of summer, are cold as snow; these same waters rarely freeze in the rigorous winters of these climates even when the sea is frozen.

The products of the land about the lake vary according to the different soils. On the eastern side are to be seen only forests of rickety, warped maples, which grow almost horizontally in sand; on the north, everywhere that the bare rock permits vegetation in some gorge or on some slope of a valley, there can be seen bushes of thornless currants and garlands of a kind of vine that bears a fruit similar to the raspberry but of a paler pink. Here and there rise isolated pine trees.

Among the great number of sites afforded by these solitudes, two are particularly noteworthy. Upon entering Lake Superior by the strait of Sainte Marie, one sees at the left some islands curving in a half-circle, which, covered with flowering trees, look like bouquets whose stems are dipping into the water; on the right, the capes of the mainland advance into the waves. Some are covered with a lawn that unites its green to the double azure of the sky and the wave. The others, composed of red and white sand, resemble, on the background of the bluish lake, the threads of a tapestry or the contrasting pieces of an inlay. Between these long bare capes appear great promontories covered with woods which are reflected upside down in the crystal below. Sometimes the closely spaced trees form a thick curtain on the coast; at times widespread, they border the land as along avenues, and then their spaced trunks open up miraculous vistas. The plants, the rocks, the colors diminish in size or change hue as the scene is more or less distant.

These islands in the south and these promontories in the east, jutting out in a western direction toward one another, form and envelop a vast roadstead which is tranquil when the storms stir up the other regions of the lake. Here frolic thousands of fish and aquatic birds: the black duck of Labrador perches on the point of a breaker; the waves surround this solitary mourner with festoons of their white froth; diving birds disappear, show themselves again, disappear once more;

the bird of the lakes glides on the surface of the water, and the kingfisher flutters his azure wings to fascinate his prey.

Beyond the islands and the promontories enclosing this roadstead, at the mouth of the strait of Sainte Marie the eye discovers the endless fluid plains of the lake. The moving surface of these plains rises and gradually is lost in the distance: from emerald green it changes to pale blue, then ultramarine, then indigo. Each hue melting into the next, the last one ends at the horizon, where it is joined to the sky by a bar of somber azure.

This site on the lake itself is a summer site, to be enjoyed when nature is calm and laughing; the second scene is, on the contrary, a winter scene: it requires a stormy and barren season.

Near the Nipigon River rises an enormous and isolated rock, which dominates the lake. To the west stretches a chain of rock formations, some horizontal, others upright in the ground. The latter pierce the air with their arid peaks; the former, with their rounded summits. Their green, red, and black slopes, hold snow in their crevices and thus mix alabaster with the colors of the granites and the porphyry.

There grow some of those pyramidal trees which nature incorporates into its tableaux, which resemble great architectural works or masses of ruins. The trees are like the columns of edifices, standing or fallen: the pine rises on the plinths of the rocks, and grasses, bristling with frost, hang sadly from their cornices.[58] It resembles the debris of a city in the deserts of Asia—pompous monuments, which before their fall dominated the woods and which now bear forests on their fallen crests.

Behind the chain of rock formations that I have just described, there is a valley dug like a furrow. The Tomb River passes through the center of it. This valley offers in summer only a flaccid yellow moss; filaments of fungus with tops of various colors mark the spaces between the rocks. In the winter, in this solitude covered with snow, the hunter can make out the birds and the quadrupeds painted with the whiteness of the frost only by the colored beaks of the former, the black muzzles and blood-red eyes of the latter. At the end of the valley and far beyond can be seen the summits of the hyperborean mountains, where God placed the source of the four greatest rivers of North America. Born in the same cradle, after a course of 1,200 leagues they go to mix with four great oceans at the four points of the horizon: the Mississippi loses itself to the south in the Mexican Gulf; the Saint Lawrence, to the east, throws itself into the Atlantic; the Ottawa rushes north into the polar seas; and the River of the West bears its tribute to the Ocean of Nontouka.[59]

After this view of the lakes, there comes a beginning of a diary which bears only the indication of the hours.

DIARY WITHOUT DATES

The sky is pure over my head, the water limpid under my boat, which is flying before a light breeze. On my left are some hills rising like cliffs and flanked with rocks from which hang the morning glory with white and blue blossoms, festoons of begonias, long grasses, rock plants of all colors; to my right reign vast prairies. As the boat advances new scenes and new views open up: at times solitary and laughing valleys, at times bare hills; here the somber porticoes of a cypress forest, there the sun playing in a light maple forest as if shining through a piece of lace.

Primitive liberty, I find you at last! I pass as that bird who flies before me, who travels haphazardly, who has only an embarrassment of riches among the shadows. Here I am as the Almighty created me, the sovereign of nature, borne triumphantly by the waters, while the inhabitants of the rivers accompany my course. The peoples of the air sing me their hymns, the animals of the earth salute me, and the forests bend their upmost branches over my passage. Is it on the forehead of the man of society or on mine that is engraved the immortal seal of our origin? Run and shut yourselves up in your cities; go and subject yourselves to your petty laws; earn your livelihood by the sweat of your brow, or devour the pauper's bread;

42

slaughter one another over a word, over a master; doubt the existence of God, or adore him in superstitious forms. I shall go wandering in my solitudes. Not a single beat of my heart will be constrained, not a single one of my thoughts will be enchained; I shall be free as nature; I shall recognize as sovereign only Him who lit the flame of the suns and who with one movement of His hand set in motion all the worlds.[60]

Seven o'clock in the Evening.
We passed the fork of the river and followed the southeast branch. We had been seeking an inlet where we could disembark along the channel. We entered a small bay thrust in by a promontory covered with a grove of tulip trees. After we had pulled our boat up on the land, some of us gathered dry branches for our fire, and others prepared the *ajoupa*. I took my gun and penetrated into the nearby forest.

I had not taken a hundred paces when I saw a flock of turkeys busy eating the berries of the ferns and the fruits of the service tree. These birds are rather different from those of their race domesticated in Europe: they are larger; their plumage is slate colored, tipped at the neck, on the back, and at the extremity of the wings with a copper red color; with the proper lighting this plumage shines like burnished gold. The wild turkeys often gather in great flocks. In the evening they perch on the tops of the highest branches. In the morning they let their repeated cry be heard from the tops of the trees; a little after sunrise their clamors cease, and they descend into the forests.

We got up early in order to leave during the coolness of the morning; the baggage was again stowed away; we unfurled our sail. On both sides we had high ground covered with forests. The foliage offered all the hues imaginable: scarlet blending into red, yellow into brilliant gold, vivid brown into light brown, green, white, and azure, washed in a thousand shades, a thousand intensities. Near us was all the variety of the prism; far from us, in the meanderings of the valley, the colors blended together into velvety backgrounds. The trees harmonized their forms: some spread out in fans, others rose in cones, others were rounded in balls, and others were shaped into pyramids. But one must be content with enjoying this spectacle without seeking to describe it.

Ten o'clock in the Morning.

We are advancing slowly. The breeze has stopped, and the channel is beginning to become narrow. The weather is becoming cloudy.

Noon.

It is impossible to go farther upstream in the boat; we must now change our manner of travel; we are going to draw our boat ashore, take our provisions, our arms, our furs for the night, and penetrate into the forest.

Three o'clock.

Who can tell the feeling one has on entering these forests as old as the world, which alone give the idea of creation as it left the hands of God? The daylight, falling from on high through a veil of foliage, spreads through the depths of the woods a changing and mobile half-light which gives fantastic size to things. Everywhere we must climb over fallen trees, above which rise new generations of trees. In vain I seek some outlet from this solitude. Misled by a brighter light, I advance through the grasses, the nettles, the mosses, the lianas, and the thick humus composed of vegetable debris; but I arrive only at a clearing formed by some fallen pines. Soon the forest becomes somber again; the eye sees only trunks of oaks and walnuts which follow one upon another and seem to come closer together as they recede into the distance. I become aware of the idea of infinity.

Six o'clock.

I had once again glimpsed a bright spot and had walked toward it. Here I am at the point of light, a sad field more melancholy than the forests which surround it! This field is a former Indian cemetery. Let me rest a moment in this double solitude of death and of nature. Is there any asylum where I would rather sleep forever?

Seven o'clock.

Being unable to get out of the woods, we have camped there. The flickering of our fire extends into the distance; lit from beneath by the scarlet light, the foliage seems bloodstained, and the trunks of the nearest trees rise like columns of red granite; but those more distant, scarcely touched by the light in the depths of the woods, resemble pale phantoms arranged in a circle on the edge of deep night.

Midnight.

The fire is beginning to go out, the circle of its light, diminishing. I listen. A formidable calm weighs upon these forests; one would say that silences follow upon silences. I seek vainly to hear in a universal tomb some noise betraying life. Whence comes that sigh? From one of my companions. He is complaining, although asleep. Thou livest; therefore thou sufferest: such is man.

Half past Midnight.

The repose continues, but the decrepit tree cracks and falls. The forests bellow; a thousand voices are raised. Soon the noises weaken and die in almost imaginary distance. Silence once again invades the wilderness.

One o'clock in the Morning.

Here is the wind: it is rushing over the tops of the trees, shaking them as it passes over my head. Now it is like the waves of the ocean breaking sadly on the shore.

The sounds have awakened sounds. The forest is all harmony. Do I hear the deep sounds of the organ, while lighter sounds wander through the vaults of verdure? A short silence follows: the aerial music begins anew; everywhere sweet complaints, murmurs that contain within them other murmurs; every leaf speaks a different language, each blade of grass gives off its own note.

An extraordinary voice resounds: it is that frog who imitates the bellowing of the bull. From all sides in the forest, the bats hanging from the leaves raise their monotonous song. It seems like a continual tolling, the funeral sounding of a bell. Everything brings us back to some idea of death because that idea is at the base of life.

Ten o'clock in the Morning.
We have continued our trip. When we descended into a flooded valley, branches of oak-willow laid from clump to clump of reeds served us as a bridge to cross the swamp. We are preparing our dinner at the foot of a hill covered with woods; we shall soon climb the hill to discover the river that we are seeking.

One o'clock.
We have started walking again; the woodcocks promise us a good dinner for tonight. The road is becoming steep, the trees are becoming rare; a slippery briar covers the side of the mountain.

Six o'clock.
Here we are at the summit. Beneath us can be seen only the tips of the trees. A few isolated rocks rise up out of this sea of verdure as reefs rise above the surface of the water. The carcass of a dog hung from a pine branch indicates the Indian sacrifice offered to the genie of this wilderness. A torrent rushes at our feet and loses itself in a little river.

Four o'clock in the Morning.
The night was peaceful. We have decided to return to our boat because we have no hope of finding a trail in this forest.

Nine o'clock.
We broke our fast under an old willow covered with morning glory and studded with toadstools. Without the mosquitoes, this place would be very agreeable; we had to make a great smoking fire with green wood to drive away our enemies. The guides announced the visit of some travelers who might still be two hours' march away from where we were. This sharpness of the ear is prodigious. There are Indians who hear the footfall of another Indian four and five hours away if they put their ears to the ground. And indeed two hours later we saw an Indian

family arrive. They cried the call of welcome; we answered joyfully.

Noon.

Our guests have informed us that they had been hearing us for two days; they knew we were palefaces, since the noise that we made walking was greater than the noise made by the redskins. I asked them the cause of this difference; they answered me that it came from the manner of breaking branches and clearing a trail. The white man also reveals his race by the weight of his step; the noise he produces does not increase regularly. The European goes in circles; the Indian walks in a straight line.

The Indian family is composed of two women, a child, and three men. When we had returned together to the boat, we built a great fire at the edge of the river. A mutual benevolence reigns among us. The women prepared our supper composed of salmon trout and a large turkey. We "warriors" are smoking and chatting together. Tomorrow our guests will help us carry our boat to a river that is only five miles from the place where we are.

The diary finishes here. A later stray page transports us to the middle of the Appalachians. Here is that page.

These mountains, unlike the Alps and the Pyrenees, are not mountains regularly piled up one upon the other, lifting their snow-covered summits above the clouds. To the west and the north they resemble perpendicular walls several thousand feet high, from whose top rush the rivers that flow into the Ohio and the Mississippi. In this kind of great chasm, one can see paths winding in the midst of precipices with the torrents. These paths and torrents are bordered by a kind of pine whose top is sea-green, and whose trunk, almost lilac, is marked with dark patches produced by flat black moss.

But on the south and the east, the Appalachians can scarcely continue to bear the name of mountains. Their summits decline

47

gradually right up to the land bordering the Atlantic coast; they pour on this ground other rivers which fecundate forests of live oak, maple, walnut, mulberry, chestnut, pine, fir, sweet gum, magnolia, and a thousand flowering shrubs.

After this short fragment comes a fairly extended portion on the course of the Ohio and the Mississippi from Pittsburgh to Natchez. The piece opens with the description of the monuments of the Ohio. *The Genius of Christianity* has a passage and a note on these monuments, but what I wrote in that passage and note differs on many points from what I say here.[61]

Imagine the remains of fortifications or monuments occupying an immense extent of space. Four kinds of works are to be noticed: square bastions, moons, half moons, and tumuli. The bastions, moons, and half moons are regular, the moats wide and deep, the entrenchments made of earth with parapets having inclined planes; but the angles of the mounds correspond to those of the moat and are not parallelograms inscribed in polygons.

The tumuli are tombs of circular form. Some of these tombs have been opened; there has been found inside each a grave formed of four stones, in which there were human skeletons. This tomb was surmounted by another tomb containing another skeleton, and so on to the top of the pyramid, which might have a height of 20 to 30 feet. These constructions cannot be the work of the present nations of America; the peoples who raised them must have had a knowledge of the arts superior even to that of the Mexicans and the Peruvians.[62]

Must these works be attributed to the modern Europeans? I have found only Hernando de Soto who penetrated the Floridas in the early days, and he never advanced beyond a village of the Chickasaws, on one of the branches of the Mobile; moreover, with a handful of Spaniards, how would he have moved all that earth, and for what purpose?

Was it the Carthaginians or the Phoenecians who, long ago, in their commerce around Africa and the Cassiterides, were drawn to the American regions? But before penetrating farther west, they must have established themselves on the Atlantic coast; then why does one find not the least trace of their passage through Virginia, the Georgias, and the Floridas? Neither the Phoenecians nor the Carthaginians buried their dead as are buried the dead of the Ohio fortifications. The Egyptians did something similar, but the mummies were embalmed, and those of the American tombs are not; it could not be said that the ingredients were lacking: the gums, resins, camphors, and salts are everywhere here.

Might Plato's Atlantis have existed? Unknown centuries ago did Africa join America? However that may be, an unknown nation, a nation superior to the Indian generations of today, passed through these wildernesses. What was this nation? What revolution destroyed it? When did this event happen? These are questions which throw us into that immensity of the past where the centuries are swallowed up like dreams.

The works of which I speak are found at the mouth of the Big Miami, at the mouth of the Muskingum, at Tomb Creek, and on one of the branches of the Scioto: those which border this river occupy the space of two hours' march as one descends toward the Ohio. In Kentucky, along the Tennessee, in the Seminole country, you cannot take a step without seeing some vestiges of these momuments.

The Indians are in agreement in saying that their fathers came from the west; they found the works of the Ohio just as they are to be seen today. But the date of this migration of the Indians from the west to the east varies according to the nations. The Chickasaws, for example, arrived in the forts that cover the mounds scarcely more than two centuries ago. They took seven years to accomplish their trip, marching only once each year, taking with them horses stolen from the Spaniards before whom they were retreating.

Another tradition claims that the works of the Ohio were raised by the *white* Indians. These white Indians, according to the red Indians, were to have come from the east; and when they left the lake without shores (the sea), they came dressed like the palefaces of today.

On the basis of this weak tradition, it has been told that

about 1170, Ogan, prince of Wales, or his son Madoc, embarked with a great number of his subjects[63] and that he landed in unknown territory to the west. But is it possible to imagine that the descendants of these Welshmen could have built the works of the Ohio, and that at the same time, having lost all the arts, they found themselves reduced to a handful of warriors wandering in the woods like the other Indians?

It has also been claimed that at the source of the Missouri numerous and civilized peoples live in military fortifications similar to those on the edges of the Ohio, that these people use horses and other domestic animals, that they have cities and public roads, that they are governed by kings.[64]

The religious tradition of the Indians about the monuments of their wilderness is not in conformity with their historical tradition. They say there is a cavern in the midst of these works; this cavern is that of the Great Spirit. The Great Spirit created the Chickasaws in that cavern. The land was then covered with water; when the Great Spirit saw this, he built walls of earth on which to put the Chickasaws out to dry.

Let us turn to the description of the course of the Ohio. The Ohio is formed by the union of the Monongahela and the Allegheny, the first river finding its source in the south in the Blue Mountains or Appalachians, the second in another chain of these mountains to the north between Lake Erie and Lake Ontario. By means of a short portage the Allegheny communicates with the first lake. The two rivers join below the fort formerly called Fort Duquesne, today Fort Pitt, or Pittsburgh. Their confluence is at the foot of a tall hill of coal; mixing their waters they lose their names and are henceforth known only as the Ohio, which means, and with good reason, "beautiful river."

More than 60 tributaries bring their riches to this river; those whose courses come from the east and the south leave the highlands that divide the tributary waters of the Atlantic from those descending to the Ohio and the Mississippi. Those which are born in the west and the north flow from the hills whose two slopes feed the lakes of Canada and supply the Mississippi and the Ohio. The space where this last river flows generally presents a wide valley bordered with hills of equal height; but as one travels downstream, such is no longer the case.

Nothing is so fertile as the lands watered by the Ohio. They produce on the hills forests of red pines, laurels, myrtles, sugar maples, oaks of four varieties; the valleys offer walnut, service tree, ash, and dogwood; the swamps bear birch, aspen, poplar, and bald cypress. The Indians make cloth with the bark of the poplar; they eat the second bark of the birch; they use the sap of the black alder to heal the fever and to drive away snakes; the oak furnishes them with arrows, the ash with canoes.

The grasses and plants are extremely varied, but those which cover all the countryside are buffalo grass seven to eight feet high, the three-leafed grass [clover], rye-grass or wild rice, and indigo.

At a depth of five or six feet beneath the everywhere fertile soil, one finds generally a bed of white stone, base for an excellent humus; however, approaching the Mississippi, one finds first at the surface a stiff black earth, then a layer of chalk of various colors, and then entire forests of bald cypress buried in the mud.

On the edge of the Chanon, 200 feet above[65] the water, some have claimed they saw characters traced on the walls of a precipice: it has been concluded from that fact that once the water flowed at that level, and that unknown nations wrote these mysterious letters as they passed on the river.

A sudden transition of temperature and climate is noticed on the Ohio. Around the Kanawha, the bald cypress ceases to grow, and the sassafras disappears; the forests of oak and elm multiply. Everything takes on a different color; the greens are deeper, their hues darker.

There are, so to speak, only two seasons on the river: the leaves fall suddenly in November, the snows follow them closely, the northwest wind begins, and winter reigns. A dry cold continues with a clear sky until March; then the wind turns to the northeast, and in less than two weeks the trees loaded with frost are covered with flowers. Summer blends into the spring.

Hunting is abundant. Striped ducks, blue linnets, cardinals, and dark red finches shine in the verdure of the trees; the *whet-shaw*[66] imitates the sound of the saw; the catbird meows, and the parrots who learn a few words around the habitations repeat them in the woods. A great number of these birds live on insects—the green tobacco caterpillar, the worm of a kind of white mulberry, the fireflies, and the water spider serve as their principal food—but the parrots gather in large flocks and lay waste to the sown fields. A bounty is offered for each bird head as well as for each squirrel head.

The Ohio affords about the same fish as the Mississippi. It is fairly common to catch trout from it weighing 30 to 35 pounds and a kind of sturgeon whose head is shaped like the blade of a paddle.

As one descends the course of the Ohio he passes a little river called Big Bone Lick. In America *licks* are beds of white, somewhat claylike earth, which the buffalo take pleasure in licking; they dig furrows in it with their tongues. The excrement of these animals is so impregnated with the earth of the lick that it resembles pieces of lime. The buffalo seek the licks because of the salts they contain. These salts cure the ruminants of the colic caused by the raw grasses. However, the earth of the Ohio valley is not salty to the taste; it is, on the contrary, quite insipid.

The lick of the Lick River is one of the largest known; the vast trails that the buffalo have traced through the grass to reach it would be frightening if one did not know that these wild bulls are the most peaceful of all creatures. There has been discovered in this lick part of a mammoth's skeleton. The thigh bone weighed 70 pounds, the ribs were curves 7 feet long, and the head 3 feet long; the molars were 5 inches wide and 8 high, the tusks 14 inches from the root to the tip.

Such remains have been found in Chile and Russia. The Tartars maintain that the mammoth still exists in their country at the mouths of rivers. It is also claimed that hunters have pursued them west of the Mississippi. If the race of these animals has perished, as we are to believe, when did this destruction come about in countries so diverse and climates so different? We know nothing of it, and yet every day we ask God to account for his works!

The Big Bone Lick is about 30 miles from the Kentucky River and 108 miles approximately from the rapids of the Ohio. The banks of the Kentucky River rise in wall-like cliffs. Here can be seen a buffalo trail that descends from the top of a hill, springs of bitumen that can be burned in place of oil, caves embellished with natural columns, and a subterranean lake that extends for unknown distances.

At the confluence of the Kentucky and the Ohio there unfolds an extraordinary grandeur: there, from the summit of the cliff, herds of deer watch one pass along the river; here clumps of old pines extend out horizontally over the waters; smiling plains stretch as far as the eye can see, while curtains of forests veil the base of a few mountains whose crests appear in the distance.

Yet this magnificent country is called Kentucky from the name of its river, which means "river of blood." It owes this grim name to its very beauty. For more than two centuries the nations allied with the Cherokees and those allied with the Iroquois nation fought each other over hunting rights there. No tribe dared settle on this battlefield: the Shawnees, the Miamis, the Piankashaws, the Wayaoes, the Kaskaskias, the Delawares, the Illinois came in turn to do battle. It was only toward 1752 that the Europeans began to learn something positive about the valleys located to the west of the Allegheny Mountains, called first the Endless Mountains, or Kittatinny Mountains, or Blue Mountains. However Charlevoix had spoken of the course of the Ohio in 1720; and Fort Duquesne, today Fort Pitt (Pittsburgh), had been laid out by Frenchmen at the junction of the two rivers that form the Ohio. In 1752 Lewis Evant[67] published a map of the land around the Ohio and the Kentucky; James Macbrive[68] traveled through this wilderness in 1754; Jones Finley[69] reached there in 1757; Colonel Boone[70] explored the whole territory in 1769 and settled there with his family in 1775. It has been said that Doctor Wood[71] and Simon Kenton[72] were the first Europeans to descend the Ohio, in 1773, from Fort Pitt to the Mississippi. The national pride of the Americans leads them to attribute to themselves the majority of the discoveries to the west of the United States; but it must not be forgotten that the French of Canada and Louisiana, arriving from the north and the south, had roamed these regions long before the Americans, who came from the east and who were impeded in their route by the confederation of the Creeks and by the Spaniards in the Floridas.

This country is beginning (1791) to be settled by the colonies of Pennsylvania, Virginia, and Carolina, and by some of my unfortunate compatriots, fleeing before the first storms of the revolution.

Will the European generations be more virtuous and freer on these shores than the American generations they have exterminated? Will not slaves till the soil under the whip of the master in this wilderness where man paraded his liberty? Will not prisons and scaffolds replace the open cabin and the tall oak, which bears only the nests of the birds? Will not the riches of the soil bring about new wars? Will Kentucky cease to be the "land of blood," and will the edifices of man better embellish the banks of the Ohio than the monuments of nature?

From the Kentucky to the Ohio Rapids is about 80 miles. These rapids are formed by a layer of rock extending under the water in the river bed; the descent of these rapids is neither dangerous nor difficult, the average fall being scarcely four to five feet in the space of a third of a league. The river is divided into two channels by some islands grouped in the middle of the rapids. When one goes with the current, it is possible to pass without lightening the boats, but it is impossible to go up the rapids without lessening the load.

The river is a mile wide at the rapids. As one glides along the magnificent channel, attention is drawn some distance below the falls to an island covered with a forest of elms woven together with garlands of lianas and virgin vines.

To the north can be made out the hills of Silver Creek. The first of these hills dips perpendicularly into the Ohio; its cliff, cut in great red facets, is decorated with plants; other parallel hills crowned with forests rise behind the first hill; and as they recede, they rise ever higher into the sky until their summits struck by the light become the color of the heavens and disappear.

To the south are savannas sprinkled with woods and covered

with buffalo, some lying down, others wandering, some grazing, some gathered in groups, confronting each other with their
lowered heads. In the midst of this tableau, the rapids, depending on how they are struck by the sun's rays, repulsed by the
wind, or shaded by the clouds, rise in golden bubbles, whiten
with foam, or roll in darkened waves.

At the foot of the rapids is a little island where bodies
petrify. This island is covered with water at the time of flood; it
is claimed that the petrifying virtue is confined to this little
corner of land and does not extend to the nearby river bank.

From the rapids to the mouth of the Wabash is 316 miles.
This river communicates by means of a nine-mile portage with
the Miami of the Lake, which flows into Lake Erie. The shores
of the Wabash are high; a silver mine has been discovered
there.

Ninety-four miles below the mouth of the Wabash com-
mences a cypress swamp. From there to the Yellow Banks, still
descending the Ohio, is 56 miles. The mouths of two rivers are
passed on the left; they are only 18 miles from one another.

The first river is the Cherokee or the Tennessee; it comes out
of the mountains that separate the Carolinas and the Georgias
from what are known as the Western Territories; it flows first
from east to west at the foot of the mountains. In this first part
of its course it is rapid and tumultuous; then it suddenly turns
to the north; enlarged by several tributaries, it spreads out and
holds back its waters as if to rest after a precipitous flight of
400 leagues. At its mouth it is 4,000 feet wide, and in a place
called the Great Bend it forms a sheet of water a league across.

The second river, the Shanawon or the Cumberland, is the
companion of the Cherokee or Tennessee. They spend their
childhood together in the same mountains and descend together into the plains. Toward the middle of her course,
obliged to leave the Tennessee, she hastens to traverse the
wilderness; and the twins, approaching one another toward the
end of their lives, expire at a short distance from one another in
the Ohio, which unites them.

The country these rivers water is generally broken up by
hills and valleys freshened by a multitude of streams. However,
there are some fields of cane on the Cumberland and several

large cypress swamps. Buffalo and deer abound in this country still inhabited by savage nations, particularly the Cherokees. The Indian cemeteries are frequent, a sad proof of the former populations of this wilderness.

From the great cypress swamp on the Ohio to the Yellow Banks, I have said the route is estimated at about 56 miles. The Yellow Banks are so named because of their color. Located on the northern bank of the Ohio, one must hug them closely because the water is deep on that side. The Ohio has almost everywhere a double shore, one in flood season, the other in dry season.

The distance from the Yellow Banks to the mouth of the Ohio at the Mississippi, at a latitude of 36° 51', is about 35 miles.

To visualize the confluence of the two rivers properly, you must imagine that you are starting from a little island off the eastern bank of the Mississippi and that you want to head into the Ohio: at the left you will see the Mississippi, at this point flowing almost east to west, its waters troubled and tumultuous; on the right, the Ohio, more transparent than crystal, more peaceful than the air, coming slowly from north to south, describing a graceful arc. In the intermediate season they are both about two miles wide at the moment of their meeting. The volume of their waters is almost the same; the two rivers, opposing one another with an equal resistance, slow their course and seem to sleep together for a few leagues in their common bed.

The point where they unite their waters is raised some 20 feet above them. Composed of mud and sand, this swampy cape is covered with wild hemp and vines crawling along the ground or climbing up the shafts of buffalo grass; oak-willows also grow on this tongue of land that disappears during the great floods. The rivers, overflowing their banks and joining together, resemble a vast lake.

The confluence of the Missouri and the Mississippi presents something that is perhaps more extraordinary yet. The Missouri is a spirited river with frothy and muddy waters; it rushes into the pure and tranquil Mississippi with violence. In the spring it detaches from its banks vast clumps of earth. These floating islands descending the course of the Missouri, with their trees covered with leaves or blossoms, some still standing, others half-fallen, offer a marvelous spectacle.

From the mouth of the Ohio to the iron mines on the eastern bluff of the Mississippi is scarcely more than 15 miles; from the iron mines to the mouth of the Chickasaw is 67 miles. One must travel 400 miles to reach the hills of Margette, watered by the small river of that name; it is an area filled with game.

Why do we find so much charm in primitive life? Why does the man who is most accustomed to exercise his thought forget himself joyously in the tumult of a hunt? Running through the woods, pursuing wild animals, building his hut, lighting his fire, preparing his own meal next to a spring, is certainly a very great enjoyment. A thousand Europeans have known this pleasure and wished for none other, while the Indian dies if he is shut up in one of our cities. That proves that man is rather an active being than a contemplative one, that in his natural condition he needs little, and that simplicity of soul is an inexhaustible source of happiness.

From the Margette River to the Saint Francis River one travels 70 miles. The Saint Francis River received its name from the French and is still a hunting rendezvous for them.

It is 108 miles from the Saint Francis River to the Arkansas or Akansas. The Arkansas are still very attached to us. Of all the Europeans, my compatriots are the most loved by the Indians. That comes from the gaiety of the Frenchmen, their brilliant valor, their predilection for the hunt and even for the primitive life—as if the greatest civilization approached the state of nature.

The Arkansas River is navigable in small boats for more than 450 miles. It flows through a beautiful country, its source seemingly hidden in the mountains of New Mexico.

From the Arkansas River to the Yazoo River is 158 miles. This latter river is 650 feet wide at its mouth. In the rainy season large boats can go up the Yazoo for more than 80 miles; a small cataract necessitates only one portage. The Yazoos, the Choctaws, and the Chickasaws formerly inhabited the different branches of this river. The Yazoos and the Natchez formed a single nation.

The distance from the Yazoo country to the Natchez country by the river is divided thus: from the Yazoo hills to Black Bayou, 39 miles; from Black Bayou to the Stony River, 30 miles; from Stony River to Natchez, 10 miles.

From the Yazoo bluffs to Black Bayou, the Mississippi is full of islands and makes wide bends; its width is almost two miles, its depth eight to ten fathoms. It would be easy to diminish the distances by cutting through some of these bends. The distance from New Orleans to the mouth of the Ohio, which is only 460 miles as the crow flies, is 856 on the river. One could shorten this distance by 250 miles at least.

From Black Bayou to the Stony River can be seen stone quarries. They are the first to be found between the mouth of the Mississippi and the little river that has taken its name from these quarries.

The Mississippi is subject to two periodic floods, one in the spring, the other in autumn. The first is the greater; it begins in May and ends in June. The current of the river flows at the rate of five miles an hour then, and the opposite movement of the countercurrents is approximately at the same speed: admirable foresight of nature! For, without these countercurrents, boats could scarcely go up river.[73] At this period, the water rises to a great height, inundates its banks, and does not return to the river it has left. As with the Nile, it stays on the land or filters through the soil on which it lays a fertile sediment.

The second flood takes place with the October rains; it is not as considerable as the spring one. During these inundations the Mississippi roars and carries down great quantities of wood. The ordinary speed of the river is about two miles an hour.

The somewhat elevated lands that border the Mississippi from New Orleans to the Ohio are almost all on the left bank; but their distance from the water varies so that sometimes between the heights and the river there are savannas several miles in width. The hills do not always run parallel with the bank; at times they spread out to great distances and open up the view of valleys where a thousand kinds of trees grow; at times they converge on the river and form a multitude of capes which reflect in the waters. The right bank of the Mississippi is level, swampy, and uniform, with only a few exceptions. In the midst of high green or golden cane, which decorates the bank, one can see bounding buffalo or the shining waters of a multitude of pools filled with aquatic birds.

The fish of the Mississippi are the perch, the pike, the sturgeon, and the colles.[74] Enormous crabs have also been caught there.

The soil around the river furnishes rhubarb, cotton, indigo, saffron, wax plant, sassafras, wild flax. A worm of the region spins a fairly strong silk. In some streams, dredges bring up large pearl oysters, but not of the first water. A quicksilver mine is known, another of lapis lazuli, and some iron mines.

The continuation of the manuscript contains the descriptions of the Natchez country and the course of the Mississippi to New Orleans. These descriptions have been entirely carried over into *Atala* and *The Natchez*.

Immediately after the descriptions of Louisiana in the manuscript come some extracts from the *Travels* of Bartram, which I had translated with a fair amount of care. Mixed in with these extracts are my corrections, my observations, my reflections, my additions, my own descriptions, just about as was the case with M. Ramond's notes in his translation of Coxe's *Travels in Switzerland*. But in my work, everything is much more close-knit, so that it is almost impossible to separate what is mine from what is Bartram's, or even to recognize it frequently. Therefore I leave the piece as it is under this title:

DESCRIPTION OF A FEW SITES
IN THE INTERIOR OF THE FLORIDAS

We were driven by a cool wind. The river was going to lose itself in a lake opening before us to form a basin of about nine leagues' circumference. Three islands rose from the middle of this lake; we sailed toward the largest, where we arrived at eight o'clock in the morning.

We disembarked on the edge of a plain circular in form; we

put our boat in the shelter of a group of chestnuts that grew almost in the water. We built our hut on a small rise. The easterly breeze was blowing and cooled the lake and the forests. We broke our fast with corncakes and scattered through the island, some to hunt, others to fish or to gather plants.

We noticed a kind of hibiscus. This enormous plant, which grows in low and humid parts, rises to more than ten or twelve feet and ends in a sharp pointed cone; the leaves, smooth and slightly furrowed, are enlivened by beautiful crimson flowers, which can be seen from great distances.

The *Agave vivipara* rose still higher in the salty inlets, and formed a forest of grasses 30 feet high. The ripe seed of this grass sometimes germinates on the plant itself, so that the young seedling falls to earth already formed. As the *Agave*

vivipara often grows at the edge of running water, its bare seed borne away by the waters would be exposed to perish: nature has prepared them while still on the old plant for those specific circumstances, so they are able to fix themselves by their little roots when they escape from the maternal bosom.

The American cypress was common on the island. The stem

of this cypress resembles that of a knotty reed, and its leaves resemble a leek: the savages call it *apoya matsi*. The Indian girls of loose morals crush this plant between two stones and rub their breasts and arms with it.[75]

We crossed a field covered with yellow-flowered jacobaea, pink-blossomed althea, and obelia, whose crown is dark red. Light winds playing on the tips of these plants broke them into waves of gold, pink, and dark red, or dug long furrows in the verdure.

The senega, which is abundant in the swampy lands, resembled in form and color shoots of red willow; some branches crawled along the ground, others rose into the air. Senega has a slightly bitter and aromatic taste. Near it grew the Carolina morning glory, whose leaf imitates an arrowhead. These two plants are to be found everywhere the rattlesnake exists: the one heals the snake's bite; the second is so powerful that the savages, after having rubbed their hands with it, handle with impunity these fearsome reptiles. The Indians tell that the Great Spirit took pity on the redskin warriors with bare legs, and he himself sowed these salutary herbs in spite of the protestations of the souls of the snakes.

We recognized serpentaria on the roots of the great trees— the toothache tree, whose trunk and thorny branches are covered with protruberances as large as pigeon eggs; arctosa or canneberge,[76] whose red cherry grows among the mosses and cures liver trouble. The black alder, which has the property of driving away vipers, was growing vigorously in the stagnant waters covered with scum.

An unexpected sight struck our eyes: we discovered an Indian ruin. It was situated on a hillock at the edge of the lake; on the left there was an earthen cone 40 to 45 feet high; from this cone started an old trail that ran through a magnificent forest of magnolias and live oaks and ended in a savanna. Fragments of vases and utensils of diverse nature were scattered here and there mixed in with fossils, shells, petrified plants, and animal bones.

The contrast between these ruins—these monuments of man in a wilderness where we thought ourselves the first to penetrate—and the youthful appearance of nature caused a strong reaction in our hearts and minds. What people had inhabited this island? Their name, race, the time of their existence—all of it is unknown; they lived perhaps when the world which hid them in its breast was still unknown to the three other parts of the earth. The silencing of this people is perhaps contemporary with the clamor made by the great European nations that fell in turn into silence and left of themselves only debris.

We examined the ruins. From the sandy fragments of the tumulus grew a kind of pink-flowered poppy, weighing down the end of a long, bending, pale green stem. The Indians draw from the root of this poppy a soporific drink; the stem and the flower have an agreeable smell which remains attached to the hand when one touches them. This plant was made to decorate the tomb of a savage: its roots procure sleep, and the perfume of the flower, which outlives the flower itself, is a rather pleasant image of the memory that an innocent life leaves in the wilderness.

Continuing our way and observing the mosses, the hanging gramineous plants, the disheveled shrubs, and all the host of plants of melancholy demeanor which decorate ruins, we observed a kind of pyramidal primrose seven to eight feet high, with greenish black oblong serrated leaves; its flower is yellow. In the evening this flower begins to open; it spreads wide during the night; dawn finds it in all its splendor; toward the middle of the morning it withers; it falls at noon. It lives only a few hours, but it passes these hours beneath a serene sky. So of what importance is the brevity of its life?

A few steps from there was spread out a border of mimosa or sensitive plant; in the songs of the savages, the soul of the maiden is often compared to that plant.⁷⁷

Returning to our camp, we crossed a stream edged with dionaeas; a multitude of ephemera buzzed about them. There were also on this expanse three kinds of butterflies: one white as alabaster, another black as jet with wings crossed by yellow bands, the third having a forked tail and four golden wings barred with blue and spotted with dark red. Attracted by the plants, insects alighted on the dionaeas. But no sooner had they touched the leaves than they closed up and enveloped their prey.

Upon our return to our *ajouppa*, we went fishing to console ourselves for the lack of success on the hunt. We embarked in the boat with lines and nets and skirted the coast of the eastern part of the island at the edge of the covering of algae and along the shaded capes. The trout were so voracious that we caught them on unbaited hooks; the fish called gold fish were abundant. There is nothing more beautiful than this little king of the waters: he is about five inches long; his head is ultramarine; his sides and belly sparkle like fire; a longitudinal brown stripe crosses his sides; the iris of his wide eyes shines like burnished gold. This fish is carnivorous.

At some distance from the shore, in the shade of a bald cypress, we noticed little mud pyramids rising beneath the water up to the surface. A legion of gold fish patrolled the approaches of this citadel in silence. Suddenly the water boiled; the gold fish fled. Crayfish armed with pincers, coming out of the assaulted place, overcame their brilliant enemies. But soon the scattered bands returned to the charge, vanquished the besieged in turn, and the brave but slow garrison backed into the fortress to gather strength.

The crocodile, floating like the trunk of a tree, the trout, the pike, the perch, the cannelet, the bass, the bream, the drumfish, the gold fish, all mortal enemies of one another, swam pellmell in the lake and seemed to have called a truce in order to enjoy together the beauty of the evening. The azure fluid was painted in changing colors. The waters were so pure that it seemed possible to touch with the finger the actors of this scene being played 20 feet deep in their crystal grotto.

To regain the inlet where we had our camp we had only to abandon ourselves to the current and the breezes. The sun was approaching its setting. In the foreground of the island appeared live oaks whose horizontal branches formed a parasol, and azaleas shining like coral formations.

Behind this foreground rose the most charming of all trees, the papaya. Its straight, grayish, carved trunk 20 to 25 feet high, supports a tuft of long ribbed leaves that are shaped like the gracious S of an ancient vase. The fruit, shaped like a pear, is distributed around the stem: you would take them for glass crystals;[78] the whole tree resembles a column of chased silver surmounted by a Corinthian urn.

Finally, in the background the magnolias and the sweet gums rose gradually into the air.

The sun was setting behind the curtain of trees on the plain. As it descended, the movements of shade and light spread something magical over the scene: there a ray shone through the dome of a great tree and sparkled like a carbuncle set in the somber foliage; here, the light diverged among the trunks and branches and cast on the grass growing columns and moving trellises. In the skies were clouds of all colors, some motionless, resembling great promontories or old towers next to a torrent, others floating in pink smoke or in flakes of white silk. A moment sufficed to change the aerial scene. One could see the flaming maws of furnaces, great heaps of coals, rivers of lava, burning landscapes. The same hues were repeated without mixing; fire stood out on fire, pale yellow on pale yellow, purple on purple. Everything was brilliant, everything was enveloped, penetrated, saturated with light.

But nature laughs at the paintbrush of man. When she seems to have attained her greatest beauty, she smiles and becomes even more beautiful.

To our right were the Indian ruins; to our left, our hunting camp; the island spread before us its landscapes engraved or modeled in the waters. To the east, the moon, touching the horizon, seemed to rest motionless on the faraway hills; to the west, the vault of heaven seemed blended into a sea of diamonds and sapphires in which the sun, half-plunged, seemed to be dissolving.

The animals of creation were, as we, attentive to this great spectacle: the crocodile, turned toward the luminary of day, spewed from his open maw the lake water in a colored spray; perched on a dried branch, the pelican praised in his own manner the Master of nature, while the stork flew away to bless Him above the clouds!

We too shall sing Thee, God of the universe, who hast lavished so many marvels! The voice of a man will be lifted with the voice of the wilderness: Thou wilt make out the accents of the weak son of woman in the midst of the music of the spheres which Thy hand sets in motion, in the midst of the bellowing of the abyss whose doors Thou hast sealed.

Upon our return to the island, I had an excellent meal: fresh trout seasoned with canneberge tips[79] was a dish worthy of a king's table. Thus was I much more than a king. If chance had placed me on the throne and a revolution had cast me from it, instead of eking out my misery in Europe as did Charles and James, I would have said to the covetous: "You want my position, well try the job; you will see it is not so desirable. Slay one another over my old mantle; in the forests of America I shall enjoy the liberty you have given back to me."

We had a neighbor at our supper. A hole similar to the burrow of a badger was the home of a tortoise; the recluse came out of her cave and started walking gravely along the water. These tortoises are little different from sea turtles; they have a longer neck. We didn't kill the peaceful queen of the island.

After supper I sat down by myself on the shore; all that could be heard was the sound of the waves lapping along the beach; fireflies shone in the darkness and were eclipsed when they crossed a moonbeam. I fell into that kind of reverie known to all travelers. No distinct remembrance of myself remained; I felt myself living as a part of the great whole and vegetating with the trees and the flowers. That is perhaps the most pleasant condition for man, for even when he is happy there is in his pleasures a certain foundation of bitterness, an indefinable something that could be called the sadness of happiness. The traveler's reverie is a sort of plenitude of the heart and emptiness of the mind which allows one to enjoy his existence in repose: it is by thought that we trouble the felicity which God gives us: the soul is peaceful; the mind is troubled.

The Indians of Florida tell that in the middle of a lake there is an island where live the most beautiful women in the world. The Muskogees several times tried the conquest of the magical island; but the Elysian retreats, fleeing before their canoes, finally disappeared: a natural image of the time we lose pursuing our chimeras. In that country there was also a Fountain of Youth. Who would want to grow younger?

The next day before sunrise we left the island, crossed the lake, and entered again on the river by which we had descended. This river was full of alligators. These animals are only dangerous in the water, especially when one is disembarking. On land, a child could easily outdistance them walking at an ordinary pace. A way of avoiding their ambushes is to set the grasses and reeds on fire. There is then the curious spectacle of great expanses of water capped with a curtain of flame.

When the crocodile[80] of these regions has reached full growth, it measures about 20 to 24 feet from the head to the tail. Its body is as large as that of a horse. This reptile would have exactly the form of the common lizard if its tail were not compressed on the two sides as is a fish's. It is covered with bulletproof scales, except around the head and between the legs. Its head is about three feet long; the nostrils are wide; the upper jaw of the animal is the only one that moves; it opens to form a right angle with the lower jaw. Beneath the upper jaw are placed two large teeth like the tusks of a boar, which give the monster a terrible appearance.

The female of the alligator lays whitish eggs on land which she covers with grasses and mud. These eggs, sometimes as many as a hundred, form with the mud that covers them little heaps four feet high and five feet in diameter at their base. The sun and the fermentation of the clay hatch the eggs. One female does not distinguish her own eggs from the eggs of another female; she takes under her protection all the sun's broods. Is it not strange to find among the crocodiles the communal children of Plato's republic?

The heat was oppressive; we were sailing in the midst of swamps; our boats were leaking, for the sun had melted the pitch of the caulking. Often we received burning blasts from the north; our scouts predicted a storm because the savanna rat was going up and down the branches of the live oak incessantly; the mosquitoes were tormenting us frightfully. We could see swamp fire in the low spots.

We spent the night very uncomfortably without any ajouppa on a peninsula surrounded by swamps; the moon and all objects were drowned in a red fog. This morning there has been no breeze, and we reembarked to try to reach an Indian village a few miles away; but it has been impossible for us to go up the river very long, and we have had to disembark on the tip of a cape covered with trees, from where we enjoy an immense view. Clouds are rising up from beneath the horizon on the northwest and are slowly climbing into the sky. We are making a shelter for ourselves as best we can with branches.

The sun is becoming overcast, the first rolls of thunder are heard; the crocodiles answer them with a low rumble, as one thunderclap answers another. An immense column of clouds is extending to the northeast and the southeast; the rest of the sky is a dirty copper color, half-transparent and tinged with lightning. The wilderness lit by a false light and the storm suspended over our heads ready to break offer a scene full of splendor.

Here is the storm! Imagine a deluge of fire without wind or water; the smell of sulphur fills the air; nature is illuminated as if by the light of a conflagration.

Now the cataracts of the abyss open up; the raindrops are not separated from one another: a veil of water joins the clouds to the earth.

The Indians say that the noise of the thunder is caused by immense birds fighting in the air and by the efforts being made by an old man to vomit up a viper of fire. To prove this assertion they show trees where lightning has traced the image of a snake. Often the storms set fire to the forests; they continue burning until the fire is stopped by some watercourse. These burned-out forests are transformed into lakes and swamps.

The curlews, whose voices we hear in the sky in the middle of the rain and thunder, announce the end of the hurricane. The wind is tearing apart the clouds whose remnants are flying across the sky; the thunder and the lightning attached to their sides follow them; the air is becoming cold and sonorous. Of the deluge there remain only drops of water which fall like beads from the leaves of the trees. Our nets and our provisions are floating in the boats full of water up to the gunwales.

The country inhabited by the Creeks (the confederation of the Muskogees, the Seminoles, and the Cherokees) is enchanting. From place to place the ground is hollowed out by a multitude of basins called wells, more or less wide and deep.

They communicate by underground passages with the lakes, the swamps, and the rivers. All these wells are placed in the center of a hillock where grow the most beautiful trees and whose sloping sides resemble the walls of a vase filled with pure water. Brilliant fish swim in the depths of this water.

In the rainy season, the savannas become kinds of lakes above which rise, like islands, the hillocks we have just mentioned.

Cuscowilla, a Seminole village, is situated on a chain of gravel hills 2,500 feet from a lake; fir trees, at a distance from one another and touching only at the top, separate the town and the lake. Between their trunks, as between columns, could be seen cabins, the lake and its shores attached on one side to the forests and on the other to prairies. This is just about the way the sea, the plain, and the ruins of Athens are seen, I have heard,[81] through the isolated columns of the temple of Olympian Zeus.

It would be difficult to imagine anything more beautiful than the surroundings of Apalachicola, the town of peace. Starting with the Chattahoochee River, the ground rises as it withdraws toward the western horizon; it is not a uniform slope but kinds of terraces stacked one upon another.

As you climb from terrace to terrace, the trees change according to the elevation. On the edge of the river are oak-willows, laurels, and magnolias; higher, sassafras and plane trees; higher yet, elms and walnuts. Finally the last terrace is covered with a forest of oaks, among which can be noted the species from which hang long growths of white moss. Bare broken rock rises above this forest.

Streams wind down from these rocks, flow among the flowers and greenery, or fall in sheets of crystal. When from the other side of the Chattahoochee River one observes these great steps crowned by the architecture of the mountains, he would think he was seeing the temple of nature and the magnificent steps leading to that monument.

At the foot of this amphitheater is a plain where graze flocks of European bulls, squadrons of Spanish horses, hordes of deer and stags, battalions of cranes and turkeys, marbling the green background of the savanna with white and black. This association of domestic and wild animals and the Seminole huts, where one sees the progress of civilization through Indian ignorance, give the final touches to this tableau the likes of which could be found nowhere else.

Here finishes, strictly speaking, the *Itinerary*, or account of places visited; but there remains in the divers parts of the manuscript, a multitude of details on the manners and customs of the Indians. I have gathered these details together in chapters by subject, after carefully reviewing them and bringing my narrative up to date. The 36 years that have passed since my trip have brought much enlightenment and changed many things in the Old and the New World; these years have necessarily modified the ideas and rectified the judgments of the writer. Before passing to the manners of the savages, I shall place before the eyes of the readers some sketches of the natural history of North America.

Natural History

§ *Beavers* §   When one sees the works of the beavers for the first time, one cannot help admiring Him who taught a poor little animal the art of the architects of Babylon and who often sends man, so proud of his genius, to the school of an insect. The astonishing creatures, as soon as they have found a valley where a stream is flowing, dam up the stream; the water rises and soon fills the interval between the two hills. It is in this reservoir that the beavers build their dwelling places. Let me describe in detail the construction of the dam.

From the two opposite sides of the hills that form the valley, begin rows of palisades laced with branches and covered with mortar. This first row is fortified by a second row placed 15 feet behind the first. The space between the two palisades is filled in with earth.

The levee thus continues from the two sides of the valley until there is only an opening of about 20 feet in the center; but here at the center, since the action of the current operates in all its force, the engineers change materials. They reinforce the middle of their hydraulic substructure with trunks of trees piled up on one another and bound together by a cement similar to that of the palisades. Often the whole dike is 100 feet long, 15 feet high, and 12 feet thick at the base; diminishing in thickness in mathematical proportion as it rises, it has no more than three feet of horizontal surface at the top. The side of the dam holding the water slopes down; the outside edge is perpendicular.

Everything is foreseen. The beaver knows by the height of the levee how many floors he must have in his future house; he knows that beyond a certain number of feet he no longer needs fear being flooded, because then the water would pass over the dike. Consequently a room that is higher than the dike furnishes him a retreat at high water; sometimes he installs a floodgate in the dam, a gate that he opens and closes at will.

The manner in which the beavers fell trees is most curious. They always choose trees at the edge of a river. Workers proportionate to the extent of the task gnaw continuously at the roots. The tree is never cut on the land side but on the water side, so that it will fall into the current.[82] A beaver stationed at some distance whistles to warn the woodsmen when he sees the top of the tree bending, so that they may take shelter from the falling tree. The workers drag the floating trunk to their cities, just as the Egyptians, for the embellishment of their cities, hewed obelisks from the quarries of Elephantine and floated them down the Nile.

The palaces of this Venice of the wilderness constructed in the artificial lake have two, three, four, and five stories, according to the depth of the lake. The edifice, built on pilings, stands with two thirds of its structure out of the water. The pilings are six in number; they support the first flooring, which is made of birch logs laid at angles. On this flooring stands the vestibule of the monument; the walls of the vestibule curve to form a vault covered with a clay that is as polished as plaster. In the floor of the portico is installed a trapdoor through which the beavers descend to get their bath or to get the aspen branches for their food. These branches are stacked under the water in a common storehouse among the pilings of the different dwellings. The first floor of the palace is topped by three other stories constructed in the same manner but divided into as many apartments as there are beavers. There are ordinarily ten or twelve of them, divided in three families. These families gather in the vestibule, which has already been described, and take their meals there together. The greatest cleanliness rules everywhere. Besides the bath door, there are exits that serve the different needs of the inhabitants; each room is floored with young pine branches, and the slightest uncleanliness is not allowed. When the proprietors go to their country home, built on the lake's edge and constructed like those of the city, no one usurps their place; their apartment remains empty until their return. When the snows melt, the citizens retire to the woods.

71

Just as there is a floodgate for the overflow waters, there is a secret route for the evacuation of the city, just as in the Gothic castles there would be an underground passage under the towers leading out into the country.

There are nurses for the sick. And it is a weak and formless animal who achieves all these works, who makes all these calculations!

Toward July the beavers have a general council: they examine whether it is expedient to repair the old city and dam or whether it would be better to build a new fortress and dike. Should food be lacking in that place, should water and hunters have done too much damage to the works, it is decided to form another establishment. On the other hand, should it be judged that the first one can still serve, the old dwellings are renovated, and the beavers then busy themselves with provisions for the winter.

The have a regular government: councillors are chosen to police the republic. During the general work, sentinels forestall any surprise. If some citizen refuses to bear his part of public duties, he is exiled; he is obliged to live alone, covered with shame, in a hole. The Indians say that this punished idler is thin and he has his back stripped of fur as a sign of infamy. Of what use is so much intelligence to these industrious animals? Man lets the ferocious beasts live and exterminates the beavers, as he suffers tyrants and persecutes innocence and genius.

Unfortunately war is not unknown to the beavers. Sometimes there arises among them civil discord, independent of the foreign entanglements they have with the muskrats. The Indians say that if a beaver is surprised marauding in the territory of a tribe other than his own, he is brought before the chief of that tribe and punished for the purpose of rehabilitation; for a second offense, they cut off his useful tail, which is both his cart and his trowel. He returns thus mutilated to his friends, who assemble to do vengeance for his injury. Sometimes the quarrel is settled by a duel between the chiefs of the two troops, or by single combat, 3 against 3, 30 against 30, as in the combat of the Curiatii and the Horatii, or the 30 Bretons against the 30 Englishmen. The general battles are bloody: the savages who come up to skin the dead often have found more than fifteen lying on the field of honor. The victorious beavers take possession of the vanquished beavers' city, and as the case may be, they establish a colony there or set up a garrison.

The female of the beaver bears two or three, sometimes as many as four young; she feeds them and teaches them for a year. When the population becomes too numerous, the young beavers go to form a new establishment, like a swarm of bees escaped from the hive. The beaver lives chastely with a single female; he is jealous and sometimes kills his wife for infidelity or a suspicion of it.

The average length of the beaver is two and a half to three feet; its width from one haunch to the other, about 14 inches; he can weigh up to 45 pounds; his head resembles that of a rat; his eyes are little, his ears short, bare inside, furry outside; his forepaws are scarcely three inches long and are armed with sharp concave claws; his back paws, webbed like a swan's, help him swim; the tail is flat, an inch thick, covered with hexagonal scales laid down like tiles in the manner of fish scales; he uses this tail as a trowel and a sled. His extremely strong jaws close like the blades of scissors; each jaw is furnished with ten teeth, of which two are incisors two inches long: it is the instrument with which the beaver cuts down the trees, squares off the trunks, tears off their bark, and crushes the tender wood on which he feeds.

The animal is black, rarely white or brown. It has two kinds of fur—the first, long, hollow and shiny; the second, a kind of down which grows under the first, is the only fur used in felt. The beaver lives 20 years. The female is larger than the male, and her fur is more gray on the belly. It is not true that when he is captured alive by hunters the beaver mutilates himself to prevent having offspring destined to become slaves. Another etymology must be sought for his name castor.

The flesh of the beavers is worthless, no matter how it is prepared. The savages preserve it, however, after having smoked it; they eat it when they lack supplies. The beaver skin is fine without being warm; thus the hunting of the beaver had no importance formerly with the Indians. The hunting of the bear, in which they saw advantage and peril, was the most honorable. They were content to kill a few beavers to wear their pelts as a decoration, but entire nations were not wiped out. The price that the Europeans have set on this pelt has by itself brought on the extermination in Canada of these quadrupeds, who by their instinct held the first rank among animals. Now one must travel very far in the direction of Hudson Bay to find beavers; moreover, they no longer exhibit the same industry because the climate is too cold. Diminished in number, they have fallen in intelligence and no longer develop the faculties which are born of association.[83]

These republics formerly counted 100 to 150 citizens; some were even more populous. There was to be seen near Quebec a pool formed by beavers which was sufficient to drive a sawmill. The reservoirs of these amphibians were often useful in preserving enough water for canoes to go upstream during the summer. Thus beavers did in New France for savages what an ingenious mind, a great king, and a great minister[84] performed in Old France for civilized man.

§ *Bear* § Bears are of three kinds in America: the brown or yellow bear, the black bear, and the white bear. The brown bear is small and frugivorous; he climbs trees.

The black bear is larger; he feeds on flesh, fish, and fruits, and he fishes with a singular adeptness. Sitting on the edge of a river, he seizes with his right paw the fish he sees passing in the water and throws it on the shore. If after having satisfied his hunger there remains something of his repast, he hides it. He sleeps part of the winter in dens or in hollow trees where he retires. In the first days of March when he comes out of hibernation, his first action is to purge himself with cathartic herbs. *Il vivoit de régime et mangeoit à ses heures.*[85]

The white bear or marine bear frequents the coasts of North America from the region of Newfoundland to the reaches of Baffin Bay, ferocious guardian of those frozen wildernesses.

§ *Deer* § The Canada deer is a kind of reindeer that can be tamed. His female, which has no antlers, is charming; and if her ears were shorter, she would fairly closely resemble a light English mare.

§ *Moose* §   The moose has the muzzle of the camel, the flat antlers of the fallow deer, the legs of the stag. Its coat is mixed gray, white, red, and black; its gait is rapid.

According to the savages, the moose have a king called the Great Moose; his subjects render him all sorts of services. This great moose has such long legs that eight feet of snow do not hinder him at all. His hide is invulnerable; he has an arm that comes out of his shoulder and which he uses the same way men use their arms.

The medicine men maintain that the moose has in his heart a little bone which, reduced to powder, calms the pain of childbirth; they say also that the left hoof of this quadruped, applied on the heart of epileptics, effects a radical cure. The moose, they add, is himself subject to epilepsy; when he feels an attack coming on, he draws blood from his left ear with his left hoof and is relieved.

§ *Bison* §   The bison carries his short black horns low; he has a long hairy beard; a similar tuft of hair hangs down in straggly fashion between his two horns all the way to the eyes. His chest is wide, his hindquarters slender, his tail thick and short; his legs are thick and turned outward; a hump of long reddish hair rises on his shoulders, like the dromedary's hump. The rest of his body is covered with a black wool which the Indians spin to make wheat sacks and blankets. The animal has a ferocious appearance but is very gentle.

There are varieties of bison, or if you wish, of buffalo, a Spanish word that has been anglicized. The largest are those found between the Missouri and the Mississippi; they approach the stature of a medium-sized elephant. They resemble the lion by the mane, the camel by the hump, the hippopotamus or the rhinoceros by the tail and the skin of the hindquarters, the bull by the horns and the legs.

In this species, the number of females by far surpasses that of the males. The bull courts the heifer by galloping around her. Motionless in the middle of the circle, she bellows softly. The savages imitate this play in their propitiatory games; they call it the Dance of the Bison.

75

The bison has irregular times of migration. It is not too well known where he goes; but presumably he goes far north in the summer since he is found on the shores of Slave Lake, and he has been found even on the islands of the Polar Sea. Perhaps he also reaches the valleys of the Rocky Mountains to the west and the plains of New Mexico to the south. The bison are so numerous in the green steppes of the Missouri that when they emigrate, the herd sometimes takes several days to file past, like an immense army. Their march is heard from a distance of several miles, and the earth can be felt shaking.

The Indians expertly tan the bison hide with the bark of the birch. The shoulder bone of the killed animal serves as their scraper. The meat of the bison, cut in wide thin slices and dried in the sun or smoked, is very savory; it keeps several years, like ham. The humps and the tongues of the cows are the most succulent parts to eat fresh. Bison dung produces glowing coals when burned, and it is of great use in the savannas where wood is lacking. This useful animal furnishes at the same time the food and the fire for the feast. The Sioux find in his hide both bed and clothing. The bison and the savage, placed on the same ground, are the bull and man in a state of nature: both seem to await only the plowing of a furrow to domesticate the one and to civilize the other.

§ *Skunk* §   The American skunk has near the bladder a little sack filled with a reddish liquid: when the animal is pursued, it ejects this water as it flees; the odor is such that hunters and even dogs abandon the prey. The smell becomes attached to the clothing and causes blindness. It is a kind of penetrating musk that makes one dizzy. The savages maintain that it is a prime remedy for headache.

§ *Fox* §   Canadian foxes are of the common species, except they have a shiny black tip to their fur. The way they catch aquatic birds is well known. La Fontaine, first of the naturalists, did not forget it in his immortal scenes.[86]

The Canadian fox makes a thousand jumps and capers on the edge of a lake or a river. The geese and ducks, charmed as they are, approach to watch him more closely. Then he sits down on his hindquarters and slowly waves his tail. The birds, more and more captivated, land and advance, waddling toward the sly quadruped, who pretends as much stupidity as they show. Soon the stupid creatures become bold enough to come peck at the tail of the past master, who pounces on his prey.

§ *Wolf* § There are in America different kinds of wolves: the one called *cervier* [lynx] comes during the night to howl around dwellings. He never cries more than once in the same place; his speed is so great that in less than a few minutes his voice can be heard at a prodigious distance from the spot where he was first heard.

§ *Muskrat* § The muskrat lives on young shoots of bushes in the spring and in summer on strawberries and raspberries; he eats heather berries in autumn and in winter feeds on the roots of nettles. He builds and works like the beaver. When the savages have killed a muskrat, they seem very sad. They smoke around his body and surround it with Manitous, deploring their parricide: the female muskrat is known to be the mother of mankind.

§ *Wildcat* § The wildcat is a kind of tiger or great cat. The way he hunts the moose with his confederate the fox is famous. He climbs a tree, lies down flat on a low branch, and wraps himself in his furry tail which goes around his body three times. Soon there are heard distant yelps, and a moose is seen to appear driven by three foxes who maneuver him toward the wildcat's ambush. At the moment when the flushed animal passes under the fatal tree, the wildcat falls upon it, holds it with his tail wrapped around its neck, and seeks to cut the jugular vein with his teeth. The moose jumps, beats the air with its antlers, kicks up the snow beneath its feet. It drags itself on its knees, flees in a straight line, backs up, crouches, moves jerkily, shakes its head. Its strength is ebbing, its sides heave, blood trickles along its neck, its legs tremble and give way. The three foxes arrive for the spoils. An equitable tyrant, the wildcat divides the prey equally between himself and his satellites. The savages never attack the wildcat and the foxes at that

77

moment. They say that it would be unjust to take from these four hunters the fruit of their work.

§ *Birds* §   Birds are more diversified and numerous in America than had been thought at first. So it was with Africa and Asia. The first travelers had been struck upon their arrival only by the large and brilliant feathered creatures which are like flowers in the trees; but in the intervening time, a host of little songbirds has been discovered whose voice is as sweet as that of our linnets.

§ *Fish* §   The fish in the lakes of Canada, and especially the lakes of Florida, are of an admirable beauty and brilliance.

§ *Snakes* §   America is so to speak the homeland of snakes. The water snake resembles the rattlesnake, but it has neither rattle nor venom. It is found everywhere.

I have spoken several times in my works of the rattlesnake. It is well known that the fangs it uses to spread its poison are not those with which it eats. The former can be drawn out, and it is then no more than a fairly handsome snake, full of intelligence, that passionately loves music. In the heat of midday, in the deepest silence of the forests, the male shakes his rattle to call the female. This love signal is the only sound which then strikes the traveler's ear. The female often bears 20 young; when they are pursued, they enter the mother's maw, as if they were returning into the maternal breast.

Snakes in general, and especially rattlesnakes, are held in great veneration by the American aborigines, who attribute to them a divine spirit. They tame them to the point of having them come in winter to sleep in boxes placed on the hearth of the hut. These singular Penates leave their demesne in spring to return to the woods.

A black snake that has a yellow ring at its neck is fairly dangerous; another completely black snake, nonpoisonous, climbs trees and gives chase to the birds and squirrels. He charms the birds by his gaze; that is, he frightens them. This effect of fear, which many have denied, is today proved without doubt: fear freezes a man's legs; why would it not do the same to a bird's wings?

The ribbon snake, the green snake, and the spotted snake take their names from their colors and the designs of their skins; they are perfectly harmless and of remarkable beauty.

The most remarkable of all is the one called glass snake because of the fragility of its body, which breaks at the slightest contact. This reptile is almost transparent and reflects colors like a prism. It lives on insects and does no harm. Its length is that of a small viper.

The two-headed snake is very little known. It rather resembles a viper; however, its heads are not flattened.

The hissing snake is very widespread in Georgia and the Floridas. It is 18 inches long; its skin is sprinkled with black on a green background. When it is approached, it flattens, changes color, and opens its maw, hissing. One must take care not to enter the atmosphere that surrounds it; it has the power to decompose the surrounding air. This air imprudently breathed causes one to languish. The victim wastes away, his lungs are corrupted, and at the end of a few months he dies of consumption: this is the claim of the inhabitants of the country.

§ *Trees and Plants* §   The trees, shrubs, plants, and flowers that have been transported into our woods, fields and gardens already announce the variety and richness of the vegetable kingdom in America.[87] Who today does not know the rose-crowned laurel called magnolia; the chestnut, which bears a veritable hyacinth, the catalpa, which reproduces the orange blossom; the tulip tree, which takes its name from its flower; the sugar maple, the red beech, the sassafras, and among the green resinous trees, the Lord Weymouth pine, the Virginia cedar, the Gilead balsam, and the Louisiana cypress, with its knotty roots, enormous trunk, and leaves resembling lace made of moss. The lilacs, azaleas, and pompadouras have enriched our springtime; the hart-wort, wisteria, begonia, Decumaria, and celustris have blended their flowers, their fruits, and their perfumes with the greenery of our ivies.

The flowering plants are without number: the Virginia

ephemeris, Helonias, the Canada lily, the superb lily, the multi-colored tiger lily, the pink Achillea, the dahlia, the autumn hellenia, and all the species of phlox are today mingled with our native flowers.

Finally, we have almost everywhere exterminated the savage population; and America gave us the potato, which eliminates forever famine among the peoples who were the destroyers of the Americans.

§ *Bees* §   All these plants feed brilliant insects. Among these has been received our honeybee, which came to discover these savannas and fragrant forests, subject of so many marvelous tales. It has been observed that the settlers are often preceded in the Kentucky and Tennessee woods by bees: forerunners of the plowmen, they are symbols of the industry and civilization they announce. Foreign to America, arriving in the wake of Columbus's ships, these pacific conquerors have taken from a new world of flowers only those treasures whose use was unknown to the inhabitants; they used these treasures only to enrich the earth from which they had drawn them. How fortunate it would be if all the invasions and all the conquests resembled those of these daughters of the skies!

However, the bees had to repulse myriads of mosquitoes who attacked their swarms in the tree trunks; their genius triumphed over these envious, evil, and ugly enemies. The bees were recognized queens of the wilderness, and their administrative monarchy was established in the forests beside Washington's republic.

Manners of the Indians

There are two equally faithful and unfaithful ways of painting the savages of North America: one is to speak only of their laws and their manners, without entering into details of their bizarre customs and their habits which are often disgusting to civilized men. Then all you will see will be Greeks and Romans, for the laws of the Indians are grave and their manners often charming.

The other way consists in representing only the habits and customs of the savages, without mentioning their laws and their manners; then you will see only the smoky, filthy cabins to which retires a kind of monkey endowed with human speech. Sidonius Apollinaris complained of being forced to listen to the raucous language of the German and to frequent the Burgundian who rubbed his hair with butter.[88]

I do not know if the hut of old Cato in the land of the Sabines was much cleaner than that of an Iroquois. Sly Horace might leave us some doubts on that score. Also, if one gives the same traits to all the savages of North America, the portrait will be unrealistic; the savages of Louisiana and Florida differed in many ways from the savages of Canada. Without giving the individual history of each tribe, I have gathered together everything I have learned of the Indians under these headings: *Marriages, children, funerals; Harvests, feasts, dances, and games; The year, division and regulation of time, the natural calendar; Medicine; Indian languages; Hunting; War; Religion; Government.* A general conclusion shows America as it is today.

MARRIAGES, CHILDREN, FUNERALS

There are two kinds of marriages among the savages. The first is by a simple agreement between the woman and the man; the contract is for a longer or shorter period, such as the marrying couple has been pleased to determine it. When the term of the contract has expired, the two spouses separate. Such was more or less the legal concubinage in Europe in the eighth and ninth centuries.

The second marriage is likewise made in virtue of the consent of the man and the woman, but the parents intervene. Although this marriage is not limited, as is the first, to a certain number of years, it can still be broken. It has been observed that among the Indians the second marriage, the legitimate marriage, was preferred by the girls and the old men, and the first by the old women and the young men.

When a savage has resolved on a legal marriage, he goes with his father to make the request of the wife's parents. The father puts on clothing that has never been worn before, decorates his head with new feathers, washes the old paint off his face, puts on new coloring, and changes the rings hanging from his nose or ears; in his right hand he takes a pipe with a white bowl and a blue stem feathered with birds' tails; in his left hand he holds his unstrung bow in the manner of a stick. His son follows him laden with skins of bear, beaver, and moose; he carries also two porcelain necklaces of four strands and a live dove in a cage.

The suitors go first to the girl's oldest relative; they enter his cabin, sitting before him on a mat, and the father of the young warrior, opening the conversation, says: "There are some skins. The two necklaces, the blue pipe, and the dove ask for your daughter in marriage."

If the presents are accepted, the marriage is concluded, for the consent of the grandfather or the oldest Sachem of the family takes precedence over the paternal consent. Age is the source of authority among the savages. The older a man is, the greater his influence. These people believe the divine power to be derived from the eternity of the Great Spirit.

Sometimes the old relative, while accepting the presents, attaches some restriction to his consent. This restriction is indicated if, after having three times drawn on the pipe, the smoker releases the first cloud of smoke instead of swallowing it, as in absolute consent.

From the old relative's cabin they go to the home of the girl's mother. When the girl's dreams have been unfavorable, her fear is great. The dreams in order to be favorable must not have represented spirits, ancestors, or the homeland, but should have shown cradles, birds, and white doves. There is however an infallible means of conjuring away fatal dreams by hanging a red necklace on the neck of an idol of oak. Among civilized men too, hope has its red necklaces and idols.

After this first request, everything gives the appearance of being forgotten; a considerable wait ensues before the conclusion of the marriage—the prime virtue of the savage is patience. In the most immediate perils, everything happens as usual. When the enemy is at the gates, a warrior who neglected to smoke his pipe calmly, seated crosslegged in the sun, would be labeled an old woman.

Whatever the young man's passion, then, he is obliged to affect an air of indifference and to await the orders of the family. According to the ordinary custom, the couple must first live in the cabin of their oldest relation; but often individual arrangements are opposed to the observance of this custom. Then the future husband builds his cabin. He almost always chooses to place it in some solitary valley near a stream or a spring and hidden under trees.

Like the heroes of Homer, the savages are all doctors, cooks, and carpenters. To construct the marriage hut four poles a foot in circumference and 12 feet in height are driven into the ground. They are destined to mark the four corners of a parallelogram 20 feet long by 18 wide. Notches cut in these posts receive crossbeams which form the four walls of the cabin when the space between them is filled with earth.

In the two longitudinal walls two openings are constructed: one serves as the entrance to the whole building; the other leads to a second room similar to the first, but smaller.

The groom is left to construct by himself the foundation of his dwelling, but he is aided in the rest of the work by his companions. They arrive singing and dancing and bring mason's tools made of wood; the shoulder blade of some quadruped serves them as a trowel. They slap the hand of their friend, jump on his shoulders, make jokes about marriage, and finish the cabin. By climbing on the posts and the beginnings of the walls, they raise the roof of birchbark and corn shucks; they mix wild animal hair and chopped wild oat straw with red clay and spread this mastic on the interior and exterior walls. In the center or at one of the extremities of the large room, the workmen plant five long poles which they cover with dried grass and mortar. This kind of cone becomes the chimney and allows the smoke to escape through an opening made in the roof. All this work is done in the midst of jokes and satirical songs, most of which are coarse; some are not lacking a certain grace: "The moon hides her face under a cloud: she is ashamed, she blushes; it is because she has just left the bed of the sun. So will . . . hide herself and blush the morning after her wedding, and we shall say to her: Let us see your eyes."

The blows of the hammer, the noise of the trowels, the cracking of broken branches, the laughter, the cries, and the songs are heard at a distance, and the families come out of their villages to take part in these frolics.

Once the cabin is finished on the outside, the interior is finished with plaster when the country supplies it and with clay when plaster is lacking. The sod remaining on the ground inside is removed. The workers, dancing on the damp ground, have soon smoothed and leveled it. Mats and reeds then cover the floor of this space as well as the walls of the dwelling. In a few hours is finished a hut which often hides under its bark roof more happiness than is covered by the arches of a castle.

The next day the new house is filled with all the furnishings and provisions of the proprietor: mats, stools, earthen and wooden vessels, pots, pails, bear and elk hams, dry cakes, sheaves of corn, plants for food or medicine. These diverse objects are hung on the walls or spread on planks; in a hole lined with split cane is thrown the corn and wild oats. Fishing, hunting, war and agricultural instruments, plows, traps, nets made with the pith of the false palm, hooks made from beaver teeth, bows, arrows, tomahawks, hatchets, knives, firearms, powder horns, *chichikoués*,[89] drums, fifes, pipes, thread made of sinews of buck, cloth made from the mulberry or the birch, feathers, beads, necklaces, black, azure, and vermillion coloring for decoration, a multitude of skins, some tanned, the others with their fur—such are the treasures with which the cabin is enriched.

A week before the celebration of the marriage, the young woman retires to the cabin of purifications, a place apart where the women enter and remain three or four days per month and where they go for childbirth. During the week of the retreat the engaged warrior hunts. He leaves the game in the place where he kills it; the women gather it up and carry it to the parents' cabin for the wedding feast. If the hunt has been good, the augury is favorable.

Finally the great day arrives. The medicine men and the principal Sachems are invited to the ceremony. A troop of young warriors goes to get the groom at his dwelling; a troop of girls likewise goes to get the bride in her cabin. The bride and groom are decked out in their finest and most brilliantly colored plumes, necklaces, and furs.

The two troops, by opposite roads, arrive at the same time at the hut of the oldest relation. A second door is made in this hut, opposite the ordinary one. Surrounded by his companions, the groom presents himself at one of the doors. The bride, surrounded by her companions, presents herself at the other. All the Sachems invited to the feast are seated in the cabin, pipe in mouth. The bride and groom advance and sit on rolls of skins at one end of the cabin.

Then the nuptial dance begins outside, performed by the two choruses left at the doors. The girls, armed with bent sticks, imitate the various actions of tilling the soil; the young warriors stand guard around them, their bows in hand. Suddenly an enemy party coming out of the forest attempts to carry off the women, who throw down their hoes and take flight; their brothers fly to their aid. A simulated battle begins, and the assailants are repulsed.

Following this pantomime come other scenes drawn with natural vivacity which paint domestic life, the household tasks, maintenance of the cabin, the pleasures and work of the home —touching occupations of a housewife. This spectacle ends with a round in which the girls turn in a direction opposite to that of the sun and the young warriors turn in the direction of the apparent movement of that luminary.

The feast follows: it is composed of soups, game, corncakes, canneberges (a kind of vegetable), mayapples (a kind of fruit borne by an herb), fish, grilled meats, and roasted birds. From large gourds they drink the sap of the maple or the sumac, and from little cups of beechwood they drink a cassina preparation, a hot drink served like coffee. The beauty of the feast lies in the profusion of dishes.

After the feast the crowd retires. There remain in the cabin of the oldest relative only twelve persons, six Sachems of the husband's family, six matrons of the wife's family. These twelve persons seated on the ground form two concentric circles, with the men forming the outer. The man and woman are

placed at the center of the two circles; they hold horizontally, each by one end, a reed six feet long. The groom has in his right hand a buck's foot; in her left hand the bride lifts a sheaf of corn. The reed is painted with different hieroglyphs which mark the age of the united couple and the moon in which the marriage takes place. At the wife's feet are laid the presents of the husband and his family, consisting of a complete outfit with mulberry bark skirt and bodice, a mantle of bird feathers or marten pelts, mocassins embroidered with porcupine quills, shell bracelets, and rings or beads for the nose and ears; with these clothes are included a reed cradle, a piece of agaric, rifle flints to light the fire, a cauldron for boiling the meat, a leather collar for bearing burdens, and a hearth log. The cradle stirs the heart of the bride; the cauldron and the collar do not frighten her. She looks with submission upon these marks of domestic slavery.

The husband does not remain without object lessons. A tomahawk, a bow, and a paddle announce his duties to him: fighting, hunting, and canoeing. With some tribes, a green lizard, of the kind whose movements are so rapid that the eye

can scarcely seize them, and dead leaves piled in a basket make the bridegroom understand that time is fleeting and that man falls. These people teach the morality of life by emblems, which recall the share of duties that nature has distributed to each of her children.

The couple, enclosed in the double circle of the twelve relatives, having declared that they wish to be joined, the oldest relative takes the six-foot reed. He separates it into 12 pieces, which he distributes to the 12 witnesses. Each witness is obliged to return his portion of reed to be reduced to ashes if the couple one day asks for a divorce.

The girls who brought the bride to the cabin of the oldest relative accompany her with songs to the marriage hut; the young warriors in turn lead the groom there. The guests of the celebration return to their villages. As a sacrifice to the Manitous they throw bits of their clothing into the river and burn part of their food.

In Europe they marry in order to escape the military laws; among the savages of North America no one could marry before having fought for the homeland. A man was not judged worthy of being a father until he had proved that he could defend his children. As a consequence of the manly custom, a warrior did not begin to enjoy public consideration until the day of his marriage.

The plurality of wives is permitted; a contrary abuse sometimes delivers one wife to several husbands. Coarse hordes offer their wives and daughters to strangers. It is not depravity but the deep sense of their misery which drives these Indians to that sort of infamy; they think that they will make their family happier by changing the paternal blood.

The savages of the Northwest wanted to join to their bloodline the first Negro that they saw. They took him for an evil spirit and hoped that in naturalizing him among them they would acquire intelligence and protectors among the black genies.

Adultery in the wife was formerly punished among the Hurons by the mutilation of the nose, for they wanted the fault to remain engraved on the face. In case of divorce the children are adjudged to the wife. Among the animals, say the savages, it is the female who feeds the young.

They tax with incontinence a woman who becomes pregnant the first year of her marriage; sometimes she takes the juice of a kind of rue to destroy the premature fruit; however (by an inconsistency natural to man), a woman is only esteemed when she becomes a mother. As a mother, she is called to public deliberations; the more children she has, especially sons, the more she is respected.

A husband who loses his wife marries his wife's sister when she has a sister, as a woman who loses her husband marries the brother of that husband if he has a brother. Such was more or less the Athenian law. A widow burdened with many children is much sought after.

As soon as the first symptoms of pregnancy appear, all relations cease between the couple. Toward the end of the ninth month the wife retires to the purification hut, where she is assisted by the matrons. The men, including even the husband, cannot enter this hut. The wife remains there 20 or 30 days after giving birth, depending on whether she has given birth to a girl or a boy.

When the father has received the news of the birth of his child, he takes a peace pipe whose stem he winds with virgin vines and runs to announce the happy news to the different members of the family. He goes first to the maternal parents because the child belongs exclusively to the mother. Approaching the oldest Sachem after having smoked to the four cardinal points, he presents the pipe to him, saying: "My wife is a mother." The Sachem takes the pipe, smokes in turn, and says as he takes the pipe from his mouth: "Is it a warrior?"

If the reply is affirmative, the Sachem smokes three times toward the sun; if the response is negative, the Sachem smokes only once. The father is accompanied ceremoniously to a greater or lesser distance, depending on the sex of the child. A savage who has become a father takes on a quite different authority in the nation; his dignity as a man begins with his paternity.

After the 30 or 40 days of purification, the mother prepares to return to her cabin, and the relatives assemble there to impose a name on the child. The fire is extinguished; the old ashes of the hearth are thrown to the winds, and a fire of sweet-smelling woods is prepared. The priest or medicine man, a torch in his hand, keeps himself ready to light the new fire; the place is purified all around by being sprinkled with spring water.

Soon the young mother advances. She comes alone dressed

in new clothing; she must wear nothing that she has used before. Her left breast is uncovered; she holds to it her completely naked child; she places a foot on the threshhold of her door.

The priest sets fire to the logs; the husband advances and receives his child from the hands of his wife. He recognizes him first and declares it aloud. Among some tribes only the relatives of the same sex as the child are present at the homecoming. After kissing the lips of his child, the father hands him to the oldest Sachem; the newborn passes through the hands of the whole family and receives the blessing of the priest and the good wishes of the matrons.

They then proceed to the choice of a name. The mother still remains on the threshold of the cabin. Each family has ordinarily three or four names which recur, but only names from the maternal side are considered. According to the opinion of the savages, it is the father who creates the child's soul; the mother engenders only his body:[90] they find it just that the body should have a name that comes from the mother.

When they wish to show great honor to the child, he is given the oldest name of the family, that of his grandmother, for example. From that moment the child occupies the place of the woman whose name he has received; in speaking to him they give him the relationship that his name resuscitates. Thus an uncle can greet a nephew with the title of "Grandmother," a custom that would be a cause for laughter, were it not infinitely touching. It gives back life, so to speak, to the ancestors; it reproduces in the weakness of the first years the weakness of old age; it binds together and brings close the two extremities of life, the beginning and the end of the family; it communicates a kind of immortality to the ancestors, by supposing them present in the midst of their posterity; it augments the attention the mother gives childhood by reminding her of the attention given hers: filial tenderness redoubles maternal love.

After the giving of the name, the mother enters the cabin; her child is returned to her and henceforth belongs only to her. She puts him in a cradle. This cradle is a little board of the lightest wood, covered with a bed of moss or wild cotton. The child is placed nude on this bed; two bands of a soft leather hold him there and keep him from falling without keeping him from moving. Above the head of the newborn is a hoop over which is stretched a veil to keep away the insects and to give coolness and shade to the little creature.

I have spoken elsewhere[91] of the Indian mother; I have told how she carries her children; how she hangs them on the branches of trees; how she sings to them; how she decks them out, puts them to sleep, and wakes them up; how, after their death, she mourns them; how she goes to spill her milk on the grass of their tomb, or gather their souls in flowers.[92]

After marriage and birth, it is fitting to speak of death, which ends the scenes of life; but I have so often described the funerals of the savages that the subject is almost exhausted. Therefore I shall not repeat what I have said in *Atala* and in *The Natchez* relative to the manner in which they dress the deceased, paint him, converse with him, etc. I shall add only that, among all the tribes, it is customary to ruin oneself for the dead: the family distributes what it possesses to the guests of the funeral repast; they must eat and drink all that is to be found in the cabin. At sunrise, they utter great shrieks over the bark coffin in which lies the body; at sunset, the shrieks begin anew; that lasts three days, at the end of which the deceased is buried. He is covered with the burial mound; if he was a renowned warrior, a post painted red marks his grave.

Among several tribes the relatives of the dead man wound themselves on the arms and legs. For a month the cries of grief at sunset and sunrise are continued, and for several years the same cries greet the anniversary of the loss they have suffered.

When a savage dies in winter on the hunt, his body is preserved on the branches of the trees; last honors are given him only after the return of the warriors to his tribe's village. Such was the practice formerly among the Muscovites.

Not only do the Indians have prayers and ceremonies that are different according to the degree of relationship, station, age, and sex of the person deceased but also they have times of public exhumation[93] and general commemoration.

Why are the savages of America the ones who, of all peoples, have the most veneration for the dead? In national calamities the first thing thought of is saving the treasures of the tombs; lawful property is recognized only where the ancestors are buried. When the Indians have argued their rights of possession, they have always used this argument, which seemed unanswerable to them: "Shall we say to our fathers: Arise, and follow us to a foreign land?" When this argument was not heeded, what did they do? They carried away the bones since they could not follow by themselves.

The reason for this extraordinary attachment to holy relics is easily found. Civilized people have monuments of letters and arts to preserve the memories of their homeland; they have cities, palaces, towers, columns, obelisks; they have the furrows in the fields they have cultivated; their names are engraved on bronze and marble; their actions are preserved in chronicles.

The savages have nothing of all that: their names are not written on the trees of the forests; their hut, built in a few hours, perishes in a few moments; their simple plowing stick, which has only grazed the earth, has not even been able to raise a furrow; their traditional songs vanish with the last memory that retains them, with the last voice that repeats them. Therefore for the tribes of the New World there is only one monument: the tomb. Take away from the savages the bones of their fathers, and you take away from them their history, their law, and even their gods; in the eyes of posterity you strip these men of the proof of their existence as well as the proof of their nothingness.

HARVESTS, CELEBRATIONS, MAPLE SUGAR MAKING, FISHING, DANCES, AND GAMES

§ *Harvests* §   It has been believed and said that the savages did not make use of the soil: that is a mistake. They are principally hunters, to be sure, but they all devote themselves to some kind of cultivation; they all know how to use the plants and trees to satisfy the needs of life. Those who occupied the fine country which forms today the states of Georgia, Tennessee, Alabama, and Mississippi were in this respect more civilized than the natives of Canada.

Among the savages all public works are celebrations. When the last of the cold weather has passed, the Seminole, Chickasaw, and Natchez women arm themselves with hickory crooks and place on their heads divided baskets filled with corn, beans, and watermelon and sunflower seeds. They go to the common field, usually placed in an easily defended place, such as a tongue of land between two rivers or inside a circle of hills.

At one end of the field, the women line up and begin to stir up the earth with their crooks, walking backward. While they thus freshen the old plowing without forming a furrow, other Indian women follow them seeding the land prepared by their companions. The beans and the corn are thrown together on the plowed land; the cornstalks being destined to serve as stakes for the climbing vegetable.

Girls busy themselves making beds of black washed earth; they spread squash and sunflower seeds on these beds; around the beds they light fires of green wood to hasten the germination by means of smoke. The Sachems and medicine men preside over the work while the young men would range around the common field driving off the birds with their cries.

§ *Celebrations* §   The Feast of the Green Corn took place in June. They collected a certain quantity of corn while the grains were still milky. From these grains, excellent at that point, they kneaded out *tossomanony*, a kind of cake that serves as provision on war expeditions or hunting trips.

The ears of corn, put to boil in spring water, are taken out half cooked and placed over embers. When they have taken on a russet color, they are shelled into a *poutagan* or wooden mortar. The grains are moistened and ground. This dough, cut in slices and dried in the sun, keeps indefinitely. When one wished to use it, he needed only to dip it in water, hickory milk,[94] or maple sap; thus soaked, it offers a nourishing and agreeable food.

The greatest feast of the Natchez was the Feast of the New Fire, a kind of jubilee in honor of the sun at the time of the great harvest. The sun was the principal divinity of all the peoples neighboring on the Mexican empire.

A public crier went through the villages announcing the

ceremony to the sound of a conch shell. He caused these words to be heard: "Let every family prepare virgin vases, clothing that has never been worn; let the cabins be washed; let the old grain, the old clothing, the old utensils be thrown out and burned in a common fire in the center of each village; let the malefactors return: the Sachems forget their crimes."

This amnesty, accorded to men at the moment when the earth lavishes its treasures, this generous call to the happy and the unfortunate, the innocent and the guilty, to the great banquet of nature, was a touching holdover from the primitive simplicity of the human race.

The crier reappeared the second day, prescribed a fast of 72 hours, a rigorous abstinence from all pleasure, and at the same time ordered purification medicine. All the Natchez would immediately take a few drops from a root that they called blood root. This root belongs to a kind of plantain; from it is distilled a red liquid that is a violent emetic. During the three days of abstinence and prayer, deep silence was observed; they tried to detach themselves from worldly things to think only of Him who ripens the fruit on the tree and the grain in the stalk.

At the end of the third day, the crier proclaimed the opening of the celebration, fixed for the next day. Scarcely had dawn lightened the sky when were seen advancing all over the paths bright with dew, the girls, the young warriors, the matrons, and the Sachems. The temple of the sun, a great cabin that received light only through two doors, one facing west and one east, was the gathering place; the eastern door was opened; the interior walls of the temple were covered with fine mats painted and decorated with various hieroglyphs. Baskets arranged in orderly fashion in the sanctuary held the bones of the oldest chiefs of the nation, like the tombs in our Gothic churches.

On an altar, placed opposite the eastern door so as to receive the first rays of the rising sun, stood an idol representing a *chouchouacha*.[95] This animal, the size of a suckling pig, has the hair of a badger, the tail of a rat, the feet of a monkey; the female has under her belly a pocket where she nourishes her young. To the right of the image of the *chouchouacha* was the figure of a rattlesnake, to the left a crudely fashioned grotesque figure. In a stone vase before the symbol an oak bark fire was tended and never allowed to go out, except on the eve of the feast of new fire or of the harvest. The firstfruits were hung around the altar; the participants were arranged thus in the temple: The Great Chief or Sun, to the right of the altar; to the left, the Squaw Chief, who, alone of all the women, had the right to penetrate into the sanctuary; beside the Sun were stationed successively the two war chiefs, the two officers for treaties, and the principal Sachems. Beside the Squaw Chief sat the aedile or inspector of public works, the four heralds of the festivities, and then the young warriors. On the ground before the altar lengths of dried cane, laid at an angle on one another to the height of 18 inches, traced concentric circles whose ultimate revolutions departing from the center had a diameter of 12 to 13 feet.

The high priest at the door of the temple kept his eyes fixed on the east. Before presiding over the feast he had three times plunged into the Mississippi. A white robe of birchbark covered him, attached around the waist by a snakeskin. The old stuffed owl that he formerly wore on his head had given way to a young owl. The priest slowly rubbed together two pieces of dry wood and whispered magic words. At his sides, two acolytes lifted up by the handles two goblets filled with a kind of black sherbet. Each of the women, back to the east, one hand resting on the plowing crook, the other holding her small children, stood in a great circle at the door of the temple.

This ceremony had something august about it: the true God makes Himself felt even in the false religions, and the man who prays is worthy of respect; the prayer that is addressed to the Divinity is so holy in its nature that it gives something sacred to the one who says it, whether he is innocent, guilty, or unfortunate. It was a touching spectacle, that of a nation assembled in a wilderness at harvest time to thank the Almighty for his bounty, to sing the Creator who perpetuates the memory of creation each morning by ordering the sun to rise over the earth.

Meanwhile a profound silence reigned in the crowd. The high priest attentively watched the variations in the sky. When the colors of the dawn, transformed from rose to deep red, began to be pierced by rays of pure fire and became brighter and brighter, the priest hurried the rubbing of the two pieces of dry wood. A sulfured elderberry pith fuse was prepared to receive the spark. The two masters of ceremonies advanced in measured step, one toward the Great Chief, the other toward the Squaw Chief. From time to time they bowed; and stopping finally before the Great Chief and the Squaw Chief, they remained completely motionless.

Torrents of flame escaped from the east, and the upper portion of the sun's disc appeared above the horizon. At that instant the high priest cried the sacred oath, the fire shot forth from the wood heated by the rubbing, the sulfured fuse ignited, the women outside the temple turned around suddenly and all at once raised toward the orb of day their newborn children and the plowing crook.

The Great Chief and the Squaw Chief drank the black sherbet, which the masters of ceremonies presented to them; the medicine man transferred the fire to the circles of reeds: the flame wound about following their spiral. The oak bark was lighted on the altar, and this new fire then gave a new life to the dead hearths of the village. The Great Chief intoned the hymn to the sun.

When the circles of reed were consumed and the canticle terminated, the Squaw Chief would leave the temple and place herself at the head of the women, who in a line would go to the common field of the harvest. It was not permitted for the men to follow. The women went to gather the first sheaves of corn to offer them to the temple and to knead out of the rest the unleavened bread for the night's banquet.

When they arrived at the fields, the women pulled from the plot allowed to their family a certain number of the finest sheaves of corn, a superb plant whose seven-foot stalks, surrounded by green leaves and surmounted by a cluster of golden beads, resemble the staff surrounded by ribbons which our peasant girls consecrate in the village churches. Thousands of blue thrushes, of little doves the size of a blackbird, and of rice-paddy birds, whose gray plumage is mixed with brown, light on the stems of the sheaves and fly away at the approach of the American harvesters, entirely hidden in the avenues of the great stalks. The black foxes sometimes ravage these fields.

These women came back to the temple bearing the firstfruit of the harvest in a bundle on their heads; the high priest received the offering and deposited it on the altar. The eastern door of the sanctuary was closed, and the western door was opened.

Gathered at the western door as the day was to end, the crowd would trace a crescent whose two points were turned toward the sun; those present, their right arms raised, would offer the unleavened bread to the heavenly body. The medicine man sang the hymn of the evening; it was the praise of the sun at its setting: its nascent rays had made the corn grow, its dying rays had sanctified the cakes formed of the grain from the harvested stalk.

When night had come, fires were lit; bear cubs were roasted; fattened on wild grapes, they made a delicious dish at this season of the year. Grilling over the coals were turkeys of the savannas, black partridges, and a kind of pheasant larger than those of Europe. The birds thus prepared were called the food of white men. The drinks and the fruits served at these repasts were the juice of smilax, maple, plane, and white walnut, and mayapples, plankmines, and nuts. The plain was resplendent with the flame of the fires; on all sides were heard the sounds of the *chichicoué*, the drum, and the fife, mingled with the voices of the dancers and the applause of the crowd.

In these celebrations, if some unfortunate was standing apart staring at the plain, a Sachem would seek him out to inquire after the cause of his sadness; he would remedy his ill, if it was not beyond remedy, or would at least comfort him if it was hopeless.

The corn harvest consists in pulling up the stalks or cutting them off two feet above the ground. The grain is kept in skins or in holes lined with reeds. Whole stalks are kept too; they are shelled as needed. To reduce the corn to flour, it is crushed in a mortar or between two stones. The savages also use handmills bought from the Europeans.

The harvest of wild oats or wild rice immediately follows that of the corn. I have spoken elsewhere of this harvest.[96]

§ *Maple Sugar Making*[97] § The gathering of maple sap was done, and is still done, among the savages twice a year. The first harvest takes place toward the end of February, March, or April, according to the latitude of the country where the sugar maple grows. The liquid gathered after the light freeze of the night is converted to sugar by boiling it over a high fire. The quantity of sugar obtained by this process varies according to the quality of the tree. This sugar, which is easily digestible, is of a greenish color, of an agreeable and slightly acid taste.

The second harvest takes place when the sap of the tree does not have so thick a consistency. This sap is condensed into a kind of molasses which diluted with spring water produces a cool drink during the heat of summer.

They maintain with great care the forests of maples of the red and white varieties. The most productive maples are those whose bark appears black and mangy. The savages think they have observed that these accidents are caused by the redheaded black woodpecker, who pierces the maple whose sap is most abundant. They respect this woodpecker as an intelligent bird and good genie.

Approximately four feet from the ground they open in the maple trunk two holes three quarters of an inch deep, inclined downward to facilitate the flow of the sap. These first two incisions are turned to the south; two other similar ones are made on the north side. These four cuts are then dug out, as the tree gives its sap, to a depth of two and one-half inches. Two wooden troughs are placed on the two sides of the tree, north and south, and tubes of elder introduced into the cuts serve to direct the sap to the troughs.

After 24 hours the sap that has run out is collected and carried into bark-covered sheds; it is boiled in a stone basin and skimmed the while. When it is reduced to half by the action of a lively fire, it is poured into another basin, where it is again boiled until it has the consistency of syrup. Then, removed from the fire, it is allowed to set for 12 hours. At the end of this time it is cast into a third basin, care being taken not to stir up the sediment that has fallen to the bottom of the liquid.

This third basin is in turn put on glowing embers. A little grease is thrown into the syrup to keep it from overflowing the edges of the container. When it begins to spin threads, it must quickly be turned into a fourth and last basin of wood, called the cooler. A strong woman stirs it continuously with a cedar staff until it has taken on the grain of sugar. Then she pours it into molds of bark, which give the solidified liquid the form of little conical loaves. The operation is completed. When it is a question of molasses, the process stops at the second firing.

The flow of the maples lasts two weeks, and these two weeks are a continuous celebration. Every morning the Indians go to the maple forest, which ordinarily has a stream running through it. Groups of men and women are scattered at the feet of the trees, young people dance or play at different games, and children bathe under the watch of the Sachems. From the gaiety of the savages, their seminudity, the liveliness of their dances, the no less noisy battles of the bathers, the movement and coolness of the water, and the age of the shade trees, one would think he was in attendance at one of those scenes of fauns and dryads described by the poets.

> Tum vero in numerum Faunosque ferasque videres
> Ludere.[98]

§ *Fishing* §   The savages are as skillful in fishing as they are adroit in hunting. They catch fish with hooks and nets, but also know how to take fish by draining ponds. They have great public fishing expeditions. The most famous of these was the sturgeon fishing, which took place on the Mississippi and its tributaries.

It opened by the marriage of the net. Six warriors and six matrons bearing the net would advance into the midst of the spectators on the public square and ask for two girls whom they pointed out, as wives for their son, the net. The relatives of the girls gave their consent, and the girls were married by the medicine man with the customary ceremonies. The Doge of Venice married the sea!

Characteristic dances followed the marriage. After the marriage of the net, they would go to the river, at whose edge were assembled the boats and the canoes. The new brides, wrapped in the net, were carried at the head of the procession. The participants embarked after arming themselves with pine torches and stones to kindle a fire. The net, his wives, the medicine man, the Great Chief, four Sachems, and eight warriors to man the oars would get into a great canoe, which took the lead of the flotilla.

The flotilla sought out some bay frequented by the sturgeon. On the way, they fished for all the other kinds of fish: trout by the net, the armored fish by the hook. The sturgeon is struck with a dart attached to a rope knotted to the inside crossbar of the boat. The wounded fish swims away dragging the boat along; but little by little his pace slackens, and he comes to die at the surface of the water. The different attitudes of the fishermen, the play of the oars, the movement of the sails, the position of the canoes, grouped or dispersed, exposing the side, the bow or the stern, all that is a most picturesque sight. The earth's landscapes form the motionless backdrop to this moving scene.

At nightfall, torches were lit in the canoes, reflecting their light on the surface of the waters. The fast-moving boats threw masses of shadow on the reddened waves; one would take these Indian fishermen, moving about in their vessels, for their Manitous, those fantastic beings, creations of the savages' superstitions and dreams.

At midnight, the medicine man would give the signal to withdraw, declaring that the net wished to retire with his two wives. The canoes drew up in two lines. A torch was placed symmetrically in a horizontal position between each pair of oarsmen on the edge of the canoes; the torches, parallel to the surface of the river, appeared and disappeared from sight with the motion of the waves and resembled flaming oars plunging into the water to propel the boats.

Then was sung the epithalamium of the net: the net, in all the glory of a new bridegroom, was declared conqueror of the sturgeon who wears a crown and is 12 feet long. They painted the ruin of the entire piscatorial army. The lencornet, whose barbs serve to entwine his enemy, the chaousaron, provided with a serrated lance, hollow and pierced at the end, the artimegue who flies a white flag, the crayfish who precede the warrior-fish to clear the way—all were conquered by the net.

Then came stanzas which told of the grief of the fish widows: "In vain these widows learn to swim, for they will no more see those with whom they loved to wander through the forests under the surface of the water; no more will they rest with them on beds of moss beneath transparent arches." The net is invited, after so many exploits, to sleep in the arms of his two wives.

§ *Dances* § Dancing among the savages, as among the ancient Greeks and most primitive peoples, is combined with all the actions of life. They dance for marriages, and women take part in that dance; they dance to receive a guest, to smoke a peace pipe; they dance for the harvest; they dance for the birth of a child; they dance above all for the dead. Each hunt has its dance, which consists of the imitation of the movements, habits, and cries of the animal whose hunt is decided upon: they climb like a bear, build like a beaver, gallop around like a bison, bound like a buck, howl like a wolf, and yelp like a fox.

In the dance of the braves or war dance, the warriors, completely armed, line up in two rows; a child walks before them, a *chichicoué* in his hand; he is the child of dreams, the child who has dreamed under the influence of the good or bad Manitous. Behind the warriors comes the medicine man, the prophet or augur-interpreter of the dreams of the child.

The dancers soon form a double circle, growling quietly, while the child remains in the center of the circle; his eyes lowered, he mutters some unintelligible words. When the child lifts his head, the warriors jump and growl more loudly. They consecrate themselves to Athaënsic, Manitou of hate and vengeance. A kind of coryphaeus marks the beat by striking a drum. Sometimes the dancers attach to their feet little bells bought from the Europeans.

If they are on the point of leaving for an expedition, a chief takes the place of the child, harangues the warriors, strikes with a club an image representing a man or the enemy's Manitou, coarsely drawn on the ground. The warriors start dancing again, and with convulsions and screaming likewise assail the image, imitate the attitudes of the fighting man, brandish their clubs or hatchets, handle their muskets or bows, and wave their knives.

Upon returning from the expedition, the war dance is even more frightful: heads, hearts, mutilated members, and bleeding scalps are hung on pikes planted in the ground. They dance around these trophies, and the prisoners who are to be burned are present at the spectacle of these horrible pleasures. I shall speak of other dances of this nature in the article on war.

§ *Games* § Games are an activity common to mankind; they have three sources: nature, society, passions. Therefore they are of three kinds: the games of childhood, the games of virility, the games of idleness or passion.

The games of childhood, invented by the children themselves, are to be found throughout the world. I have seen the little Indian, the little Bedouin, the little Negro, the little Frenchman, the little Englishman, the little German, the little Italian, the little Spaniard, the little oppressed[99] Greek, and the little Turk his oppressor, throw balls and roll hoops. Who showed these children who are so diverse in language, so different in their races, their manners, and their country, who taught them the same games? The Master of men, the Father of the great and same family. He taught these amusements to innocence as a development of strength, a need of nature.

The second class of games includes those which, by serving to teach an art, fulfill a social necessity. Among these must be classed the gymnastics, chariot races, and naumachia of the ancients, the jousts, tilts, feats of arms, and tournaments of the Middle Ages, and finally the tennis, fencing, horse races, and games of skill of the moderns. The theater with its splendor is a thing apart, and genius demands it as one of its recreations. So it is with some mental combinations, such as checkers and chess.

Games of the third kind are games of chance, those in which man exposes his fortune, his honor, sometimes his liberty and his life, with a fury that approaches delirium; it is a need of the passions. Dice among the ancients, cards among the moderns, bones among the savages of North America are among these regrettable recreations.

The three kinds of games I have just mentioned are to be found among the Indians. The games of their children are those of our children; they have the ball and the racket, races, archery for the young people, and also the feather game, which recalls an old game of the days of chivalry.

The warriors and girls dance around four posts on which are attached feathers of different colors. From time to time a young man leaves the quadrilles and takes a feather of the color worn by his mistress; he attaches this feather to his hair and returns to the dancing groups. By the arrangement of the feather and the kind of step, the Indian girl guesses the place her lover is indicating for a rendezvous. There are warriors who take feathers of a color worn by no dancer; this act means the warrior does not love or is not loved. Married women are admitted only as spectators at this game.

Among the games of the third kind, the games of idleness or of the passions, I shall describe only the game of bones. In this game, the savages bet their wives, their children, their liberty; and when they have played on their word and have lost, they keep their promise. A strange thing! Man, who often fails to observe the most sacred oaths, who laughs at law, who unscrupulously deceives his neighbor and sometimes his friend, who prides himself on ruse and duplicity, is honorbound to fulfill the obligations of his passions, to keep his word in crime, to be sincere toward the often guilty authors of his ruin and the accomplices of his depravity.

In the game of bones, also called the plate game, only two players take part; the other players bet for or against. The two adversaries each have a person who is their marker. The game is played on a table or simply on the grass. The two active players are provided with six or eight dice or bones resembling apricot stones cut with six unequal faces. The two largest faces are painted, one white, the other black. The bones are mixed in a slightly concave dish of wood; the player spins the dish; then, striking the table or the grass, he makes the bones jump into the air. If all the bones fall with the same color up, the one who has played wins five points. If five bones out of six or eight have the same color up, the player earns only one point the first time; but if the same player repeats the same play, he makes a clean sweep and wins the game, which is for forty points. As a player wins points, they are deducted from the adversary's score. The winner continues to play; the loser cedes his place to one of the bettors on his side called at will by his side's marker. The markers are the principal participants in this game; they are chosen with great precaution, and those are especially preferred whose Manitou is believed strongest and most adroit.

The designation of the markers brings about violent debates. If one side has named a marker whose Manitou, that is to say, fortune, is known as redoubtable, the other side opposes this nomination. They sometimes greatly appreciate the idea of the power of the Manitou belonging to a man they detest; in this case, interest prevails over passion, and that man is adopted for marker in spite of the hatred they bear him.

The marker holds in his hand a little board on which he notes the plays in red chalk. The savages press tightly around the players; all eyes are attached on the dish and the bones; each one offers vows and makes promises to the good spirits. Sometimes the sums bet on the play are immense for the Indians. Some have pledged their cabins; others have stripped themselves of their clothes and bet them against those of the opposing party; others who have already lost everything they possess finally propose their liberty against a small bet; they offer to serve for a certain number of months or years the one who wins a game from them.

The players prepare for their ruin by religious observances: they fast, they keep vigil, they pray; the young men withdraw from their mistresses, the married men from their wives; the dreams are observed with care. The interested parties arm themselves with a bag in which they put all the things they have dreamed of, little bits of wood, leaves of trees, teeth of fish, and a hundred other Manitous deemed propitious. Anxiety is painted on their faces during the day, for the assembly would not be more moved were the fate of the nation at stake. They crowd around the marker; they seek to touch him, to put themselves under his influence; it is a veritable frenzy; each play is preceded by a profound silence and followed by a lively acclamation. The applause of those who win, the imprecations of those who lose, are directed at the markers, and men, ordinarily chaste and moderate in their speech, spew out oaths of remarkable coarseness and atrocity.

When the play is to be decisive, it is often halted. The bettors of one or the other of the parties declare that the moment is fatal, that the bones must no longer be thrown. A player, apostrophizing the bones, reproaches them with their wickedness and threatens to burn them; another does not want the affair to be decided until he has thrown a bit of petun[100] in the river; several people with loud cries ask for the throwing of the bones; but one opposing voice is enough to stop the play as a matter of prerogative. When it would seem they were at the final moment, one of those present cries: "Stop. Stop! The furnishings of my cabin are bringing me bad luck!" He runs to his cabin, breaks and throws out the door all his furniture, and returns saying, "Play! Play!"

Often a bettor imagines that a certain man is bringing him bad luck; this man must leave the game if he is not taking part, or there must be found another man whose Manitou in the judgment of the bettor can overcome that of the man who brings bad luck. It has happened that French commanders in Canada, witnesses of these deplorable scenes, have seen themselves forced to withdraw to satisfy the caprice of an Indian. And these caprices must not be treated lightly; the whole nation would be up in arms on behalf of the player; religion would take a hand in the affair, and blood would flow.

Finally, when the decisive play is made, few Indians have the strength to bear the sight of it; most of them throw themselves on the ground, close their eyes, stop up their ears, and wait for the decree of fortune as one would await a sentence of life or death.

YEAR, DIVISION AND ORDERING
OF TIME, NATURAL CALENDAR

§ *Year* § The savages divide the year into 12 moons, a division that strikes all men; for the moon, disappearing and reappearing 12 times, visibly cuts the year into 12 parts, while the solar year, the true year, is not indicated by variations in the sun's disk.

§ *Division of Time* §   The 12 moons draw their names from the labors, the blessings, and the evils of the savages, and from the gifts and accidents of nature; consequently these names vary according to the country and the ways of the diverse peoples; Charlevoix quotes a great number of them. A modern traveler[101] gives thus the months of the Sioux and the Chippewas:

SIOUX MONTHS		SIOUX LANGUAGE
March	Moon of the eye sickness	Wisthociasia-onì
April	Moon of game	Mograhoandì-onì
May	Moon of nests	Mograhochandà-onì
June	Moon of strawberries	Wojusticiascià-onì
July	Moon of cherries	Chamoasciä-onì
August	Moon of buffaloes	Tantankakiocu-onì
September	Moon of wild oats	Wasipi-onì
October	Moon of the end of wild oats	Sciwostapi-onì
November	Moon of the buck	Takiouka-onì
December	Moon of the buck losing his horns	Ah esciakiouska-onì
January	Moon of valor	Ouwikari-onì
February	Moon of wildcats	Owiciata-onì

CHIPPEWA MONTHS		ALGONQUIAN LANGUAGE
June	Moon of strawberries	Hode ï min-quìsìs
July	Moon of burned fruit	Mikin-quìsìs
August	Moon of yellow leaves	Wathebaqui-quìsìs
September	Moon of falling leaves	Inaqui-quìsìs
October	Moon of passing game	Bina-hamo-quìsìs
November	Moon of snow	Kaskadino-quìsìs
December	Moon of the Little Spirit	Manito-quìsìs
January	Moon of the Great Spirit	Kitci manito-quìsìs
February	Moon of arriving eagles	Wamebinni-quìsìs
March	Moon of hard snow	Ouabanni-quìsìs
April	Moon of snow shoes	Pokaodaquimi-quìsìs
May	Moon of flowers	Wabigon-quìsìs

The years are counted by snows or flowers. The old man and the girl find thus the symbol of their age in the number of their years.

§ *Natural Calendar* § In astronomy, the Indians scarcely know anything other than the north star; they call it the motionless star; it serves as their guide at night. The Osages have observed and named some constellations. During the day the savages have no need of a compass; in the savannas the grass tips leaning toward the south, in the forests the moss attached to the tree trunks on the north side, show them the north and the south. They know how to draw on bark geographical maps where the distances are indicated by the number of nights of march. The limits of their territory are rivers, mountains, a rock where a treaty has been concluded, a grave on the edge of a forest, a cave of the Great Spirit in a valley.

The birds, the quadrupeds, and the fish serve as barometers, thermometers, and calendars for the savages; they say that the beaver taught them to build and to govern themselves, the wildcat to hunt with dogs as he hunts with wolves, the water plover to fish with an oil which attracts fish.

The pigeons with their countless flights and the American woodcocks with their ivory beaks announce autumn to the Indians; the parrots and the woodpeckers predict rain with vibrating calls.

When the maukawis, a kind of quail, makes his song heard in April from sunrise to sunset, the Seminole rests assured that the cold is past; the women sow the summer grains; but when the maukawis perches at night on a cabin, the inhabitant of the cabin prepares to die.

If the white bird plays high in the air, he announces a storm; if he flies at night before the traveler, throwing himself first on one wing then another, as if frightened, he predicts danger.

In the great events of the nation, the medicine men affirm that Kit-chi-manitou shows himself above the clouds borne by his favorite bird, the wakon, a kind of bird of paradise with brown wings whose tail is decorated with four long green and red feathers.

The harvests, the games, the hunts, the dances, the assemblies of Sachems, the ceremonies of marriage, birth, or death —everything is regulated by a few observations drawn from the story of nature. One feels how much grace and poetry these customs must spread throughout the ordinary language of these peoples. Our people frolic in the wading pond, climb the maypole, harvest in mid-August, plant onions on Saint Fiacre's day, marry on Saint Nicholas's day.

MEDICINE

The science of the doctor is a kind of initiation among the savages: it is called the great medicine; one becomes affiliated with it as with freemasonry; it has its secrets, its dogma, its rites.

If the Indians could ban from the treatment of the ill the superstitious customs and the quackery of the priests, they would know all the essentials of the art of healing; one could even say that this art is almost as advanced among them as among the civilized peoples.

They know a multitude of specifics proper for closing wounds; they know the use of the *garent oguen*, which they also call *abasoutchenza*, because of its form; it is the ginseng of the Chinese. With the second bark of the sassafras they calm intermittent fevers; the roots of the ivy-leafed lychnis is beneficial to them in reducing distention of the stomach; they use the Canada Bellis, six feet high, with thick and fluted leaves, for gangrene: it completely cleans out the sores, whether it is reduced to powder, or applied raw and crushed.

The three-leafed hedisaron, with its red flowers arranged in a spike, has the same virtue as the Bellis.

According to the Indians, the forms of the plants have analogies and resemblances with the different parts of the human body which these plants are destined to cure or with the harmful animals whose venom they neutralize. This observation would merit consideration. The simple peoples, who disdain less than we the indications of Providence, are less subject than we to being mistaken.

One of the great treatments used by the savages in many sicknesses is the steam bath. For this purpose they build a cabin that they call the sweat cabin. It is constructed with branches fixed in the ground to form a circle and gathered together at the top to form a cone; they are then covered on the outside with skins of different animals. A small opening is made at the ground level through which one can crawl. In the middle of this sweating room is a basin full of water that they boil by throwing in stones heated red hot in the fire;[102] the steam which rises from this basin is burning hot, and within a few minutes the patient is covered with sweat.

Surgery is not nearly as advanced as medicine among the Indians. However, they have managed to substitute for our instruments ingenious inventions. They understand very well the application of bandages to simple fractures; they have bones as pointed as lancets to use to bleed and to scarify rheumatic members; they suck the blood by means of a horn and draw out the prescribed quantity. Gourds full of combustible material which they set on fire take the place of cupping glasses. They open blisters with the sinew of a buck and make siphons with the bladders of various animals.

The principle of the fumigatory box, used for a time in Europe in the treatment of drowned persons, is known to the Indians. They use for this purpose a large intestine closed on one end, open on the other and ending in a little wooden tube. This intestine is blown up with smoke, and the smoke is passed into the intestines of the drowned person.

In each family they keep what is called the medicine sack; it is a sack filled with Manitous and different specifics of great power. This sack is carried to war. In the camps it is a palladium, in the cabin one of the Lares.

The women during their lying-in retire to the cabin of purifications; they are aided there by matrons. These, in the ordinary births, have sufficient knowledge, but in the difficult births they suffer from the lack of instruments. When the child is presented badly and they cannot turn him around, they suffocate the mother, who, struggling against death, delivers her fruit by the effort of a last convulsion. They always inform the woman in labor before having recourse to this means; she never hesitates to sacrifice herself. Sometimes the suffocation is not complete; at the same time they save the child and his heroic mother.

It is also the practice in desperate cases to cause a great fear to the woman in confinement; a band of young men approach in silence the cabin of purifications and suddenly utter a war cry. This clamor fails in its effect with the courageous women, and there are many of them.

When a savage falls ill, all his relatives go to his hut. The word *death* is never pronounced in the presence of a friend of the sick person. The most outrageous insult that can be made to a man is to say to him: "Your father is dead."

We have seen the serious side of the savages' medicine; now we shall see the amusing side, the side an Indian Molière would have painted, if there were not something sad about that which recalls the moral and physical infirmities of our nature.

If the patient has fainting spells, in the intervals when he might be considered dead, the relatives, seated according to degree of relationship around the dying man's mat, utter screams that could be heard from half a league away. When the patient regains his senses, the screams cease, to begin again at the first crisis.

Meanwhile the medicine man arrives; the patient asks him if he will return to life. The medicine man does not fail to answer that he is the only one who can restore him to life. Then the patient who thinks himself near death harangues his relatives, consoles them, invites them to banish sadness and to eat well.

The patient is covered with grasses, roots, and bits of bark; with a pipestem they blow on the parts of the patient's body where the illness is supposed to be residing; the medicine man speaks into his mouth to conjure, if there is still time, the infernal spirit.

The patient orders the funeral meal himself. All food that remains in the cabin must be consumed. They begin to slaughter the dogs so they can go to inform the Great Spirit of the imminent arrival of their master. With all this childishness, the simplicity with which a savage accomplishes the last act of life has nonetheless something sublime about it.

By declaring that the patient is going to die, the medicine man protects his science against the effect of an unfortunate event and causes admiration for his art if the patient recovers his health. When he sees that the danger is passed, he says nothing, but begins his adjurations.

First he pronounces words that no one understands; then he

cries: "I shall discover the evil spell; I shall force Kitchi-Manitou to flee before me."

He goes out of the hut; the relatives follow him; he runs into the sweating cabin to receive divine inspiration. Arranged in mute terror around the sweating room, the relatives hear the priest scream, sing, and cry, accompanying himself with the *chichicoué*. Soon he comes out completely nude from the opening of the hut, frothing at the mouth, his eyes crossed. He dives, dripping with sweat, into icy water, rolls on the ground, plays dead, revives, and flies to his hut, ordering the relatives to go wait for him at the patient's hut. Soon he is seen to return, holding a smouldering ember in his mouth and a snake in his hand.

After new contortions around the patient, he drops the ember and cries: "Awake, I promise you life; the Great Spirit has caused me to know the spell which was killing you." The frenzied priest throws himself on the arm of his dupe, tears it open with his teeth, taking out of his own mouth a little bone that he had kept hidden there: "There," he cries, "is the spell which I have torn from your flesh!" Then he asks for a deer and some trout to make a feast, or else the sick man could not get well. The relatives are obliged to go hunting and fishing immediately.

The doctor eats the dinner; that does not suffice. The patient is threatened with a relapse if they do not obtain within an hour the cloak of a chief who resides two or three days' march from there. The medicine man knows it; but as he prescribes at the same time the rule and the dispensations, for the consideration of four or five profane cloaks furnished by the relatives, he releases them from supplying the sacred cloak demanded by heaven.

The fantasies of the patient, who quite naturally returns to life, increase the bizarre nature of this cure. The patient escapes from his bed, drags himself on his hands and feet behind the furnishings of the cabin. Vainly is he questioned; he continues his round and utters strange cries. He is seized and put back on his mat; he is believed to be subject to an attack of his illness; he remains quiet a moment and then gets up without warning and dives into a pond; he is removed from it only with

111

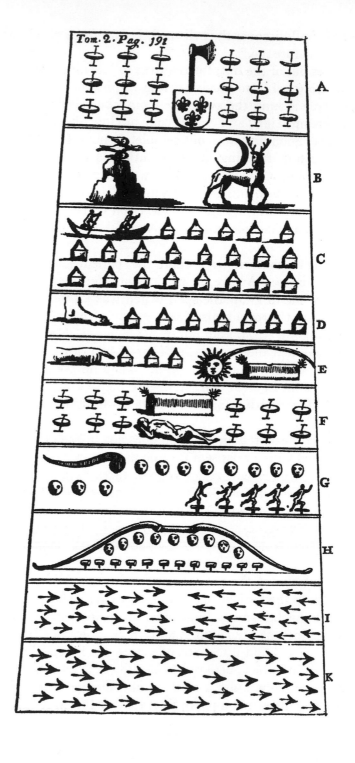

difficulty; he is presented with a drink: "Give it to that moose," he says, pointing to one of his relatives.

The doctor seeks to penetrate the cause of the new delirium of the patient. "I fell asleep," is the reply, "and I dreamed that I had a bison in my stomach." The family is in consternation, but suddenly those present cry out that they are also possessed by an animal: one imitates the cry of the caribou, another the barking of a dog, a third the howling of a wolf; the patient in turn imitates the bellow of the bison: it is a frightful charivari. The dreamer is made to sweat with an infusion of sage and pine branches; his imagination is cured by the consideration of his friends, and he declares that the bison has gone out of his body. These follies, mentioned by Charlevoix, recur every day among the Indians.

How can the same man, who rose so high when he thought himself on the brink of death, fall so low when he is sure of living? How can wise old men, reasonable young men, sensible women, submit themselves to the caprices of a deranged mind? Those are the mysteries of man, the double proof of his greatness and his misery.

INDIAN LANGUAGES

Four principal languages seem to divide North America: Algonquian and Huron in the north and east, Sioux in the west, and Chickasaw in the south; but the dialects differ somewhat from tribe to tribe. The Creeks of today speak Chickasaw mixed with Algonquian. The old Natchez was merely a softer dialect of Chickasaw.

Natchez, like Huron and Algonquian, knew only two genders, masculine and feminine; it rejected the neuter. That is natural among peoples who endow everything with senses, who hear voices in every rustling, who attribute hatred and love to plants, desires to the waters, immortal souls to the animals, spirits to the rocks. Nouns in Natchez were not declined; they simply took in the plural the letter *k* or the syllable *ki*, if the noun ended with a consonant.

The verbs were distinguished by the characteristic, the suffix, and the prefix. Thus the Natchez said: *T-ija*, I walk; *ni*

Tija-ban, I walked; *ni-ga Tija,* I shall walk; *ni-ki Tija,* I have walked.

There were as many verbs as there were nouns exposed to the same action; thus *to eat* corn was another verb from *to eat* deer; *to walk* in a forest was said in another way from *to walk* on a hill; *to love* one's friend was rendered by the verb *napiti-lima,* which means *I esteem; to love* one's mistress was expressed by the verb *nisakia,* which can be translated by "I am happy." In the languages of the peoples near nature, the verbs are either greatly multiplied or vary their meanings; the father, mother, son, wife, and husband sought different expressions to express their diverse feelings; they modified according to human passions the primitive speech which God gave man with existence. Intonation was everything; man has drawn from it the languages with their variations and riches, languages where one can find nonetheless a few words with the same roots, which have remained as a type or proof of a common origin.

Chickasaw, the root of Natchez, lacks the letter *r,* except in the words derived from the Algonquian, such as *arrego,* "I wage war," which is pronounced with a kind of rending of the sound. Chickasaw has frequent aspirations for the language of violent passions, such as hate, anger, jealousy; in the tender feelings, in the descriptions of nature, its expressions are full of charm and beauty.

The Sioux, whom their tradition declares to have come from Mexico to the upper reaches of the Mississippi, have extended the empire of their language from that river to the Rocky Mountains on the west and as far as the Red River on the north; there are found the Chippewas, who speak a dialect of Algonquian, and are enemies of the Sioux.

The Sioux language is sibilant to the point of being rather disagreeable to the ear; it is the language that named almost all the rivers and all the places in the west of Canada: the Mississippi, the Missouri, the Osage, etc. Nothing is yet known of its grammar, or almost nothing.

Algonquian and Huron are the mother tongues of all the peoples of the part of North America included between the sources of the Mississippi, Hudson Bay, and the Atlantic, as

114

far as the coast of Carolina. A traveler who knew these two languages could travel through more than 1,800 leagues of this country without an interpreter and make himself understood to more than 100 peoples.

The Algonquian language began at Acadia and the Gulf of St. Lawrence; turning from the southeast by the north toward the southwest, it embraced an extent of 1,200 leagues. The natives of Virginia spoke it; beyond, in the Carolinas to the south, the Chickasaw language dominated. The Algonquian idiom to the north stopped among the Chippewas. Farther yet to the north appears the language of the Eskimo; in the west the Algonquian language touched the west bank of the Mississippi; on the right bank reigns the Sioux language.

Algonquian has less energy than Huron; but it is softer, more elegant, and clearer. It is ordinarily used in treaties and is considered the polite or classic language of the wilderness.

Huron was spoken by the people of that name and by the Iroquois, a colony of that people. Huron is a complete language having its verbs, nouns, pronouns, and adverbs. The simple verbs have a double conjugation, one absolute, the other reciprocal; the third persons have two genders, and the numbers and tenses follow the mechanism of the Greek language. The active verbs are multiplied infinitely, as in the Chickasaw language.

Huron is without labials; they speak from the gullet, and almost all the syllables are aspirated. The diphthong *ou* forms an extraordinary sound which is expressed without any movement of the lips. The missionaries, not knowing how to indicate it, wrote it with the figure *8*.

The genius of this noble language consists particularly in personifying the action, that is, expressing the passive by the active. Thus, the example is quoted by Father Rasle:[103] "If you asked a European why God created him, he would tell you: it is to know Him, love Him, serve Him, and by this means merit eternal glory." A savage would answer you in the Huron Language: "The Great Spirit thought of us: let them know me, let them love me, let them serve me, then I shall make them enter into my illustrious felicity."

The Huron or Iroquois language has five principal dialects. This language has only four vowels, *a, e, i, o,* and the diphthong *8*, which has something of the consonant and the value of the English *w;* it has seven consonants, *g, h, k, n, r, s, t*.[104]

In Huron, almost all the nouns are verbs. There is no infinitive; the root of the verb is the first person of the present indicative. There are three basic tenses from which all the others are formed: the present indicative, the indefinite preterite, and the simple affirmative future. There are practically no abstract nouns; if some are found, they have obviously been formed afterwards from the concrete verb, modifying one of its persons.

Huron has a dual, as in Greek, and two first persons plural and dual; it has no auxiliary to conjugate the verbs, no participles, no passive verbs; ideas are expressed in the active: *I am loved*, is expressed by *One loves me*, etc. It has no pronouns to express the relationships of the verbs: they are recognized simply by the first letter of the verb, which is modified as many different times and in as many different manners as there are possible relationships among the persons of the three numbers, which is enormous. Thus these relationships are the key to the language. When you understand them (they have fixed rules), you are no longer held back.

A singular thing is that in the verbs, the imperatives have a first person.

All the words of the Huron language compound with one another. It is generally true, with few exceptions, that the object of the verb, when it is not a proper name, is included in the verb itself and forms only a single word; but then the verb takes the conjugation of the noun, for all the nouns belong to a conjugation. There are five.

This language has a great number of expletives which mean nothing alone, but which, spread through the discourse, give it great strength and clarity. The particles are not always the same for men and women. Each gender has its own.

There are two genders, the noble gender for the men, and the nonnoble gender for the women and male or female animals. In saying of a coward that he is a woman, the word *woman* is made masculine; in saying of a woman that she is a man, the word *man* is made feminine.

116

The mark of the noble and nonnoble gender, of the singular, of the dual, and the plural, is the same in nouns as in verbs, which all have in each tense and each number two third persons, noble and nonnoble.

Each conjugation is absolute, reflexive, reciprocal, and relative. I shall give an example here:

Absolute Conjugation

SINGULAR PRESENT INDICATIVE

Iks8ens—I hate, etc.

DUAL

Tenis8ens—You and I, etc.

PLURAL

Te8as8ens—You and we, etc.

Reflexive Conjugation

SINGULAR

Katats8ens—I hate myself, etc.

DUAL

Tiatats8ens—We hate ourselves, etc.

PLURAL

Te8atats8ens—You and we, etc.

For the reciprocal conjugation, *te* is added to the reflexive conjugation, changing *r* to *h* in the third persons of the singular and plural.

Thus you will have: Tekatats8ens—I hate myself *mutuo*, with someone.

Relative Conjugation of the same verb, same tense

SINGULAR

Relation of the First Person to the Others

Kons8ens—I hate you, etc.

Relation of the Second Person to the Others

Taks8ens—You hate me.

Relation of the Third Person Masculine to the Others
Rask8ens—He hates me.
Relation of the Third Person Feminine to the Others
8aks8ens—She hates me, etc.
Relation of the Indefinite Third Person One
Ionks8ens—One hates me.

DUAL

Dual subject in combination with dual object use the plural verb forms. We shall give then only the relation of the dual to the singular.

Relation of the Dual to the Other Persons
Kenis8ens—We two hate you, etc.

The third persons dual to the others are the same as the plurals.

PLURAL

Relation of the First Person Plural to the Others
K8as8ens—We hate you, etc.
Relation of the Second Person Plural to the Others
Tak8as8ens—You hate me.
Relation of the Third Person Plural Masculine to the Others
Ronks8ens—They hate me.
Relation of the Third Person Plural Feminine to the Others
Ionsks8ens—They hate me.

Conjugation of a Noun

SINGULAR

Hieronke—My body
Tsieronke—Your body
Raieronke—His body
Kaieronke—Her body
Ieronke—Someone's body

118

Tenïeronke—Our (*meum et tuum*)

Iakeniieronke—Our (*meum et illum*)

Seniieronke—Of you two

Niieronke—Of the two of them

Kaniieronke—Of the two of them (feminine)

Te8aieronke—Our (*nost. et vest.*)

Iak8aieronke—Our (*nost. et illor.*)

And so on with all the nouns. In comparing the conjugation of this noun with the absolute conjugation of the verb *iks8ens*, "I hate," you see that there are absolutely the same modifications in the three numbers: *k* for the first person, *s* for the second, *r* for the third noble, *ka* for the third nonnoble, *ni* for the dual. For the plural you reduplicate *te8a, se8a, rati, konti*, changing *k* to *te8a, s* to *se8a, ra* to *rati, ka* to *konti*, etc.

Family relationships are always from the greater to the smaller. Example:

> My father, *rakenika*, "he who has me for son" (Relation of the third person to the first).
> My son, *rienha*, "he whom I have for son" (Relation of the first to the third person).
> My uncle, *rakenchaa, rak* . . . (Relation of the third person to the first).
> My nephew, *rion8atenha, ri* . . . (Relation of the first to the third person, as in the preceding verb).

The verb *to want* can not be translated in Iroquois. They use *ikire*, "to intend," thus:

> I want to go there.
> *Ikere etho iake.*
> I intend to go there.

The verbs that express a thing which no longer exists at the moment of speaking have no perfect, but only an imperfect, as *ronnhek8e*, "he has lived, he no longer lives." By analogy to

119

this rule: if I have loved someone and still love him, I shall use the perfect *kenon8ehon*. If I no longer love him, I shall use the imperfect *kenon8esk8e*: "I used to love him, but I no longer love him." So much for the tenses.

As for the persons, the verbs that express a thing which is not done voluntarily have no first persons, but only a third relative to the others. Thus, "I sneeze," *te8akitsionk8a*, relation of the third to the first person: that sneezes me or causes me to sneeze.

"I yawn," *te8akskara8ata*, same relation of the third person nonnoble to the first *8ak*, "that opens my mouth." The second person, *you yawn, you sneeze*, will be the relation of the same third person nonnoble to the second *tesatsionk8a, tesaskara8ata,* etc.

For the indirect objects of verbs and prepositional phrases, there is a sufficient variety of modifications of endings which express them intelligibly; these modifications are subject to fixed rules.

Kninons, "I buy." *Kehninonse*, "I buy for someone." *Kehninon*, "I buy from someone." *Katennietha*, "I send." *Kehnieta*, "I send by someone." *Keiatennietennis*, "I send to someone."

From the examination of these languages alone, it is clear that the peoples named by us as *savages* were far advanced in that civilization which involved the combination of ideas. The details on their government will confirm this truth more and more.[105]

HUNTING

When the old men have decided on the beaver or bear hunt, a warrior goes from door to door in the villages, saying: "The chiefs are going to leave; let those who wish to follow them paint themselves with black and fast to learn from the Spirit of dreams where the bears and beavers are hiding this year."

At this announcement all the warriors daub their faces with soot mixed with bear oil, and the fast of eight nights begins. It is so rigorous that they must not even swallow a drop of water, and they must chant incessantly in order to have favorable dreams. When the fast is over, the warriors bathe, and a great feast is served. Each Indian makes a recital of his dreams: if the greatest number of these dreams designates the same place for the hunt, it is there that they resolve to go. They offer an expiatory sacrifice to the souls of the bears killed in the preceding hunts and beg them to be favorable to the new hunters; that is, they ask the dead bears to let the living bears be struck down. Each warrior sings of his former exploits against the wild beasts.

The songs finished, they leave completely armed. When they have arrived at the edge of a river, the warriors, holding paddles in their hands, sit down two by two in the bottom of the canoes. At the signal given by the chief the canoes form a straight line; the one at the head serves to break the force of the water when they have to navigate against the current. On these expeditions they take packs of hounds and carry with them snares, traps, and snowshoes.

When they have arrived at the assembly point, the canoes are drawn up on the shore and enclosed in a palisade covered with sod. The chief divides the Indians into companies made up of the same number of individuals. After the division of the hunters, they proceed to the division of the hunting grounds. Each company builds a hut in the center of the portion allotted to it.

The snow is cleared, pikes are driven into the ground, and birch bark strips are placed against these pikes. Above the strips of bark that form the walls of the hut, other strips of bark are placed sloping toward each other to form the roof of the building; a hole cut in the roof lets out the smoke of the hearth. Outside, the snow stops up the chinks of the shack and serves as its plaster or stucco. A fire is lit in the middle of the cabin, furs cover the ground, and the dogs sleep at the feet of their masters; far from suffering from the cold, they are stifled. Smoke is everywhere. The hunters, seated or reclining, try to place themselves beneath this smoke. They wait until snow has fallen, until the northeast wind, clearing the sky, has brought a dry cold, before they begin the beaver hunt. But during the days preceding the clearing weather, they busy themselves with some intermediate hunts, such as that of the otter, the fox, and the muskrat.

The traps used for these animals consist of planks of varying thickness and size. A hole is made in the snow; one end of the plank is placed on the ground, the other is lifted on three pieces of wood arranged in the shape of a figure 4. The bait is attached to one of the legs of this figure; the animal that wants to seize it, enters below the plank, draws the bait to him, springs the trap, and is crushed. The bait differs according to the animal. For the beaver it is a bit of aspen wood; for the fox and wolf, a strip of flesh; for the muskrat, walnuts and various dry fruits.

Traps are set for wolves at the entrance of runs and at the entrance of a thicket; for foxes, on the incline of hills at some distance from the warrens; for muskrats, in thickets; for otters, in ditches of the field and the reeds of the pond.

The traps are inspected in the morning; the hunters leave the hut two hours before daylight. They walk on the snow with shoes that resemble tennis rackets; these rackets are 18 inches long by 8 wide;[106] oval in form in front, they end in a point behind; the curve of the ellipse is made of birch, bent and hardened in the fire. The longitudinal and transversal cords are of leather strips, six in each direction, reinforced by willow shoots. The racket is held to the foot by three bands. Without these ingenious contraptions it would be impossible to take a step in winter in this climate; but they hurt and are tiring at first because they oblige one to walk with the knees turned in and the legs out.

When the Indians go about inspecting the traps in November and December, it is ordinarily in the midst of blizzards, sleet, and wind: they can scarcely see six inches before them. The hunters walk in silence, but the dogs, who smell the prey, howl. All the wisdom of the savage is necessary to find the buried traps when the paths are covered with frost.

At a stone's throw from the traps the hunter stops to await the break of day. He stands motionless in the midst of the storm, his back turned to the wind, his fingers stuck in his mouth; on each hair of the furs with which he is covered there forms a needle of frost, and the tuft of hair that crowns his head becomes a plume of ice.

At the first light of day, when they see the sprung traps, they close in on the animal. A wolf or a fox, his hindquarters broken, shows his white teeth and his black maw to the hunters; the dogs finish off the wounded animal.

They clear away the new snow and reset the trap; they put in new bait, taking care to place the trap on the leeward side. Sometimes the traps are sprung without any game being caught. This accident is the effect of the slyness of the foxes, who attack the bait by extending the paw from the side of the plank rather than entering under the trap; completely safe, they carry off the booty.

If the first emptying of the traps has been good, the hunters return triumphant to the hut. The noise they make then is unbelievable: they tell of the morning's take, invoke the Manitous, and cry out without hearing one another; they go wild with joy, and the dogs are not silent. From this first success they draw the most favorable omen for the future.

When the snow has ceased falling and the sun shines on its hardened surface, the beaver hunt is proclaimed. First a solemn prayer is made to the Great Beaver, and they present him with an offering of tobacco. Each Indian arms himself with a club to break the ice and with a net to envelop the prey. But whatever the rigor of the winter, certain little ponds never freeze in Upper Canada. This phenomenon is due to the abundance of hot springs or to the particular exposure of the ground.

These reservoirs of unfreezing water are often formed by the beavers themselves, as I have said in the article on natural history. Here is how the hunters destroy the peaceful creatures of God. In the dam of the pond where the beavers live, the hunters make a hole that is large enough for the water to drain off and for the marvelous town to be left dry. Standing on the dam, a club in their hands, their dogs behind them, the hunters are attentive; they see the inhabitants uncovered as the water lowers. Alarmed by this rapid flow the amphibian people, not knowing the cause but judging that a breach has been made in the dam, busy themselves immediately with closing it. All swim about vying with one another: some advance to examine the nature of the damage, others reach the bank to seek materials, and others go to the country houses to warn the citizens. The unfortunates are surrounded on all sides; at the dam, the club strikes dead the worker who was trying to repair the damage; the inhabitant taking refuge in his country house is no safer: the hunter throws at him a powder that blinds him, and the dogs strangle him. The cries of the conquerors resound in the woods, the water runs out, and they march to assault the citadel.

The manner of taking beavers in the frozen ponds is different. Holes are made in the ice; imprisoned under their crystal vault, the beavers hurry to come and breathe at these openings. The hunters are careful to cover the broken spot with reeds; without that precaution, the beavers would discover the ambush. So they approach the breathing hole; the ripple they make swimming betrays them. The hunter plunges his arm into the hole, drags out the animal by a paw, and throws him on the ice, where he is surrounded by a circle of assassins, dogs and men. Soon attached to a tree, he is skinned half alive by a savage so that his fur can go beyond the seas to cover the head of an inhabitant of London or Paris.

When the expedition against the beavers is terminated, the warriors return to the hunting hut singing hymns to the Great Beaver, to the sound of the drum and the *chichicoué*.

The skinning is a communal operation. They plant stakes. Two hunters stand at each pole which holds two beavers hung by the rear legs. On the order of the chief, they open the belly of the slaughtered animals and skin them. If a female is found among the victims, the consternation is great; not only is it a religious crime to kill the females of the beaver, but it is also a political crime, a cause of war between tribes. However, the love of gain, the passion for strong liquors, and the need for firearms have won out over the strength of superstition and established right; females in great numbers have been hunted down, which will sooner or later cause the extinction of their species.

The hunt finishes with a feast composed of the flesh of the beavers. An orator gives the eulogy of the dead as if he had not contributed to their death: he tells all that I have transcribed of their manners; he praises their wit and wisdom. "You will no more hear," he says, "the voice of the chiefs who commanded you and that you had chosen among all the beaver warriors to give you laws. Your language, which the medicine men know perfectly, will no longer be spoken at the bottom of the lake; you will no longer wage battles with the otters, your cruel enemies. No, beavers! But your pelts will serve to buy arms, we shall carry your smoked hams to our children, and we shall prevent our dogs from breaking your bones, which are so hard."

All the speeches, all the songs of the Indians, prove that they associate themselves with the animals, that they attribute to them a character and a language, that they regard them as their tutors, as beings endowed with an intelligent soul. The Scriptures often offer the instinct of animals as an example to man.

The bear hunt is the most renowned hunt among the savages. It begins with long fasts, sacred purges, and feasts; it takes place in winter. The hunters follow frightful paths along lakes and between mountains whose precipices are hidden under the snow. In the dangerous gorges they offer the sacrifice reputed to be the most powerful with the genius of the wilderness: they hang a live dog from the branches of a tree and let it die there, mad. Huts raised hurriedly each night give only a poor shelter: one is frozen on one side and burned on the other in them. To defend themselves against the smoke, the inhabitants have no other resource than to lie on their stomachs, their faces buried in skins. The famished dogs howl and pass back and forth over the bodies of their masters. When the masters think they will be able to manage a miserable meal, the dog, more alert, swallows it down.

After unheard-of fatigue they arrive at plains covered with pine forests, the lair of the bears. The fatigue and the perils are forgotten as the action begins.

The hunters divide and, placing themselves at some distance from one another, spread out over a great circular space. Scattered on the different points of a circle, they walk at a fixed time along a radius leading to the center, examining with care the old trees that hide the bears. The animal betrays himself by the mark that his breath leaves in the snow.

As soon as the Indian has discovered the traces he is seeking, he calls his companions, climbs the pine, and 10 or 12 feet from the ground finds the opening by which the hermit has retired into his cell. If the bear is asleep, his head is split; two other hunters, climbing the tree in turn, help the first one to drag the dead animal from its den and throw it down.

The exploring and victorious warrior then hastens to descend. He lights his pipe, puts it in the maw of the bear, and blowing into the bowl of the pipe, fills the mouth of the quadruped with smoke. He then addresses the soul of the deceased; he begs him to pardon him for his death and not be contrary to him in hunts he might undertake. After this harangue, he cuts the tendon of the bear's tongue, to be burned at the village in order to discover by the way it sputters in the flame whether the spirit of the bear is or is not appeased.

The bear is not always enclosed in the trunk of a pine; he sometimes lives in a den whose entrance he has stopped up. This hermit is sometimes so replete that he can scarcely walk, although he has lived a part of the winter without food.

The warriors, who have started from the circumference of the circle and gone toward the center, finally meet, dragging along or chasing their prey. One can sometimes see young savages arrive pushing before them with a little stick a great bear lumbering through the snow. When they tire of this game, they plunge a knife into the heart of the poor animal.

The bear hunt, like all the other hunts, finishes with a sacred feast. The custom is to roast a whole bear and to serve him to the guests seated in a circle on the snow under the shelter of the pines, whose layered branches are likewise covered with snow. The head of the victim, painted red and blue, is exposed at the top of a pole. Orators address it, eulogizing the dead one while they devour its members. "How you climbed to the tops of the trees! What strength in your embraces! What constancy in your enterprises! What sobriety in your fasts! Warrior with the thick fur, in the spring the young female burned with love for you. Now you are no more, but your remains still are the delight of those who possess them."

One often sees seated helter-skelter with the savages at these feasts, dogs and tame bears and otters.

During this hunt the Indians take on obligations that they have difficulty in fulfilling. They swear, for example, not to eat before having carried the paw of the first bear they kill to their mothers or their wives, and sometimes their mothers and their wives are 300 or 400 miles away from the forest where they struck down the animal. In these cases they consult the medicine man, who by means of a present arranges the affair. The imprudent makers of vows are let off with burning in the honor of the Great Hare the part of the animal that they had dedicated to their relatives.

The bear hunt finishes toward the end of February, and it is then that the moose hunt begins. Great herds of the animals are found in the young growths of pines.

To catch them, one encloses a considerable area within two triangles of unequal size formed of high pikes placed close together. These two triangles communicate by one of their angles, at which passage lines are stretched. The base of the greater triangle is left open, and the warriors line up along it. Soon they advance making loud cries, beating on a kind of drum. The moose take flight into the enclosure of pikes. In vain they seek a way out; they finally arrive at the fatal constriction and remain caught in the nets. Those who pass through them rush into the small triangle, where they are easily pierced with arrows.

The bison hunt takes place during the summer in the savannas that border the Missouri or its tributaries. The Indians, beating the plain, push the herds toward the water. When they refuse to flee, the grass is ignited, and the bison find themselves constricted between the fire and the river. Several thousands of these heavy animals, bellowing at the same time, crossing the flame or the waters, falling struck by the bullet or pierced by the pike, offer an astonishing spectacle.

The savages also employ other methods of attack against the bison: at times they disguise themselves as wolves in order to approach them; at times they attract the cows, imitating the bellowing of the bull. During the last days of autumn, when the rivers are barely frozen, two or three tribes joined together drive the herds toward the rivers. A Sioux, dressed in the skin of a bison, crosses the river on the thin ice; the deceived bison follow him. The fragile bridge breaks under the heavy cattle, which are massacred amidst the floating fragments. On these

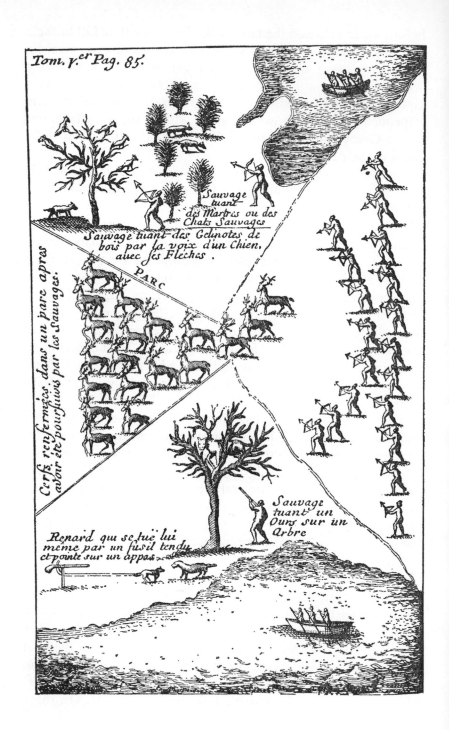

Tom. 5.er Pag. 85.

Sauvage tuant des Martres ou des Chats Sauvages

Sauvage tuant des Gelinotes de bois par la voix d'un Chien, auec ses Fleches.

PARC

Cerfs renfermés dans un parc apres auoir été pourſuivis par les Sauvages.

Sauvage tuant un Ours sur un Arbre

Renard qui se tuë lui même par un fusil tendu et pointé sur un appas.

occasions the hunters use arrows: the silent blow of that arm does not frighten the prey, and the arrow is recovered by the archer when the animal is struck down. The musket does not have that advantage: there is loss and there is noise in the use of lead and powder.

They are careful to stay downwind from the bison, who scent man at a great distance. The wounded bull backtracks, defends the heifer, and often dies for her.

The Sioux wander in the savannas on the right bank of the Mississippi from the sources of the river to Saint Anthony Falls; they raise horses of Spanish blood, with which they pursue the bison.

They sometimes have singular companions in this hunt—wolves. These attach themselves to the Indians in order to profit from their leavings, and in the melee they carry off the lost calves.

Often these wolves also hunt for themselves. Three of them amuse a cow by their gambols. While she looks at these traitors' games with naïve attention, a wolf hidden in the grass seizes her by the udder; she turns her head to free herself, and the three accomplices of the brigand jump at her throat.

At the scene of this hunt there is executed some months after a no less cruel but more peaceful hunt, that of the doves; they are taken at night by torchlight from the isolated trees where they rest during their migration from the north to the south.

The return of the warriors in the spring is a great celebration, when the hunt has been good. Getting their canoes, they repair them with bear grease and pine resin; the pelts, the smoked meats, and the baggage are put on board, and they let themselves go with the current of the rivers, whose rapids and cataracts have disappeared under the flood of the waters.

As they approach the village, an Indian who has been put ashore runs to inform the nation. The women, the children, the old men, and the warriors who had remained in the cabins, go to the river. They greet the fleet with a cry, to which the fleet replies with another cry. The canoes break their column and line up side by side, prow forward. The hunters jump onto the bank and go back to the villages in the order observed at the departure. Each Indian sings his own praise: "One must be a man to attack the bear as I have done; one must be a man to bring back such furs and food in such great abundance." The tribes applaud. The women follow bearing the spoils of the hunt.

They divide the pelts and the meats on the public square; they light the fire of the return; they throw into it the tendons from the bears' tongues; if they are thick and crackle properly, it is a most favorable augury; if they are dry and burn silently, the nation is threatened with some calamity.

After the pipe dance, they serve the last feast of the hunt: it consists of a bear that has been brought live from the forest: they put it on to cook whole with the skin and the entrails in an enormous pot. They must leave nothing of the animal, must not break its bones, a Judaic custom; they must drink to the last drop the water in which it has boiled. The savage whose stomach refuses the food calls his companions to his aid. This feast lasts eight or ten hours; the celebrants leave it in a frightful state; some pay with their lives for the horrible pleasure which superstition imposes. A Sachem closes the ceremony: "Warriors, the Great Hare has watched our arrows; you have shown the wisdom of the beaver, the prudence of the bear, the force of the bison, the speed of the moose. Withdraw, and spend the moon of fire at fishing and games." This discourse ends with an *Oah!* a religious cry thrice repeated.

The animals that furnish pelts to the savages are the badger; the gray fox; the yellow and the red fox; the pecan;[107] the gopher; the raccoon; the gray and the white hare; the beaver; the ermine; the marten; the muskrat; the tiger cat or wildcat; the otter; the lynx; the polecat; the black, the gray and the striped squirrel; the bear; and several species of wolf.

The skins for tanning are taken from the moose, the elk, the mountain sheep, the deer, the doe, the stag, and the bison.

WAR

Among the Savages all bear arms—men, women, and children; but the body of the fighters is composed in general of the fifth part of the tribe.

Fifteen is the legal age of military service. War is the great affair of the savages and the foundation of their politics; it has about it something more legitimate than war among civilized peoples because it is almost always declared for the very existence of the people who undertake it: it is a matter of preserving hunting lands or fields appropriate for farming. But by the very reason that the Indian applies himself to the art which causes death only in order to live, there result from it implacable furies among the tribes: they are fighting over the family food. The hatreds become individual; as the armies are not large and each enemy knows the name and the face of his enemy, they also fight fiercely through antipathies of character and by individual resentments; these children of the same wilderness carry into their external quarrels something of the animosity of civil disputes.

To this first and general cause of war among the savages are joined other reasons for taking up arms, drawn from some superstitious motive, from some domestic dissension, from some question of interest born out of the commerce with the Europeans. Thus, killing female beavers had become, among the hordes of the north of America, a legitimate subject for war.

War is declared in an extraordinary and terrible manner. Four warriors painted black from head to foot slip through the deepest shadows into the land of the threatened people; when they arrive at the doors of the cabins, they cast on the hearth of these cabins a tomahawk painted red, on whose handle are marked in signs known to the Sachems the motives of the hostilities. The first Romans hurled a javelin onto the enemy territory. These Indian heralds at arms immediately disappear into the night like phantoms, uttering the famous war cry or whoop. It is uttered by placing the hand on the mouth and striking the lips so that the sound which escapes intermittently, at times low, at times high, ends in a sort of bellow impossible to imagine.

When war is declared, if the enemy are too weak to wage it, they flee; if they feel strong, they accept it; immediately there commence the customary preparations and ceremonies.

A great fire is lit on the public square, and the war cauldron is placed on the pyre: it is the Janissary's pot. Each combatant throws into it something that belongs to him. They also plant two stakes from which are hung arrows, tomahawks, and feathers, all painted red. The stakes are placed at the north, the east, the south, or the west of the public square, according to the geographical point from which the battle is to come.

When that is done, they present to the warriors the war medicine, a violent emetic dissolved in two pints of water, which must be swallowed at one draught. The young men disperse in the neighborhood but not too far away. The chief who is to command them, after having rubbed his neck and face with bear grease and powdered charcoal, withdraws to the steambath, where he spends two whole days sweating, fasting, and observing his dreams. During these two days it is forbidden for women to approach the warriors; but they may speak to the chief of the expedition, whom they visit in order to obtain from him a portion of the booty taken from the enemy, for the savages never doubt the success of their enterprises.

These women bring different presents which they lay down at the feet of the chief. He notes with seeds or shells the particular desires: a sister claims a prisoner to take the place of a brother who died in battle; a matron demands scalps to console her for the loss of her parents; a widow requires a captive as a husband, or a foreign widow as a slave; a mother asks for an orphan to replace the child she has lost.

When the two days of retreat are finished, the young warriors go in turn to the war chief. They declare to him their plan to take part in the expedition; for although the council has resolved on war, this resolution binds no one; taking part is purely voluntary.

All the warriors daub themselves with black and red in the manner they think most likely to terrify the enemy. Some make longitudinal or transversal stripes on their cheeks and some, round or triangular marks; others draw figures of snakes there. The bare chest and arms of a warrior offer the history of his exploits: particular figures indicate the number of scalps he has taken, the battles in which he has found himself, the dangers he has experienced. These hieroglyphs, impressed in the skin

132

in blue points, remain permanently; they are fine pricks, burned with pine gum.

The combatants, entirely nude or dressed in a sleeveless tunic, put feathers in the single tuft of hair they have on the top of the head. In their leather belts are stuck the knives used to cut scalps; the tomahawk hangs from the same belt; in their right hands they hold the bow or the carbine; on the left shoulder they carry a quiver full of arrows or a horn full of powder and balls. The Cimbri, the Teutons, and the Franks tried thus to make themselves formidable in the eyes of the Romans.

The war chief comes out of the steam bath, a necklace of red porcelain in his hand, and addresses his brothers in arms: "The Great Spirit opens my mouth. The blood of our brothers killed in the last war has not yet been wiped away; their bodies have not been covered; we must go to protect them from the flies. I am resolved to walk by the path of war; I have seen bears in my dreams; the good Manitous have promised to aid me, and the evil ones will not be against me. I shall go thus to eat the enemy, drink their blood, and make prisoners. If I perish, or if some of those who consent to follow me lose their lives, our souls will be received in the land of spirits; our bodies will not lie in the dust or the mud, for this red necklace will belong to him who will cover the dead."

The chief throws the necklace to the ground; the most renowned warriors rush to pick it up; those who have not yet fought or who have only an ordinary reputation dare not vie for the necklace. The warrior who picks it up becomes the lieutenant general of the chief; he replaces him in command if the chief perishes on the expedition.

The warrior who possesses the necklace makes a speech. Hot water is brought in a vase. The young men wash the war chief and remove from him the black color with which he is covered; then they paint his cheeks, forehead and chest with chalks and clays of various colors and dress him in his finest robe.

During this ovation, the chief sings in a low voice that famous song of death which is sung when one is going to undergo the pain of death. "I am brave, I am intrepid, I do not

133

fear death; I laugh at the torment; how cowardly are they who fear it! Women, less than women! May fury consume my enemies! May I devour them and drink their blood to the last drop!"

When the chief has finished the song of death, his lieutenant general begins the song of war. "I shall fight for the homeland; I shall take scalps; I shall drink from my enemies' skulls, etc."

Each warrior, according to his character, adds to his song details which are more or less atrocious. Some say: "I shall cut off the fingers of my enemies with my teeth; I shall burn their feet and then their legs." Others say: "I shall let worms crawl into their wounds; I shall remove their scalps; I shall pull out their hearts and stuff them into their mouths."

These infernal songs were scarcely shouted except by the hordes of the north. The tribes of the south were satisfied with smothering the prisoners with smoke.

The warrior, having repeated his song of war, repeats his family song; it consists of the praise of his ancestors. The young men who are going to combat for the first time keep silent.

Once these first ceremonies are finished, the chief goes to the council of Sachems, who are seated in a circle, each with a red pipe in his mouth. He asks them if they persist in desiring to raise the hatchet. The deliberation begins anew, and almost always the first resolution is confirmed. The war chief returns to the public square, announces to the young men the decision of the elders, and the young men answer with a cry.

They untie the sacred dog, which was attached to a stake, and offer it to Areskoui, god of war. Among the Canadian nations they slaughter the dog, and after having boiled it in a cauldron, they serve it to the gathered men. No woman may take part in this mysterious feast. At the end of the repast, the chief declares that he will start out on a certain day, at the rise or setting of the sun.

The natural indolence of the savages is suddenly replaced by an extraordinary activity; the gaiety and martial ardor of the young men communicate themselves to the nation. There are established kinds of workshops for the manufacture of sleds and canoes.

The sleds used for the transporting of the baggage, the sick, and the wounded are made of two very thin boards, a foot and a half long by seven inches wide; turned up in front, they have edges to which are attached straps for fixing the load. The savages draw this wheelless chariot by means of a double band of leather, called *metump*, which they pass around the chest, and whose ends are fixed to the front of the sled.

The canoes are of two kinds, large and small. They are constructed in the following manner: Curved pieces unite at the ends in order to form an ellipse of about 8½ feet for the short diameter, 20 for the long diameter. On these main pieces they attach thin ribs of red cedar; these ribs are reinforced by wicker work. This canoe skeleton is covered with bark gathered in the winter from the elms and the birches by throwing boiling water on the trunks of the trees. These pieces of bark are assembled by means of extremely supple pine roots which do not dry easily. The sewing is covered inside and out with a resin whose secret is kept by the savages. When the canoe is finished and is supplied with maple paddles, it rather resembles a water spider, the graceful and light insect which walks rapidly on the surface of lakes and rivers.

A combatant must carry with him ten pounds of corn or other grain, his mat, his Manitou, and his medicine sack.

The day which precedes that of the departure, which is called the day of farewells, is given over to a touching ceremony among the members of the Huron and Algonquian nations. The warriors, who until then have camped on the public square or on a kind of Champ-de-Mars, disperse in the villages and go to say their farewells from cabin to cabin. They are received with the marks of the most tender interest; those who will remain behind want to have something that has belonged to the warriors; they take off their robes to give them better ones; they exchange pipes with them; the warriors must eat or drain a cup. Each hut has a particular wish for them, and they must answer by a like hope for their hosts.

When the warrior says his farewells in his own cabin, he stops and stands at the threshold. If he has a mother, she advances first; he kisses her eyes, her mouth, and her breasts. His sisters come next, and he touches their foreheads; his wife throws herself down before him; he commends her to the good spirits. Of all his children, he is presented only with his sons; he holds over them his hatchet or his tomahawk without saying a word. Finally, his father appears last. The Sachem, after having struck his shoulder, harangues him, inviting him to honor his ancestors; he says to him: "I stand behind you as you stand behind your son: if they come to me to insult your memory, it will be like boiling my flesh."

The day after the day of farewells is the day of departure. At the first light of dawn, the war chief leaves his hut and cries the war yell. If the least cloud obscures the sky, if a bad dream has come, if some bird or some animal of evil augury has been seen, the day of departure is put off. The camp, awakened by the death yell, gets up and arms.

The chiefs of the tribes raise the standards, formed of round pieces of bark attached to the end of long spears; on them are coarsely drawn Manitous—a tortoise, a bear, a beaver, etc. The chiefs of the tribes are like brigadier generals under the command of the general and his lieutenant. There are also captains who are not recognized by the army as a whole; they are partisans who follow the adventurers.

The census or the enumeration of the army takes place. Each warrior gives to the chief as he passes before him a small piece of wood marked with a particular seal. Up to the moment of giving over their symbols the warriors may withdraw from the expedition, but after this enlistment whoever draws back is declared infamous.

Soon the supreme priest arrives, followed by the chapter of medicine men or doctors. They bring reed baskets formed like funnels, leather bags full of roots and plants. The warriors sit on the ground in a circle, their legs crossed; the priests stand in the center.

The great medicine man calls the combatants by their names; the warrior who is called rises and gives his Manitou to the medicine man, who puts it in one of the reed baskets as he sings these words in Algonquian: *ajouh-oyah-alluya!*

The Manitous vary infinitely because they represent the caprices and the dreams of the savages. They are mouse skins stuffed with hay or cotton, little white pebbles, stuffed birds, teeth of quadrupeds or fish, bits of red cloth, branches of trees, bits of glass, or some European jewelry—in short, all the forms that the good spirits are supposed to have taken to manifest themselves to the possessors of these Manitous: happy at least to reassure themselves so cheaply and to believe themselves, sheltered by a worthless straw from the blows of fortune! Under the feudal regime[108] they took cognizance of an acquired right by the giving of a stick, a straw, a ring, a knife, etc.

The Manitous, distributed in three baskets, are confided to the guard of the war chief and the chiefs of the tribes. From the collection of the Manitous they pass on to the benediction of the medicinal plants and the surgical instruments. The great medicine man draws them one by one from the bottom of a leather or buffalo hair bag; he puts them down on the ground, dances around them with the other medicine men, strikes his thighs, discomposes his face, screams, and speaks unknown words. He finally declares that he has communicated to the simples a supernatural virtue and that he has the power to restore to life dead warriors. He cuts his lips with his teeth, applies a powder on the wound from which he carefully sucks the blood, and gives the appearance of having cured it. Sometimes he is presented with a dog considered dead; but upon applying an instrument, he makes the dog get up on his paws, and they deem it a miracle. Yet they are intrepid, these men who allow themselves to be enchanted by such coarse magic. The savage sees in the tricks of his priests only the intervention of the Great Spirit; he does not blush to call to his aid him who caused the wound and who can cure it.

Meanwhile the women have prepared the departure feast; this last meal, like the first, is made up of dog flesh. Before touching the sacred dish the chief addresses himself to the assembly: "My brothers, I am not yet a man, I know; yet you are not aware that I have sometimes seen the enemy. We have been killed in the last war; the bones of our companions have not been protected from the flies; we must go to cover them. How could we stay so long on our mats? The Manitou of my courage orders me to avenge man. Young men, take heart."

The chief intones the song of the Manitou of battle; the young men repeat its refrain. After the canticle the chief retires to the summit of an eminence and lies down on a skin, meanwhile holding in his hand a red pipe whose bowl is turned toward the enemy country. They execute the dances and the pantomimes of war. The first is called the Dance of Discovery.

An Indian advances alone slowly into the midst of the spectators; he portrays the departure of the warriors: one sees them march and then camp at nightfall. The enemy is discovered; they crawl on hands and knees to reach him: attack, melee, capture of one, death of another, precipitous or quiet retreat, sad or triumphal return.

The warrior who executes this pantomime closes it with a song in his own honor and in honor of his family: "Twenty snows ago I took twelve prisoners; ten snows ago I saved the chief. My ancestors were brave and famous. My grandfather was the wisdom of the tribe and the roar of battle; my father was a pine tree of strength. My great-great-grandmother was the mother of five warriors; my grandmother alone was worth a whole council of Sachems; my mother makes excellent *sagam-ité*. I am stronger and wiser than all my ancestors." It is the song of Sparta: "We once were young, valiant and bold."

After this warrior the others get up and sing in like manner of their high deeds; the more they boast, the more they are congratulated. Nothing is as noble, nothing is as handsome as they; they have all the qualities and all the virtues. He who said he was above everyone applauds the one who declares that he surpasses him in merit. The Spartans had this custom too. They thought that the man who praises himself publicly takes on the obligation of deserving the praise.

Little by little all the warriors leave their places to join in the dances; they execute marches to the sound of the drum, the fife, and the *chichikoué*. The movement augments; they imitate the activities of a siege, they attack a palisade. Some jump as if to clear a moat; others appear to throw themselves into the water to swim; others hold out their hands to still other companions to help them up to the assault. Tomahawk resounds against tomahawk; the *chichikoué* hastens the measure; the warriors draw their daggers and begin to whirl, first slowly, then faster, and soon with such speed that they disappear into the circle they describe. Horrible cries pierce the vault of heaven. The daggers that these ferocious men hold at one another's throat with a skill that makes one shudder, their black or striped faces, their fantastic clothing, their long yells—this whole tableau of a savage war inspires terror.

Worn out, panting, covered with sweat, the actors finish the dance and pass on to the trials of the young men. They are insulted and outrageously degraded; burning embers are poured on their hair; they are struck with whips, and hot coals are thrown at their heads. All this treatment they must bear with perfect impassivity. He who would give the least sign of impatience would be declared unworthy of raising the hatchet.

The third and last banquet of the sacred dog crowns these various ceremonies. It must last only a half hour. The warriors eat in silence; the chief presides over them; soon he leaves the feast. At this signal the guests run to the baggage and take up the arms. The relatives and friends surround them without saying a word; the mother watches the son busy loading the packets on the sleds; silent tears can be seen. Some families are sitting on the ground; others are standing; all are attentive to the tasks of the departure; one can read written on all the foreheads the same question already posed by several tender moments: "What if I were not to see him again?"

Finally the war chief comes out completely armed from his cabin. The troop is drawn up in military order. The great medicine man, bearing the Manitous, appears at the head; the war chief walks behind him; then comes the standard bearer of the first tribe, holding aloft his ensign; the men of that tribe follow their symbol. The other tribes parade after the first and draw the sleds loaded with cauldrons, mats, and sacks of corn; warriors carry on their shoulders, four by four, or eight by eight, the little and the big canoes; the painted women or courtesans with their children accompany the army. They are also harnessed to the sleds, but instead of having the *metump* passed around the chest, they have it against their foreheads. The lieutenant general walks alone on the flank of the column.

The war chief, after a few steps on the way, stops the warriors and says to them: "Let us banish sadness; when one is about to die one must be happy. Be amenable to my orders. He who distinguishes himself will receive much tobacco. I give my mat to . . . , a powerful warrior, to carry. If I and my lieutenant are put in the cauldron, it will be . . . who will lead you. Come, strike your thighs, and yell three times."

The chief then hands his sack of corn and mat to the warrior he has designated, which gives him the right to command the troop if the chief and his lieutenant perish.[109]

The march begins again. The army is ordinarily accompanied by all the inhabitants of the village as far as the river or lake where they all launch their canoes. Then the scene of farewells is repeated: the warriors strip themselves and divide their clothing among the members of their families. It is permissible at this last moment to express one's grief aloud. Each combatant is surrounded by his relatives who cover him with caresses, hold him in their arms, call him by the sweetest names there are. Before separating, perhaps forever, they pardon one another for the wrongs they may have committed toward one another. Those who remain pray the Manitous to shorten the time of absence; those who depart ask the dew to descend on the hut of their birthplace; in their wishes of happiness they do not even forget the domestic animals, guests of the paternal home. The canoes are launched onto the river, the savages embark, and the fleet departs. The women, remaining on the bank, make from afar the last signs of friendship to their husbands, fathers, and sons.

To reach the enemy country, they do not always follow the direct route; they sometimes take the longest route as the surest. The march is regulated by the medicine man according to the good or bad omens: if he has observed a hoot owl, they stop. The fleet enters an inlet; they land and raise a palisade, after which the fires are lit and the cauldrons set to boiling. When the supper is finished the camp is put under the guard of the spirits. The chief recommends to the warriors to keep their tomahawks beside them and not to snore too loudly. On the palisade they hang the Manitous, that is, the stuffed mice, the little white stones, the bits of straw, the pieces of red cloth; and the medicine man begins the prayer: "Manitous, be vigilant. Open your eyes and ears. If the warriors were surprised, that would be to your dishonor. What! The Sachems would say, the

Manitous of our nation have allowed themselves to be beaten by the Manitous of the enemy! You realize how shameful that would be; no one would give you food; the warriors would seek new dreams to get other spirits more powerful than you. It is in your interest to keep a good guard; if our scalps were taken during our sleep, we would not be to blame, but you would be in the wrong."

After this admonition to the Manitous, each warrior retires in the most perfect security, convinced that he has not the least thing to fear.

Europeans who have made war together with the savages, astonished by this strange confidence, used to ask their mat companions if they were never surprised in their encampment. "Very often," they would reply. "Wouldn't you do better in that case," the foreigners would say, "to post sentinels?" "That would be very wise," the savage would reply as he turned over to go to sleep. The Indian makes a virtue of his improvidence and his indolence by putting himself under the sole protection of heaven.

He has no fixed time for repose or movement: let the medicine man cry at midnight that he has seen a spider on a willow leaf, they must leave.

When they are in a country that abounds in game, the troop disperses; the baggage and those who carry it remain at the mercy of the first hostile party; but two hours before sunset, all the hunters return to camp with an exactness and a precision of which only the Indians are capable.

If they fall upon a blazed trail or a trade route, the dispersement of the warriors is even greater. This path is marked in the forests on the trunks of the trees, notched at the same height. It is the road that the different red nations follow to traffic with one another or with the white nations. It is a public right that this road remain neutral; they do not trouble those who have set out upon it.

The same neutrality is observed on the blood trail; this path is traced by the fire that has been set to the brush. No cabin rises on this road given over to the passage of the tribes on their distant expeditions. Even if enemy parties meet there, they never attack one another. Violating the trade route or the blood

141

trail is an immediate cause of war against the nation guilty of the sacrilege.

If a troop of Indians finds another troop asleep, one with which they are allied, they remain standing outside the palisades of the camp until the warriors wake up. When they have come out of their sleep, their chief approaches the travelers, presents them with a few scalps kept for these occasions, and says, "You are master here"; which means, "You may pass, you are our brothers, your honor is intact." The allies reply, "We are master here"; and they continue on their way. Whosoever should take for an enemy a friendly tribe and awaken them, would expose himself to reproaches of ignorance and cowardice.

If one is to cross the territory of a neutral nation, right of passage must be asked. A deputation goes with the pipe to the principal village of that nation. The orator declares that the tree of peace has been planted by their ancestors, that the hatchet is buried at the foot of the tree, that they must brighten the chain of friendship and smoke the sacred pipe. If the chief of the neutral nation accepts the pipe and smokes, the passage is granted. The ambassador returns to his people dancing.

Thus they advance toward the country where they are carrying the war, without a plan, without precautions, as if without fear. It is chance which ordinarily gives the first news of the enemy: a hunter will return in haste to declare that he has met with traces of men. They immediately order the cessation of all kind of work so that no noise will be heard. The chief leaves with the most experienced warriors to examine the tracks. The savages are able to hear sounds from infinite distances and to identify footprints on dry heather or bare rocks, where any other eye than theirs would see nothing. Not only do they discover these vestiges, but they can say which Indian tribe has left them and when they were left. If the separation of the two feet is great, they are Illinois who passed there; if the mark of the heel is deep and the impression of the toe wide, they recognize the Ojibways; if the foot bears to the side, they are sure that the Potawatomis are abroad; if the grass is barely trodden, if the bend is at the top of the plant and not near the ground, they are the fugitive tracks of the Hurons; if the feet are turned outward, if they fall 36 inches from one another, Europeans have marked their route. The Indians walk with the tip of the foot inward and with both feet on a line. They judge the age of the warriors by the heaviness or lightness, the shortness or length of the stride.

When the moss or grass no longer is damp, the tracks are of the previous day; the tracks are four or five days old when the insects are already crawling in the trodden grass or moss; they are eight, ten, or twelve days old when the vegetating force of the earth has reappeared and new leaves have grown. Thus a few insects, a few blades of grass, and a few days erase the footsteps of man and his glory.

When they have carefully recognized the tracks, they put their ears to the ground and judge by murmurs that the European ear cannot seize, how far away the enemy is.

After they return to the camp, the chief has all the fires extinguished. He forbids speaking and orders no more hunting; the canoes are drawn up on the land and hidden in the bushes. They take a great repast in silence, after which they retire.

The night that follows the first discovery of the enemy is called the Night of Dreams. All the warriors are obliged to dream and to tell the next morning what they dreamed, so that they may judge the success of the enterprise.

The camp then affords a singular spectacle: savages rise and walk in the darkness, murmuring their song of death, to which they add a few new words such as these: "I shall swallow four white snakes, and I shall tear the wings from a red eagle." It is the dream that the warrior has just had which he weaves into his song. His companions are obliged to guess the sense of this dream, or else the dreamer is freed of service. Here the four white snakes may be taken for four Europeans that the dreamer must kill and the red owl for an Indian whose scalp he must take.

A warrior in the Night of Dreams once expanded his song of death with the story of a dog with ears of fire; he was never able to obtain the explanation of his dream, and he left for his cabin. These customs, which are childish in nature, might indicate cowardice among the Europeans; but among the savages of North America they did not have that drawback. Such behavior was recognized only as an act of that free and bizarre will from which the Indian is never separated, whoever the man may be to whom he submits for a moment, by reason or caprice.

During the Night of Dreams the young men greatly fear that the medicine man has dreamed ill, that is, that he has been afraid; for the medicine man by a single dream can make the army retreat even if it has marched 200 leagues. If some warrior thinks he saw the spirits of his forefathers or imagines he heard their voices, he also obliges the camp to retreat. Absolute liberty and unenlightened religion govern the actions of the savages.

If no dream has upset the expedition, they start out again. The painted women are left behind with the canoes; the warriors send ahead a score of their number chosen among those who have sworn the oath of friends.[110] The greatest order and silence reign among the members of the troop; the warriors march in single file so that each following warrior puts his feet in the tracks of the one ahead of him. They thus avoid the multiplicity of footprints. For greater precaution the warrior who brings up the rear spreads dead leaves and dust behind him. The chief is at the head of the column. Guided by the traces of the enemy, he follows their turnings through the bushes like a wise bloodhound. From time to time they halt and listen attentively. If hunting is the image of war among the Europeans, among the savages war is the image of hunting. The Indian learns by pursuing men how to discover the bear. The greatest general in the state of nature is the strongest and most vigorous hunter; intellectual qualities, ingenious plots, perfected use of judgment are what make the great captains in the social state.

The scouts sent to reconnoiter sometimes bring back bundles of newly cut reeds; they are challenges or provocations. They count the reeds, their number indicating the number of the enemy. If the tribes that conveyed these challenges were known as were the Hurons for their military frankness, the bundles of reeds told the exact truth; on the other hand, if they were known as were the Iroquois for their political genius, the reeds increased or diminished the numerical force of the combatants.

Should the location of a camp the enemy occupied the previous night come into view, it is examined with care. According to the construction of the huts, the chiefs recognize the different tribes of the same nation and their different allies. The huts that have only a single stake at the entrance are those of the Illinois. The addition of a single beam, the degree of its incline, become indications. The round *ajoupas* are those of the Ottawas. A hut whose roof is flat and turned up announces pale-faces. It sometimes happens that the enemy, before being met by the nation seeking them, has beaten an ally of the nation; to intimidate those who are pursuing them, they leave behind them the monument of their victory. One day a large birch skinned of its bark was found. On the bare white wood was traced an oval on which stood out in black and red the following figures: a bear, a birch leaf eaten by a butterfly, ten circles and four mats, a flying bird, a moon on six sheaves of corn, a canoe and three *ajoupas*, a man's foot and 20 huts, an owl and a setting sun, an owl, three circles and a man lying down, a tomahawk and 30 heads arranged in a straight line, two men standing in a little circle, three heads in a bow with three lines.

The oval of the hieroglyphs designated an Illinois chief named Atabou; he was recognized by the distinguishing marks he had on his face; the bear was the Manitou of the chief; the birch leaf eaten by the butterfly represented the national symbol of the Illinois; the ten circles numbered 1,000 warriors, each circle being taken for 100; the four mats proclaimed four advantages gained; the flying bird marked the departure of the Illinois; the moon on the sheaves of corn meant that the departure had taken place in the moon of green grain; the canoe and the three *ajoupas* told that the 1,000 warriors had traveled three days by water; the man's foot and the 20 huts denoted 20 days' march by land; the owl was the symbol of the Chickasaws; the setting sun showed that the Illinois had arrived at the west of the camp of the Chickasaws; the owl, the three circles, and the man lying down said that 300 Chickasaws had been surprised during the night; the tomahawk and the 30 heads in a straight line declared that the Illinois had killed 30 Chickasaws. The two men standing in a little circle announced that they took away 20 prisoners; the three heads in the bow counted three dead on the side of the Illinois, and the three lines indicated three wounded.

A war chief must know how to explain rapidly and precisely these emblems; and by the knowledge he has of the strength and alliances of the enemy, he must judge the historical exactness of these trophies. If he makes the decision to advance in spite of the true or claimed victories of the enemy, he prepares for combat.

New investigators are dispatched. They advance, crouching along the bushes and sometimes pulling themselves along on their hands; they climb the highest trees. When they have discovered the hostile huts, they hasten back to camp to report to the chief the enemy's position. If this position is strong, they examine by what strategy they might make the enemy abandon it.

One of the most common elements of strategy is to imitate the cry of wild animals. Young men spread out in the brush, imitating the call of stags, the roar of buffalo, the cry of a fox. The savages are accustomed to this ruse; but such is their passion for the hunt, and such is the perfect imitation of the voices of the animals, that they are continuously taken in this trap. They leave their camp and fall into an ambush. They rally, if they can, on ground defended by natural obstacles, such as a path in a marsh, a tongue of land between two lakes.

Enclosed in this position, they then, instead of trying to break out, busy themselves with different games, as if they were in their villages. It is always only as a last resort that two troops of Indians resolve on an attack in force; they prefer to fight with patience and ruse; and as neither side has provisions, either those who block a canyon are forced to retreat, or those shut up in it must break out.

The melee is frightful; it is a great duel as in the ancient combats: man to man. There is in the human face animated by anger something contagious and terrible which spreads. The cries of death, the songs of war, the mutual outrages make the battlefield resound; the warriors insult one another as did the heroes of Homer; they know one another by name: "Don't you

146

remember," they say to one another, "the day when you wanted your feet to have the speed of the wind so you could flee before my arrow? Old women! Shall I have them bring you some new *sagamité* and burning *cassina* in a section of reed?" "Babbling chief with a big mouth," answer the others, "we can see that you are accustomed to wearing a skirt; your tongue is like the aspen leaf, it trembles ceaselessly!"

The combatants taunt one another with their natural imperfections: they call each other limping, cross-eyed, short; these words inflicted on the self-esteem augment their rage. The frightful custom of scalping the enemy heightens the ferocity of the combat. They put their foot on the neck of the one who is overcome; with the left hand they grasp the tuft of hair the Indians keep on the top of their heads; with the right hand they trace a circle on the scalp around the hair with a narrow knife. This trophy is often taken with such skill that the brain is left uncovered without having been penetrated by the point of the instrument.

When the two enemy parties meet in open country and one is weaker than the other, the weaker ones dig holes in the ground. They crawl into them and fight as in those fortified cities whose works, almost at ground level, present little surface for bullets. The besiegers launch their arrows like bombs, with such exactness that they fall on the heads of the besieged.

Military honors are accorded to those who have slain the greatest numbers of the enemy: they are allowed to wear the feathers of the killiou. To avoid injustice, the arrows of each warrior bear an individual mark. When they draw them from the body of the victim, they know the hand that launched them.

The firearm cannot bear testimony to the glory of its master. When one kills with the bullet, the tomahawk, or the hatchet, it is by the number of scalps that the exploits are counted.

During the combat it is rare for them to obey the war chief, who indeed seeks only to distinguish himself. It is rare for the victors to pursue the vanquished. They stay on the battlefield to strip the dead, to bind up the prisoners, to celebrate the triumph with dances and songs; they mourn the friends they have lost. Their bodies are exposed amidst great lamentations on the branches of the trees, while the bodies of the enemy remain lying in the dust.

A warrior dispatched from the camp bears to the nation news of the victory and announces the return of the army.[111] The old men assemble; the war chief reports to the council on the expedition; according to this report they determine whether to continue the war or negotiate peace.

If they decide on peace, the prisoners are kept as a means of concluding it; if they hold out for war, the prisoners are tortured. May I be allowed to refer my readers to the episodes of *Atala* and *The Natchez* for the details. The women ordinarily show themselves to be cruel in this vengeance: they tear the prisoners with their nails, pierce them with household instruments, and prepare meals of their flesh. This flesh is eaten grilled or boiled, and the cannibals know which are the most succulent parts of the victim. Those who do not devour their enemies at least drink their blood and daub their chests and faces with it.

But the women also have a fine privilege: they can save the prisoners by adopting them as brothers or husbands, especially if they have lost brothers or husbands in the battle. Adoption confers the rights of nature. There is no example of an adopted prisoner betraying the family of which he has become a member, and he shows no less ardor than his new compatriots in bearing arms against his former nation; thus arise the most pathetic adventures. A father fairly often finds himself face to face with his son. If the son overcomes the father, he lets him go the first time, but he says to him: "You gave me life, I give it back to you; we are even. Appear no more before me, for I shall take your scalp."

However, the adopted prisoners do not enjoy complete security. If it so happens that the tribe in which they serve suffers some loss, they are massacred: the woman who has cared for a child cuts him in two with a blow of the hatchet.

The Iroquois, renowned moreover for their cruelty towards prisoners of war, had a custom one would almost say was borrowed from the Romans, which bore evidence of the genius of a great people: they incorporated the conquered nation into their own nation without making them slaves; they did not even force them to adopt their laws; they only subjected them to their customs.

All tribes did not burn their prisoners; some were content to reduce them to servitude. The Sachems, rigid partisans of the old customs, deplored that humaneness, a degeneration, they said, of the old virtue. Christianity, spreading among the Indians, had contributed to softening ferocious characteristics. It was in the name of a God sacrificed by men that the missionaries obtained the abolition of human sacrifice. They planted the cross in place of the torture stake, and the blood of Jesus Christ redeemed the blood of the prisoner.

RELIGION

When the Europeans landed in America, they found among the savages religious beliefs which are almost wiped out today. The peoples of Florida and Louisiana almost all adored the sun, as did the Peruvians and the Mexicans. They had temples, priests or medicine men, and sacrifices; however, they mixed with this southern cult the cult and traditions of some northern divinity.

The public sacrifices took place along rivers; they were made at the change of seasons or on the occasion of peace or war. The individual sacrifices were accomplished in the huts. The Indians threw to the wind the profane ashes and lit a new fire. The offering to the good and evil spirits consisted of animal skins, household implements, arms, necklaces, all of it of little value.

But a superstition common to all Indians, and very likely the only one that has been kept, was that of the Manitous. Each savage has his Manitou, as each Negro has his fetish: it is a bird, a fish, a quadruped, a reptile, a stone, a bit of wood, a shred of cloth, a colored object, an American or European ornament. The hunter is careful never to kill or wound the animal he has chosen for Manitou. When this misfortune does take place, he seeks by all possible means to appease the shades of the dead god; but he is not entirely reassured until he has dreamed another Manitou.

Dreams play a great role in the religion of the savage; their interpretation is a science, and their illusions are held for realities. Among civilized peoples, it is often the contrary: the realities are illusions.

Among the indigenous nations of the New World the dogma of the immortality of the soul is not distinctly expressed, but they all have an idea of it, as indicated by their customs, their fables, their funeral ceremonies, their piety toward the dead. Far from denying the immortality of the soul, the savages multiply it: they seem to accord it to the souls of animals—from insects, reptiles, fishes, and birds to the greatest quadruped. Indeed, peoples who see and hear spirits everywhere must naturally suppose that they have one within themselves and that the animate beings which are companions of their solitude also have divine intelligence.

Among the nations of Canada, there existed a complete system of religious fables, and surprisingly there could be noted in those fables traces of the Greek fictions and Biblical truths.

The Great Hare one day assembled on the water his court composed of the moose, the deer, the bear, and the other quadrupeds. He drew a grain of sand from the bottom of the great lake and from it formed the earth. Then he created men from the dead bodies of different animals.

Another tradition makes of Areskoui or Agresgoué, god of war, the Supreme Being or the Great Spirit.

The Great Hare was crossed in his plans: the god of waters, Michabou, surnamed the Great Tiger Cat, opposed the enterprise of the Great Hare; the latter, having to fight Michabou, could create only six men. One of these men climbed to the sky; he had commerce with the beautiful Athaënsic, divinity of vengeance. The Great Hare, perceiving that she was pregnant, with a kick cast her to the earth; she fell on the back of a tortoise.

Some medicine men maintain that Athaënsic had two sons, one of whom killed the other; but it is generally believed that she gave birth only to a daughter, who became the mother of Tahouet-Saron and Jouskeka. Jouskeka killed Tahouet-Saron.

Athaënsic is sometimes taken as the moon and Jouskeka as the sun. Areskoui, god of war, also becomes the sun. Among the Natchez, Athaënsic, goddess of vengeance, was the squaw-chief of the evil Manitous, as Jouskeka was the squaw-chief of the good ones.

In the third generation, the race of Jouskeka became almost entirely extinct, and the Great Spirit sent a flood. Messou, otherwise Saketchak, seeing this deluge, delegated a crow to inquire after the state of things, but the crow performed his task badly; then Messou sent the muskrat, who brought him a bit of mud. Messou reestablished the land in its original state; he let fly arrows against the trunks of the trees still standing, and those arrows became branches. He then married, out of gratitude, a female muskrat; from that marriage were born all the men who today people the world.

There are variants to these fables. According to some authorities it was not Messou who caused the flood to stop but the tortoise on which Athaënsic fell from heaven. The tortoise in swimming parted the waters with his flippers and bared the land. Thus it is vengeance which is the mother of the new race of men.

The Great Beaver is, after the Great Hare, the most powerful of the Manitous. It is he who formed Lake Nipissing. The cataracts found on the Ottawa River, which flows out of Nipissing, are the remains of the dams that the Great Beaver had constructed to form the lake; but he died in the midst of his undertaking. He is buried on the top of a mountain to which he gave his own shape. No nation passes by the foot of his tomb without smoking in his honor.

Michabou, god of waters, was born at Michilimackinac, on the straits that join Lake Huron to Lake Michigan. From there he transported himself to the straits of Sainte Marie, set up a dam at the falls, and, stopping the waters of Lake Nipigon, made Lake Superior to catch beavers. Michabou learned from the spider how to weave nets and then taught the same art to men.

There are places the spirits particularly like. Two days' journey below Saint Anthony Falls is seen the great Wakon-Teebe (the cavern of the Great Spirit); it contains an underground lake of unknown depth; when a stone is thrown into this lake, the Great Hare causes a fearsome voice to be heard. Characters are engraved by the spirits on the stone of the vault.

Toward the sunset from Lake Superior are mountains formed of stone which glitters like the ice of cataracts in winter. Behind these mountains extends a lake much greater than Lake Superior; Michabou particularly likes this lake and these mountains. But it is at Lake Superior that the Great Spirit has fixed his residence; he is seen walking there by moonlight; he also likes to pick the currants which cover the southern bank of the lake. Often, seated on top of a rock, he unleashes storms. He inhabits an island in the lake that bears his name; it is there the souls of warriors fallen on the battlefield go to enjoy the pleasures of the hunt.

From the middle of the Sacred Lake there used to emerge a mountain of copper which the Great Spirit removed and transported elsewhere a long time ago; but he strewed on the bank stones of the same metal which have a singular virtue: they render invisible those who carry them. The Great Spirit does not want these stones to be touched. One day some Algonquians were bold enough to remove one; scarcely had they returned to their canoes than a Manitou more than 60 cubits high, appearing from the depths of a forest, pursued them. The water scarcely reached his waist. He obliged the Algonquians to throw into the waves the treasure they had stolen.

On the shores of Lake Huron the Great Spirit caused the white hare to sing like a bird and gave the voice of a cat to the bluebird.

On the islands of Lake Erie, Athaënsic planted flea grass. If a warrior looks at this herb, he is consumed with fever; if he touches it, a subtle fire runs over his skin. Athaënsic also planted on the shore of Lake Erie the white cedar to destroy the race of men: the vapor arising from the tree kills the child in the breast of the young mother, as rain spoils the cluster on the vine.

The Great Hare gave his wisdom to the hoot owl of Lake Erie. This bird hunts mice in the summer; he mutilates them and carries them off alive to his abode, where he is careful to fatten them for the winter. That is not too unlike the rulers of men.

At the cataract of Niagara lives the redoubtable Spirit of the Iroquois.

Near Lake Ontario male doves cast themselves in the morning into the Genesee River; in the evening they are followed by an equal number of females; they are going to seek the fair Endaé, who was recalled from the land of souls by the songs of her husband.

The little bird of Lake Ontario wages war on the black snake. Here is what gave birth to this war.

Hondioun was a famous chief of the Iroquois, the hut builders. He saw the young Almilao, and he was astonished. He danced three times in anger, for Almilao was a daughter of the Huron nation, enemies of the Iroquois. Hondioun returned to his hut saying, "It does not matter"; but the warrior's soul did not speak thus.

He lay on his mat for two suns, and he could not sleep; at the third sun he closed his eyes and saw a bear in his dreams. He prepared for death.

He arose, took his arms, crossed the forests, and arrived at the hut of Almilao in the enemy country. It was dark.

Almilao heard someone walking in her cabin; she said, "Akouessan, sit on my mat." Hondioun sat on the mat without speaking. Athaënsic and her anger were in his heart. Almilao threw an arm around the Iroquois warrior without knowing him, and sought his lips. Hondioun loved her as if she were the moon.

Akouessan of the Abnakis, allies of the Hurons, arrived; he approached in the darkness: the lovers slept. He lay next to Almilao without noticing Hondioun rolled in the skins of the couch. Akouessan enchanted the sleep of his mistress.

Hondioun awoke, stretched out his hand, touched the head of a warrior. The war cry shook the cabin. The Sachems of the Hurons rushed in. Akouessan the Abnaki was no more.

Hondioun, the Iroquois chief, was attached to the prisoners' stake; he sang his death song; he called Almilao from within the fire and invited the Huron girl to devour his heart. She wept and smiled: life and death were on her lips.

153

The Great Hare caused Hondioun's soul to enter into the black snake and that of Almilao into the little bird of Lake Ontario. The little bird attacked the black snake and struck it dead with its beak. Akouessan was changed into a merman.

The Great Hare made a cave of black and green marble in the land of the Abnakis; he planted a tree in the salty lake, the sea at the entrance of the cave. All the efforts of the palefaces have never been able to uproot that tree. When the storm blows on the shoreless lake, the Great Hare descends from the blue rock and comes under that tree to mourn Hondioun, Almilao, and Akouessan.

So it is that the fables of the savages lead the traveler from the depths of the lakes of Canada to the shores of the Atlantic. Moses, Lucretius, and Ovid seem to have left a legacy to these peoples, the first his tradition, the second his bad physics, the third his metamorphoses. You can find in all that enough religion, falsehood, and poetry, to learn, to be led astray, and to be consoled.

Government among
the Indians

THE NATCHEZ: DESPOTISM IN
THE STATE OF NATURE

Almost always the state of nature has been confused with the primitive state; from this mistake has come the misconception that the savages had no government, that each family was simply led by its chief or its father, that a hunt or a war occasionally united the families in common interest, but that once this interest was satisfied the families returned to their isolation and independence.

Those are notable errors. Among the savages there are to be found all the types of governments known to civilized peoples, from despotism to republic, passing through monarchy, limited or absolute, elective or hereditary.

The Indians of North America knew monarchies and representative republics. Federalism was one of the most common political forms used by them. The extent of their wilderness had done for the science of their government what the excess population has produced for ours.

The error into which people have fallen relative to the political existence of the savage government is all the more singular in that they should have been enlightened by the history of the Greeks and Romans: at the birth of their empire, they had very complicated institutions.

Political laws are born among men before civil laws, which would seem however to precede the first; but it is a fact that power was regulated before right, because men need to protect themselves against the arbitrary before fixing their relations with one another. Political laws are born spontaneously with man and are established without antecedents; they are to be found among the most barbarous hordes.

Civil laws, on the other hand, are formed by customs: what was a religious custom for the marriage of a girl and boy, for the birth of a child, for the death of the head of a family, is transformed into a law by the lapse of time. Private property, unknown to the hunting peoples, is another source of civil laws lacking in the state of nature. Thus there existed among the Indians of North America no code of crimes and punishments. Crimes against things and persons were punished by the family, not by the law. Vengeance was justice: natural law prosecuted among the uncivilized that which public law reaches among the civilized.

Let us assemble first the characteristics common to all the governments of the savages, then we shall enter into the details of each of the governments.

The Indian nations are divided by tribes; each tribe has a hereditary chief, who is distinct from the military chief; the latter derives his right from election, as among the old Germanic peoples.

The tribes have a particular name: the Eagle tribe, the Bear tribe, the Beaver tribe, etc. The emblems that serve to distinguish the tribes become the insignia in war and the seals at the bottom of treaties.

The chiefs of the tribes and of the divisions of tribes draw their names from some quality, some defect of their minds or their persons, from some circumstance of their lives. Thus, one is called White Bison, another Broken Leg, Flat Mouth, Dark Day, Darter, Beautiful Voice, Beaver Killer, Heart of Fire, etc.

So it was in Greece; in Rome, Cocles drew his name from his close-set eyes or from the loss of his eye, and Cicero, from the mole or the industry of his grandfather. Modern history designates its kings and warriors as The Bald, The Stutterer, The Red, The Lame, The Hammer (Martel), The Big-head (Capet), etc.

The councils of the Indian nations are composed of the chiefs of tribes, the military chiefs, the matrons, the orators, the prophets or medicine men, and the doctors; but these councils vary according to the makeup of the peoples.

The spectacle of a council of savages is very picturesque. When the ceremony of the pipe is finished, an orator takes the floor. The members of the council are seated or lying on the ground in various positions. Some, entirely nude, have only a buffalo skin to wrap themselves in; others, tattooed from head to toe, resemble Egyptian statues;[112] others mix European ornaments with savage ornaments—feathers, bird beaks, bear claws, buffalo horns, beaver bones, fish teeth. Their faces are striped with different colors or smeared with white or black. They listen attentively to the orator. Each of his pauses is received with the applauding cry of *Oah! Oah!*

Nations so simple should have nothing to debate in politics; yet the truth is that no civilized people treats of more things at once. An embassy must be sent to a tribe to congratulate it on its victories; a pact of alliance must be concluded or renewed; an explanation must be asked over the violation of a territory; a deputation must be sent to mourn the death of a chief; an opinion must be expressed at an assembly; a chief elected, a competitor driven off, mediation offered or accepted to cause two peoples to lay down their arms, a balance maintained so that a certain nation will not become too strong and threaten the liberty of the others. All these affairs are discussed with order; the reasons pro and con are clarified. Sachems have been known who were fully conversant with all these matters and who spoke with a profoundness and judgment few statesmen in Europe would be capable of.

The deliberations of the council are set down in necklaces of different colors—they are the state archives, which contain the treaties of war, peace, and alliance, with all the conditions and clauses of these treaties. Other necklaces contain the speeches delivered in the different councils. I have mentioned elsewhere the artificial memory the Iroquois used to retain a long speech. The work was divided among warriors who, by means of a few bones, learned by heart, or rather wrote in their memory, the part of the speech that they were charged with reproducing.[113]

The decrees of the Sachems are sometimes engraved on trees

in enigmatic signs. Time, which gnaws at our old chronicles, likewise destroys those of the savages, but in a different way; it extends a new layer of bark over the papyrus which guards the Indians' history. After a short number of years, the Indian and his history have disappeared in the shadow of the same tree.

Let us now go on to the history of the particular institutions of the Indians' governments, beginning with despotism.

It must first be remarked that wherever despotism has been established there reigns a kind of physical civilization, such as is found among most of the peoples of Asia and such as there existed in Peru and Mexico. The man who can no longer enter into public affairs and who delivers his life to a master as if he were a beast or a child has all the time he needs to occupy himself with his material well-being. Since the system of slavery supplies this man with other arms beside his own, those "machines" plow his field, beautify his dwelling, manufacture his clothing, and prepare his meals. But, after arriving at a certain point, that civilization of despotism remains stationary; for the superior tyrant, who is willing to permit a few particular tyrannies, always keeps the right of life and death over his subjects, and they are careful to close themselves up within a mediocrity which excites neither the cupidity nor the jealousy of power.

Under the empire of despotism there is thus a beginning of luxury and administration, but in a measure which does not permit industry to develop or the genius of man to arrive at liberty through enlightenment.

Hernando de Soto found people of this nature in the Floridas and came to die on the banks of the Mississippi. Over this great river extended the domination of the Natchez. They were of Mexican origin, leaving that country only after the fall of Montezuma's throne. The period of the emigration of the Natchez corresponds with that of the Chickasaws, who came from Peru, likewise driven from their native land by the invasion of the Spaniards.

A chief named The Sun governed the Natchez: that chief claimed to descend from the luminary of day. Succession to the throne was through the women—it was not the son of The Sun who succeeded him, but the son of his sister or his closest female relative. Squaw Chief, such was her name, had along with The Sun a guard of young men called *Allouez.*

The dignitaries beneath The Sun were the two war chiefs, the two priests, the two treaty officers, the inspector of public works and granaries—a powerful man called Flour Chief— and the four masters of ceremonies.

The harvest, done communally and placed under the guard of The Sun, was the origin and the principal cause of the establishment of tyranny. Sole depository of the public fortune, the monarch profited from it to make the subjects his creatures: he gave to some at the expense of others; he invented that hierarchy of offices which involves a host of men in power through their complicity in oppression. The Sun surrounded himself with satellites ready to execute his orders. After a few generations, classes were formed in the state. Those who descended from the generals or the officers of the *Allouez* claimed nobility; they were believed. Then was invented a multitude of laws. Each individual saw himself obliged to bear to The Sun a part of his hunt or his catch. If The Sun ordered a certain task, they were obliged to execute it without receiving any salary for it. In imposing the duty, The Sun appropriated the right of judgment. "May I be relieved of this dog," he would say, and his guards would obey.

The despotism of The Sun engendered that of the Squaw Chief and then that of the nobles. When a nation becomes enslaved, there is formed a chain of tyrants from the first class to the last. The arbitrary nature of Squaw Chief's power took on the character of that sovereign's sex; it moved into the field of manners. Squaw Chief thought herself entitled to have as many husbands and lovers as she wished. She then had the objects of her caprice strangled. In a short time it was allowed that the young Sun, upon ascending the throne, could have his father strangled when that father was not noble.

This corruption by the mother of the heir to the throne descended to the other women. The nobles could abuse the virgins and even the young wives of the whole nation. The Sun had gone as far as to decree a general prostitution of the women, as it was practiced at certain Babylonian initiations.

There remained only one more evil, superstition: the

Natchez were overburdened with it. The priests calculated to fortify tyranny by the degradation of the people's reason. It became a singular honor, a meritorious action in the eyes of heaven, to kill oneself on the tomb of a noble; there were chiefs whose funerals entailed the massacre of more than 100 victims. These oppressors seemed to abandon absolute power in life only to inherit the tyranny of death: the people still obeyed a dead body, so much were they bent on slavery! Much more, they sometimes solicited ten years in advance the honor of accompanying The Sun to the land of souls. Heaven permitted one justice: those very *Allouez* by whom servitude had been instituted, gathered the fruits of their work—opinion obliged them to stab themselves at their master's funeral. Suicide became the worthy ornament of despotism's funeral services. But of what use was it to the sovereign of the Natchez to take his guard along with him beyond life? Could they defend him against the eternal avenger of the oppressed?

When a certain Squaw Chief died, her husband, who was not noble, was strangled. The eldest daughter of the Squaw Chief, who succeeded to her office, ordered the strangling of 12 children; these 12 bodies were arranged around those of the former Squaw Chief and her husband. The 14 bodies were laid out on an elegantly decorated stretcher.

Fourteen *Allouez* carried the funeral bed. The convoy started off. The parents of the strangled children opened the line of march, two by two, carrying their dead children in their arms. Fourteen victims who had vowed themselves to death followed the funeral bed holding in their hands the fatal rope that they had woven themselves. The closest relatives of the victims surrounded them. The family of the Squaw Chief closed the line of march.

At distances of ten paces the parents who preceded the bier, would drop the bodies of their children; the men who carried the stretcher walked on these bodies, so that when they arrived at the temple, the flesh of these tender bodies was torn to shreds.

The convoy stopped at the place of entombment. They undressed the 14 victims, who then sat down on the ground; an *Allouez* sat down on the lap of each of them, another held their

160

hands behind them; they were made to swallow three pieces of tobacco[114] and drink a little water; the cord was passed around their necks, and the relatives of the Squaw Chief, singing, pulled on the two ends of the cord.

It is difficult to understand how a people among whom individual property was unknown, and who were ignorant of most needs of society, could have fallen under such a yoke. On one side naked men, the liberty of nature; on the other, demands without equal, a despotism that goes beyond the most formidable examples among civilized peoples. The primitive innocence and virtue of the political state in its cradle, the corruption and crimes of a decrepit government: what a monstrous combination!

A simple, natural, almost effortless revolution delivered the Natchez in part from their chains. Broken by the yoke of the nobles and The Sun, they were content to retreat to the forests; solitude returned their liberty to them. The Sun, remaining in the big village, no longer having anything to give to the *Allouez*, since the communal field was no longer cultivated, was abandoned by those mercenaries. The Sun had for successor a reasonable prince who did not reestablish the guards; he abolished the tyrannical customs, recalled his subjects, and caused them to love his government. A council of old men formed by him destroyed the principle of tyranny by regulating communal property in a new way.

The savage nations, under the empire of primitive ideas, have an invincible aversion to private property, the foundation of social order. Therefore among some Indians there are the communal property, the public field of harvest, the crops stored in granaries where each comes to draw according to his needs; but at the same time, it is the source of power for the chiefs who guard those treasures and who finally distribute them for the benefit of their own ambition.

The regenerated Natchez found a means of sheltering themselves from private property, without falling into the disadvantage of communal property. The public field was divided into as many lots as there were families. Each family took off the harvest from one of these lots. Thus the public granary was destroyed at the same time that the communal field remained, and as each family did not gather in specifically the product of the square that they had plowed and sown, it could not say that it had a particular right to the enjoyment of what it had received. It was not the communality of the land, but the communality of the work which caused the communal ownership.

The Natchez preserved the exterior and the forms of their old institutions: they did not cease having an absolute monarchy, a Sun, a Squaw Chief, and different orders or different classes of men; but they were only remembrances of the past, remembrances useful to the peoples, with whom it is never good to destroy the authority of the ancestors. They continued to maintain the perpetual fire in the temple; they did not even touch the ashes of the old chiefs placed in that edifice because it is a crime to violate the asylum of the dead, and, after all, the dust of tyrants presents lessons as great as that of other men.

MUSKOGEES: LIMITED MONARCHY IN THE STATE OF NATURE

To the east of the land of the despotically oppressed Natchez the Muskogees offered on the scale of savage governments the constitutional or limited monarchy.

The Muskogees form with the Seminoles in old Florida the Creek confederation. They have a chief called Mico, a king or magistrate. The Mico, recognized as the first man of the nation, receives all sorts of marks of respect. When he presides over the council, almost abject homage is paid him; when he is absent, his seat remains empty. The Mico convokes the council to deliberate on peace and war; to him the ambassadors and foreigners who arrive in the nation present themselves.

The royalty of the Mico is elective and cannot be removed. The old men name the Mico; the body of warriors confirm the nomination. One must have spilled blood in combat or have distinguished oneself by force of reason, genius, or eloquence, in order to aspire to the place of the Mico. This sovereign, who owes his power only to his merit, rises over the confederation of the Creeks like the sun, to animate and fecundate the earth.

The Mico bears no mark of distinction. Outside the council

he is a simple Sachem who mixes with the crowd, chats, smokes, drains the cup with all the warriors. A foreigner could not recognize him. In the council itself, where he receives so many honors, he has only his voice; all his influence is in his wisdom. His opinion is generally accepted, because his opinion is almost always the best.

The Muskogees' veneration for the Mico is extreme. If a young man is tempted to do something dishonest, his companion says to him, "Be careful, the Mico sees you," and the young man stops. It is the action of the invisible despotism of virtue.

The Mico enjoys, however, a dangerous prerogative. The harvests among the Muskogees are gathered in common. Each family, after having received its lot, is obliged to bear part of it to a public granary, on which the Mico draws at will. The abuse of a like privilege produced the tyranny of the Suns of the Natchez, as we have just seen.

After the Mico, the greatest authority of the state resides in the council of old men. This council decides on peace and war and executes the orders of the Mico: a singular political institution. In the monarchy of civilized peoples, the king is the executive power, and the council or national assembly wields the legislative power; here it is the opposite: the monarch makes the laws, and the council executes them. These savages thought perhaps that there was less peril in investing a council of elders with the executive power than in putting this power in the hands of a single man. On the other hand, experience having proved that a single man of mature age and of a reflective mind better elaborates laws than a deliberative body, the Muskogees have placed the legislative power in the king.

But the council of the Muskogees has a capital vice: it is under the immediate direction of the grand medicine man, who leads it through fear of enchantments and through the interpretations of dreams. The priests form in this nation a redoubtable body, which threatens to capture various powers.

The war chief, independent of the Mico, exercises an absolute power over the armed youth. Nevertheless, if the nation is in imminent peril, the Mico appears for a limited time to be the general, since he is the magistrate at home.

Such is, or rather such was the Muskogee government, considered in itself and separately. It has other ties as a federative government.

The Muskogees, a proud and ambitious nation, came from the west and seized Florida after having wiped out the Yamasees, its first inhabitants.[115] Soon after, the Seminoles, arriving from the east, contracted an alliance with the Muskogees. The latter being the stronger, they forced the Seminoles to enter into a confederation, in virtue of which the Seminoles send representatives to the great villages of the Muskogees and thus find themselves governed in part by the Mico.

The two united nations were called by the Europeans the nation of the Creeks and were divided by them into upper Creeks, the Muskogees, and lower Creeks, the Seminoles. The ambition of the Muskogees remained unsatisfied, and they carried war to the Cherokees and the Chickasaws and obliged them to enter into the common alliance, a confederation as famous in the south of North America as that of the Iroquois in the north. Is it not singular to see savages attempt the union of the Indians into a federal republic at the same place where the Europeans were to establish a government of that nature?

The Muskogees in making treaties with the whites stipulated that no brandy would be sold to their allied nations. In the villages of the Creeks only a single European trader was allowed; he lived there under public protection. The laws of the most exact probity were never violated in respect to him; he came and went in safety for his fortune as for his life.

The Muskogees are inclined to idleness and feasting; they cultivate the land, have flocks and Spanish horses, and also slaves. The serf works in the fields, cultivates the fruits and flowers in the garden, keeps the cabin clean, and prepares the meals. He is housed, dressed, and fed like his masters. If he marries, his children are free; they regain their natural right by birth. The misfortune of the parents is not passed on to their posterity; the Muskogees did not want servitude to be hereditary: a fine lesson that savages have given to civilized men!

Such is slavery nonetheless: whatever its mildness, it degraded the virtues. The Muskogee, bold, boisterous, impetuous, barely putting up with the slightest contradiction, is served by the Yamasee, timid, silent, patient, abject. This Yamasee, former master of the Floridas, is still of the Indian race; he fought like a hero to save his country from the invasion of the Muskogees, but fortune betrayed him. What made such a great difference between the Yamasee of old and the Yamasee of today? Two words: liberty and servitude.

The Muskogee villages are built in a particular way: each family has almost always four similar houses or huts. These four cabins face one another to form a square court of about half an acre which is entered at the four corners. The cabins, constructed of boards, are plastered inside and out with a red mortar that resembles brick clay. Bits of cypress bark, arranged like tortoise shells, serve as roofs for the buildings.

In the center of the principal village, and in the highest place, is a public square surrounded by four long galleries. One of these galleries is the council chamber where the council meets every day to conduct business. This chamber is divided into two rooms by a longitudinal partition; the room at the back is thus deprived of light; it can be entered only by a low door opening at the bottom of the partition. In this sanctuary are placed the treasures of religion and politics: the deerhorn beads, the medicine cup, the *chichikoués*, the peace pipe, the national standard made from the tail of an eagle. Only the Mico, the war chief, and the high priest can enter this fearsome place.

The outer room of the council chamber is cut in three parts by small transverse partitions waist high. From these balconies rise three graduated rows of seats arranged against the wall of the sanctuary. It is on these mat-covered benches that the Sachems and the warriors sit.

The three other galleries, which form with the council gallery the enclosure of the public square, are likewise divided each into three parts; but they have no longitudinal partition. These galleries are called banquet galleries. A noisy crowd can always be found there, occupied at different games.

The walls, the partitions, and the wooden columns of these galleries are covered with hieroglyphic ornaments embodying the religious and political secrets of the nation. These paintings represent men in diverse attitudes, birds and quadrupeds with heads of men, men with heads of animals. The design of the monuments is effected with boldness and in natural proportions; the color is bright but applied without art. The order of architecture of the columns varies in the villages according to the tribe: at Otasses the columns are always spiral because the Muskogees of Otasses are of the Snake tribe.

This nation has a city of peace and a city of blood. The city of peace is the capital of the Creek confederation and is called Apalachicola. In that city blood is never spilled; and when it is a question of general peace, the Creek representatives are convoked there.

The Blood town is called Coweta; it is situated 12 miles from Apalachicola. The question of war is deliberated there.

Notable in the Creek confederation are the savages who inhabit the fair village Uche, composed of 2,000 inhabitants, which can arm 500 warriors. These savages speak the Savanna or Savantica language, a language radically different from the Muskogee tongue. The allies of the village of Uche are ordinarily, in the council, of a different opinion from the other allies, who look upon them with jealousy; but they are circumspect enough on both sides to avoid a rupture.

The Seminoles, less numerous than the Muskogees, have barely nine villages, all situated on the Flint River. You cannot take a step in their country without discovering savannas, lakes, fountains, and rivers of the purest water.

The Seminole exudes gaiety, contentment, love; his step is light, his manner open and serene; his gestures betray activity and life. He speaks much and volubly; his language is harmonious and easy. This amiable and fickle character is so pronounced among these people that they can scarcely maintain a dignified appearance in the political assemblies of the confederation.

The Seminoles and the Muskogees are fairly tall, and, by an extraordinary contrast, their women are the smallest race of women known in America: they rarely attain the height of four feet two or three inches; their hands and feet resemble those of a European girl of nine or ten. But nature has compensated for this kind of injustice: their figures are elegant and gracious, their eyes black, extremely large, and full of languor and modesty. They lower their eyelids with a kind of voluptuous modesty. If you did not see them when they speak you would think you were hearing children pronouncing only half-formed words.

The Creek women work less that the other Indian women. They busy themselves with embroidery, coloring, and other small work. The slaves spare them the work of cultivating the earth; and yet they help, as do the warriors, in gathering the harvest.

The Muskogees are renowned for poetry and music. During the third night of the new corn celebration, they gather in the council galleries and compete for the singing prize. This prize is bestowed by the Mico according to majority vote: it is a branch of live oak; the Hellenes vied for an olive branch. The women take part and often obtain the crown; one of their odes is still famous:

SONG OF THE PALEFACE[116]

The paleface came from Virginia. He was rich; he had blue cloth, powder, arms, and French poison.[117] The paleface saw Tibeïma the *Ikouessen*.[118]

"I love you," he said to the painted woman. "When I approach you, I feel the marrow of my bones melt; my eyes become troubled; I feel as if I were dying."

The painted woman, who wanted the paleface's riches, answered him, "Let me engrave my name on your lips; press my breast against your breast."

Tibeïma and the paleface built a cabin. The *Ikouessen* dissipated the great riches of the foreigner and then was unfaithful to him. The paleface learned of it, but he could not stop loving her. He went from door to door begging grains of corn for Tibeïma. When the paleface could obtain a bit of liquid fire,[119] he drank it to forget his grief.

Still loving Tibeïma, still deceived by her, the white man lost his reason and started running wild in the woods. The painted woman's father, a famous Sachem, reprimanded her: the heart of a woman who has ceased loving is harder than the fruit of the papaya.[120]

The paleface returned to his cabin. He was naked and had a long bristly beard; his eyes were hollow, his lips

167

pale. He sat down on a mat to ask for hospitality in his own cabin. The white man was hungry. As he had become unbalanced, he thought he was a child and took Tibeïma for his mother.

Tibeïma, who had found riches once again with another warrior in the paleface's former cabin, held in horror the man she had loved. She drove him out. The paleface sat down on a heap of leaves at the door and died. Tibeïma died also. When the Seminole asks what are the ruins of this cabin covered with tall grass, they do not answer.

In the beautiful wilderness of Florida the Spaniards had placed a Fountain of Youth. So was I not authorized to choose this wilderness for the land of some other illusions?

We shall soon see what has become of the Creeks and what fate threatens this people making rapid strides toward civilization.

THE HURONS AND THE IROQUOIS: REPUBLIC IN THE STATE OF NATURE

If the Natchez offer an example of despotism in the state of nature and the Creeks show the first characteristics of limited monarchy, the Hurons and the Iroquois presented, in the same state of nature, the republican form of government. Like the Creeks, they had in addition to the nation's constitution itself, a general representative assembly and a federal pact.

The government of the Hurons differed a little from that of the Iroquois. Next to the council of the tribes there arose a hereditary chief, whose succession was assured through women, as with the Natchez. If the chief's line was extinguished, it was the noblest matron of the tribe who chose a new chief. The influence of the women must have been considerable in a nation whose politics and whose nature gave them so many rights. The historians attribute to this influence a portion of the good and bad qualities of the Huron.

Among the nations of Asia, the women are slaves and have no part in the government; but, burdened with the domestic tasks, they are spared in general the harshest work of the fields. Among the nations of German origin the women were free, but they remained strangers to the acts of politics, if not to the acts of courage and honor. Among the tribes of North America the women participated in the affairs of state but were employed at those painful tasks which have devolved upon man in civilized Europe. Slaves and beasts of burden in the fields and on the hunts, they became free and queenlike in the family assemblies and in the nation's councils. It is necessary to go back to the Gauls to find something of this status of women in a nation.

The Iroquois or the Five Nations,[121] called in the Algonquian language the *Agannonsioni*, were a colony of the Hurons. They separated from the Hurons at an unknown date; they abandoned the shores of Lake Huron and settled on the south bank of the Hochelaga River (the Saint Lawrence), not far from Lake Champlain. Subsequently they went up as far as Lake Ontario and occupied the country situated between Lake Erie and the sources of the Hudson River.

The Iroquois offer a great example of the change oppression and independence can effect in men's characters. After having left the Hurons, they turned to cultivating the land and became a peaceful agricultural nation, from which fact they drew their name of *Agannonsioni*.

Their neighbors, the Adirondacks, of whom we have made the Algonquians, a warlike hunter people who extended their domination over an immense country, scorned the emigrating Hurons whose harvests they bought. It so happened that the Algonquians invited a few young Iroquois on a hunt; they distinguished themselves to such an extent that the jealous Algonquians massacred them.

The Iroquois rushed to arms for the first time; initially defeated, they resolved to perish to the last man or to be free. A warrior genius, which they had not suspected, developed in them suddenly. They in turn overcame the Algonquians, who allied themselves with the Hurons, from whom the Iroquois traced their origin. It was at the most heated moment of that quarrel that Jacques Cartier and then Champlain landed in Canada. The Algonquians joined with the foreigners, and the Iroquois had to fight against the French, the Algonquians, and the Hurons.

Soon the Dutch arrived at Manhattan (New York). The

Iroquois sought the friendship of these new Europeans, procured firearms, and in a short time became more skillful in operating those arms than the whites themselves. There is no example among the civilized peoples of a war so long and implacable as that the Iroquois waged against the Algonquians and the Hurons. It lasted more than three centuries. The Algonquians were exterminated and the Hurons reduced to a tribe taking refuge under the cannon of Quebec. The French colony of Canada, on the point of succumbing itself to the attacks of the Iroquois, was saved only by a piece of political strategy on the part of these extraordinary savages.[122]

It is probable that the Indians of North America were first governed by kings, like the inhabitants of Rome and Athens, and that these monarchies changed then into aristocratic republics; in the principal Huron and Iroquois settlements noble families were found, ordinarily three in number. These families were the source of the three main tribes: one of these tribes enjoyed a sort of preeminence; the members of this first tribe called one another brother and called the members of the two other tribes cousins.

These three tribes bore the names of the Huron tribes: the Deer Tribe, the Wolf Tribe, the Tortoise Tribe. The last one was divided into two branches, the Great Tortoise and the Small Tortoise.

The government, extremely complicated, was composed of three councils: the council of the participants, the council of the elders, and the council of the warriors capable of bearing arms—that is, the body of the nation.

Each family furnished a representative to the council of participants; this representative was named by the women, who often chose a woman to represent them. The council of participants was the supreme council; thus the highest power belonged to the women, and the men called themselves only their lieutenants; but the council of elders decided in the last resort, and to it were appealed the deliberations of the council of participants.

The Iroquois had thought that they should not be deprived of the aid of a sex whose unbounded and ingenious mind is very resourceful and is capable of acting on the human heart, but they had also thought that the decrees of a council of women could be impassioned. They had wanted these decrees to be tempered and so to speak cooled by the judgment of the elders. The council of women was to be found among our forefathers, the Gauls.

The second council, or the council of elders, was the moderator between the council of participants and the council composed of the body of young warriors.

All the members of these three councils did not have the right to speak: orators chosen by each tribe dealt with the affairs of state before the councils. The orators made a particular study of politics and eloquence.

This custom, which would be an obstacle to liberty among the civilized peoples of Europe, was only a measure of order among the Iroquois. With these peoples none of the individual liberty was sacrificed to the general liberty. No member of the three councils felt himself bound individually by the deliberation of the councils. However it was unprecedented for a warrior to refuse to submit to them.

The Iroquois nation was divided into five cantons. These cantons were not dependent on one another and could make peace and war separately. The neutral cantons offered them their good offices in such cases.

The five cantons named representatives from time to time who renewed the general alliance. In this diet, held in the midst of the forests, they dealt with a few great undertakings involving the honor and safety of the whole nation. Each representative made a report relative to the canton he represented, and they deliberated on the means of creating mutual prosperity.

The Iroquois were as famous for their politics as for their arms. Placed between the English and the French, they soon perceived the rivalry of these two peoples. They understood that they would be sought after by both. They made an alliance with the English, whom they didn't like, against the French, whom they esteemed but who had united with the Algonquians and the Hurons. However, they did not want the complete triumph of either of the foreign parties; thus the Iroquois were ready to disperse the French colony of Canada when an order of the Sachems stopped the army and forced it to return; thus also the French were on the point of conquering New Jersey and driving out the English when the Iroquois had their five nations march to the aid of the English and saved them.

The Iroquois had nothing in common with the Huron except the language: the Huron, gay, witty, fickle, with a brilliant and bold valor, tall and elegant, seemed to be born to be the ally of the French.

The Iroquois was, on the contrary, heavily built with a wide chest, muscular legs, and vigorous arms. The big round eyes of the Iroquois sparkled with independence, and his entire appearance was that of a hero; there shone on his forehead the intricate combinations of thoughts and the elevated emotions of the soul. This intrepid man was not at all surprised by firearms when they were used against him for the first time; he stood firm under the whistling of the balls and the noise of the cannon, as if he had heard them all his life; he did not appear to pay any more attention to them than to a storm. As soon as he could procure a musket, he made better use of it than a European. Yet he did not abandon the tomahawk, the knife, the bow and arrow; but he added the carbine, the pistol, the dagger, and the hatchet: he seemed never to have enough arms to suit his valor. Doubly armed with the murderous instruments of Europe and America, his head ornamented with plumes, his ears notched, his face smeared with black, his arms dyed with blood, this noble champion of the New World became as fearsome to see as to fight, on the shore he defended foot by foot against the foreigner.

It was in the upbringing that the Iroquois placed the source of their virtue. A young man never sat down in front of an old man: the respect for age was equal to that Lycurgus had caused in Lacedaemon. Youth was accustomed to bear the greatest privations as well as to brave the greatest perils. Long fasts ordered by politics in the name of religion, dangerous hunts, continual training at arms, manly and virile games, had given to the character of the Iroquois something indomitable. Often little boys would tie their arms together, put a burning coal on their bound arms, and fight to see who could bear the pain the longest. If a girl did something wrong and her mother

172

threw some water in her face; that single reprimand sometimes was enough to cause the girl to hang herself.

The Iroquois scorned pain as he did life: a Sachem 100 years old braved the flames of the pyre; he excited the enemy to redouble their cruelty; he defied them to draw as much as a sigh from him. This magnanimity of age had no other purpose than to set an example for the young warriors and to teach them to be worthy of their fathers.

This greatness made itself felt everywhere among these people. Their language, almost entirely aspirated, shocked the ear. When an Iroquois spoke it was like hearing a man who, expressing himself with effort, went successively from the lowest to the highest tone.

Such was the Iroquois before the shadow and the destruction of European civilization were extended over him.

Although I have said that civil law and criminal law are almost unknown to the Indians, custom in some places has taken the place of law. Murder, which among the Franks was redeemed by a monetary settlement commensurate with the status of the persons, is redeemed among the savages only by the death of the murderer. In Italy during the Middle Ages the respective families took up everything concerning their members; that was the beginning of the hereditary vendettas which divided the nation when the enemy families were powerful.

Among the tribes of North America the family of the murderer does not come to his aid, but the relatives of the murdered man consider it their duty to avenge him. The criminal whom the law does not threaten, whom nature does not defend, finding no asylum either in the woods where the allies of the dead man pursue him, or among the foreign tribes who would give him up, or in his home which would not save him, becomes so miserable that an avenging tribunal would be a blessing to him. At least that would be a form, a manner of condemning or acquitting him; for if the law strikes down, it also preserves, like time, which sows and harvests. The Indian murderer, tired of a wandering life, finding no public family to punish him, gives himself into the hands of a particular family which immolates him; in the absence of armed force, the crime leads the criminal to the feet of the judge and the executioner.

Involuntary manslaughter is sometimes expiated by presents. Among the Abnakis, the law was specific: the body of the assassinated man was exposed on a kind of frame in the air; the assassin, attached to a stake, was condemned to take his food and spend several days in this pillory of death.

PRESENT STATE OF THE
SAVAGES OF NORTH AMERICA

If I presented the reader this tableau of savage America as the faithful picture of what exists today, I would be deceiving him. I have painted what was much more than what is. There are no doubt still to be found several of these character traits in the Indians of the wandering tribes of the New World; but the manners in general, the originality of the customs, the primitive form of the governments, in short the American genius, all this has disappeared. After having told of the past, I have yet to complete my work by sketching the present.

When one has evaluated the tales of the first navigators and colonists who reconnoitered and cleared Louisiana, Florida, Georgia, the two Carolinas, Virginia, Maryland, Delaware, Pennsylvania, New Jersey, New York, and all that which is called New England, Acadia, and Canada, one can scarcely estimate the savage population contained between the Mississippi and the Saint Lawrence at the time of the discovery of those countries at less than three million men.

Today the Indian population of all North America, including neither the Mexicans nor the Eskimo, scarcely reaches 400,000. The roll of the indigenous peoples of that part of the New World has not been called: I shall do it. Many men, many tribes will fail to answer: a last historian of those peoples, I shall open their death register.

In 1534, upon the arrival of Jacques Cartier in Canada, and at the time of the founding of Quebec by Champlain in 1608, the Algonquians, the Iroquois, the Hurons, with their allies or subjects, namely, the Etchimins, the Souriquois, the Bersiamites, the Papinachois, the Montagais, the Attikamègues, the Nipissings, the Temiscamings, the Amikouès, the Cristinaux [Crees], the Assiniboins, the Potawatomis, the Nokais, the Otchagras, and the Miamis, armed about 50,000 warriors;[123] that supposes among the savages a population of about 250,000. According to Lahontan, each of the five great Iroquois villages contained 14,000 inhabitants. Today one can find in Lower Canada only six hamlets of savages who have become Christians: the Hurons of Corette, the Abnakis of Saint François, the Algonquians, the Nipissings, the Iroquois of the Lake of the Two Mountains, and the Osouekatchies— feeble remnants of several races that are no more, and which, gathered together by religion, offer the double proof of its power to preserve, and man's power to destroy.

The remains of the five Iroquois nations is enclaved in the English and American possessions, and the number of all the Savages that I have just named is at most 2,500 to 3,000.

The Abnakis, who is 1587 occupied Acadia (today New Brunswick and Nova Scotia); the savages of Maine, who destroyed all the whites' settlements in 1675, and who continued their ravages until 1748; the same hordes who subjected New Hampshire to the same fate; the Wampanoags, the Nipmucks, who carried on pitched battles with the English, besieged Hadley and assaulted Brookfield in Massachusetts; the Indians who in the same years 1673 and 1675 fought the Europeans; the Pequots of Connecticut; the Indians who negotiated the cession of part of their territories to the states of New York, New Jersey, Pennsylvania, Delaware; the Piscataways of Maryland; the tribes who obeyed Powhatan in Virginia; the Paroustis in the Carolinas—all these peoples have disappeared.[124]

Of the numerous nations that Hernando de Soto found in the Floridas (and we must include in this name all that which forms today the states of Georgia, Alabama, Mississippi, and Tennessee), there remain only the Creeks, the Cherokees, and the Chickasaws.[125]

The Creeks, whose former manners I have painted, could not now raise more than 2,000 warriors. Of the vast countries that belonged to them they no longer possess any more than about eight square miles in the state of Georgia and a territory of about the same size in Alabama. The Cherokees and the Chickasaws, reduced to a handful of men, live in a corner of the states of Georgia and Tennessee; the latter, on the two banks of the Hiwassee.

As weak as they are, the Creeks fought the Americans valiantly in the years 1813 and 1814. Generals Jackson, White, Clayborne, and Floyd caused them to suffer great losses at Talladega, Hillabes, Autossees, Becanachaca, and especially at Entonopeka.[126] These savages had made notable progress in civilization, and especially in the art of war, using and directing artillery very well. A few years ago they judged and put to death one of their Micos, or kings, for having sold lands to the whites without the participation of the national council.

The Americans, who covet the rich territory where the Muskogees and the Seminoles still live, have wanted to force them to cede it to them for a sum of money, proposing that they be transported then to the west of the Missouri. The state of Georgia has maintained that it bought that territory; the American Congress has placed an obstacle before this claim; but sooner or later the Creeks, the Cherokees, and the Chickasaws, pressed in the midst of the white populations of Mississippi, Tennessee, Alabama, and Georgia, will be obliged to undergo exile or extermination.

Upstream along the Mississippi, from its mouth to the confluence of the Ohio, all the savages who inhabited these two banks—the Biloxis, the Torimas, the Kappas, the Sotouis, the Bayogoulas, the Kalapaoian, the Tansas, the Natchez, and the Yazoos—are no more.

In the valley of the Ohio, the nations that wandered along that river and its tributaries rose up in 1810 against the Americans. They put at their head a medicine man or prophet who predicted victory, while his brother, the famous Tecumseh,[127] fought. Three thousand savages united to recover their independence. The American general Harrison[128] marched against them with a body of troops; he met them on November 6, 1811, at the confluence of the Tippecanoe and the Wabash. The Indians showed the greatest courage, and their chief Tecumseh displayed an extraordinary skill; he was, however, overcome.

The War of 1812 between the Americans and the English

renewed the hostilities on the frontiers of the wilderness; the savages almost all rallied to the English; Tecumseh had passed into their service: Colonel Proctor,[129] an Englishman, directed the operations. Barbarous scenes took place at Chicago and forts Meigs[130] and Milden.[131] The heart of Captain Wells was devoured in a feast of human flesh. General Harrison rushed in again and overcame the savages at the Thames affair.[132] Tecumseh was killed there; Colonel Proctor owed his safety to the speed of his horse.

Peace being concluded between the United States and England in 1814, the limits of the two empires were definitively drawn. By a chain of military posts the Americans assured their domination over the savages.

From the mouth of the Ohio to the falls of Saint Anthony on the Mississippi there are to be found on the western bank of the river the Saukes, whose population attains the figure of 4,800; the Foxes, 1,600; the Winnebagos, 1,600 and the Menominees, 1,200. The Illinois are of the stock of these tribes.

Then come the Sioux, of Mexican stock divided into six nations; the first inhabits in part the upper Mississippi; the second, third, fourth, and fifth hold the banks of the St. Peter's River,[133] the sixth extends toward the Missouri. These six Sioux nations are estimated at about 45,000.

Behind the Sioux, approaching New Mexico, are some remains of the Osages, the Kansas, the Octotatas, the Nakotas, the Ajoues, and the Pawnees.

The Assiniboins wander under different names from the northern sources of the Missouri to the great Red River, which flows into Hudson Bay;[134] their population is 25,000.

The Chippewas of Algonquian race and enemies of the Sioux, hunt, 3,000 or 4,000 warriors strong in the wilderness that separates the great lakes of Canada from Lake Winnipeg.

That is all which is known positively of the population of the savages of North America. Even if we add to these known tribes the less familiar tribes that live beyond the Rocky Mountains, we shall have difficulty indeed finding the 400,000 individuals mentioned at the beginning of this census. There are travelers who do not number at more than 100,000 the Indian population on this side of the Rocky Mountains nor at more than 50,000 beyond the mountains, including the savages of California.

Pushed by the European population toward the Northwest of North America, the savage population comes by a singular destiny to expire on the very shore on which they landed in unknown centuries to take possession of America. In the Iroquois language, the Indians give themselves the name "men of forever"—*Ongoue-onoue*. These "men of forever" have gone, and the foreigner will soon leave to these legitimate heirs to a whole world, only the earth of their tombs.

The reasons for this depopulation are known: the use of strong liquors, vices, illnesses, and wars, which we have multiplied among the Indians, have precipitated the destruction of these peoples; but it is not entirely true that the social state, coming to be established in the forests, has been a sufficient cause of this destruction.

The Indian was not savage; the European civilization did not act on the pure state of nature; it acted on the rising American civilization; if it had found nothing, it would have created something; but it found manners and destroyed them because it was stronger and did not consider it should mix with those manners.

Asking what would have happened to the inhabitants of America, if America had escaped the sails of navigators, would no doubt be a vain question but still curious to examine. Would they have perished in silence as did those nations more advanced in the arts, which in all probability formerly flourished in the country watered by the Ohio, the Muskingum, the Tennessee, the lower Mississippi, and the Tombigbee?

Putting aside for a moment the great principles of Christianity, as well as the interests of Europe, a philosophical spirit could wish that the people of the New World had had the time to develop outside the circle of our institutions.

We are everywhere reduced to the worn forms of an old civilization (I do not speak of the populations of Asia, fixed for 4,000 years in a despotism which is infantile). There have been found among the savages of Canada, New England, and the Floridas, beginnings of all the customs and all the laws of the Greeks, the Romans and the Hebrews. A civilization of a nature different from ours could have reproduced the men of antiquity or have spread new enlightenment from a still unknown source. Who knows whether we would not have seen one day land on our shores some American Columbus coming to discover the Old World?

The degradation of the Indians' manners marched in step with the depopulation of the tribes. The religious traditions have become much more confused; education, first spread by the missionaries of Canada, has mixed foreign ideas with the native ideas of the inhabitants. One can see today through crude fables the Christian beliefs disfigured. Most of the savages wear crosses as ornaments, and the Protestant traders sell them what the Catholic missionaries gave them. Let us say, to the honor of our country and the glory of our religion, that the Indians became very attached to the French, that they never stopped missing them, and that a black robe (a missionary) is still venerated in the American forests. If the English in their wars with the United States saw almost all the savages enrolled under the British banner, it is because the English of Quebec still have among them descendants of the French, and they occupy the land which *Ononthio*[135] governed. The savage continues to love us in the land on which we trod, where we were his first guests, and where we left tombs: serving the new possessors of Canada, he remains faithful to France with the enemies of France.

Here is what can be read in a recent book of *Travels* to the sources of the Mississippi. The significance of this passage is all the greater in that the author in another part of his *Travels*, pauses to argue against the Jesuits of our days:

> In all justice, the French missionaries in general distinguished themselves everywhere by an exemplary life in conformity with their state. Their good religious faith, their apostolic charity, their insinuating gentleness, their heroic patience, and their shunning of fanaticism and rigorism mark in these countries edifying periods in the glory of Christianity; and while the memory of the del Vildes, the Vodillas, etc., will always be held in execration in all truly Christian hearts, that of the Daniels,[136] the Bréboeufs,[137] etc., will never lose the veneration which the

179

history of the discoveries and the missions justly confers upon them. That is the source of the preference which the savages show for the French, a preference they naturally find in the depths of their souls, nourished by the traditions which their fathers left in favor of the first apostles of Canada, then New France.[138]

That confirms what I have already written on the missions of Canada. The brilliant character of French valor, our disinterestedness, our gaiety, our adventuresome spirit were in sympathy with the genius of the Indians; but it must also be realized that the Catholic religion is more appropriate to the education of the savage than the Protestant sect.

When Christianity began in the midst of a civilized world and the spectacle of paganism, it was simple in its outward appearance, severe in its morality, and metaphysical in its arguments, because it was a question of tearing away from their error people overcome by the senses or misled by philosophical systems. When Christianity passed from the delights of Rome and the schools of Athens to the forests of Germania, it surrounded itself with pomp and images in order to enchant the simplicity of the barbarian. The Protestant governments of America occupied themselves little with the civilization of the savages: they thought only of trading with them. Now commerce, which increases civilization among peoples already civilized and among whom intelligence has prevailed over manners, produces only corruption among peoples whose manners are superior to their intelligence. Religion is obviously the primitive law: Fathers Jogues,[139] Lallemant,[140] and Brébeuf were legislators of a quite different kind from the English and the American traders.

Just as the religious notions of the savages became confused, the political institutions of these peoples have been altered by the influx of the Europeans. The mainsprings of the Indian government were subtle and delicate; time had not consolidated them; foreign politics, touching them, easily broke them. Those various councils balancing their respective authority, those counterweights formed by the members (the Sachems, the matrons, the young warriors)—all that machine was put in

180

disarray: our presents, our vices, and our arms bought, corrupted, or killed the individuals who made up these several powers.

Today the Indian tribes are simply led by a chief. Those which have confederated gather sometimes in general diets; but since no law regulates these assemblies, they almost always disperse without having decreed anything. They realize their nothingness and the discouragement that accompanies weakness.

Another cause has contributed to the degradation of the savages' government: the establishment of American and English military posts in the midst of the forests. There a commander sets himself up as the protector of the Indians in the wilderness; by means of a few presents he causes the tribes to appear before him; he declares himself their father and the envoy of the three white worlds: the savages designate thus the Spaniards, the French, and the English. The commander informs his "red children" that he is going to fix certain limits, clear certain lands, etc. The savage ends up believing he is not the real possessor of the land disposed of without his being consulted; he becomes accustomed to look upon himself as a species inferior to the white; he consents to receive orders, to hunt, to fight for masters. What need to govern oneself when one has only to obey?

It is natural that the manners and customs deteriorated with religion and politics, that everything was swept away at once. When the Europeans penetrated America, the savages lived and dressed by means of the product of their hunt and carried on no commerce among themselves. Soon the foreigners taught them to barter for arms, strong liquors, different household utensils, coarse cloth, and beads. Some Frenchmen, called *coureurs de bois*,[141] at first accompanied the Indians in their excursions. Little by little there were formed commercial companies which thrust out advance posts and placed shops in the midst of the wilderness. Pursued by the European avidity and by the corruption of civilized people even in the depths of their forests, the Indians exchange at these trading posts rich furs for objects of little value but which have become for them objects of

181

prime necessity. Not only do they deal in the hunts already accomplished, but they make disposition of the future hunts, as one sells a harvest still standing in the field.

These advances accorded by the traders plunge the Indians into an abyss of debt. Then they have all the calamities of the common man of our cities and all the distress of the savage. Their hunts, whose results they seek to increase to an exaggerated degree, are transformed into a frightful exhaustion. They take along their wives; these unfortunates, used for all the camp services, draw the sledges, go to retrieve the slain animals, tan the skins, dry the meat. They can be seen loaded with the heaviest burdens, still carrying their little children at the breast or on their shoulders. Should they be pregnant and ready to give birth, to hasten their delivery and return more quickly to the work they press their stomach against a wooden bar raised several feet off the ground; letting their head and arms hang down they give birth to a miserable creature, in all the rigor of the curse: *In dolore paries filios!*[142]

Thus civilization, entering through commerce among the American tribes, instead of developing their intelligence, stupefied them. The Indian has become perfidious, selfish, lying, and dissolute; his cabin is a receptacle for filth and dirt. When he was nude or covered with animal skins, there was something proud and great about him; today European rags, without covering his nudity, merely attest to his misery: he is a beggar at the door of a trading post; he no longer is a savage in his forests.

Finally there has been formed a kind of half-breed people, born from the commerce of European adventurers and savage women. These men, who are called *bois-brûlés*,[143] because of the color of their skin, are the businessmen and the brokers between the tribes from whom they draw their origin: speaking at the same time the languages of their fathers and their mothers, interpreters for the traders with the Indians and for the Indians with the traders, they have the vices of the two races. These bastards of civilized nature and savage nature sell themselves now to the Americans, now to the English, to deliver to them the monopoly of the pelts; they feed the rivalries of the English companies—Hudson's Bay Company and the

Northwest Company—and the American companies—Columbia American Fur Company, Missouri's Fur Company,[144] and others. They conduct hunts themselves for the account of the traders and with hunters paid by the companies.

The spectacle is then quite different from the Indian hunts: the men are on horseback; there are wagons that transport the dried meat and the furs; the women and children are carried on little carts by dogs. These dogs, so useful in the northern countries, are another burden for their masters, for since they cannot feed them during the summer, they board them on credit with keepers and thus contract new debts. The famished dogs sometimes leave their kennel and go fishing: they can be seen diving into the rivers and seizing the fish at the bottom of the water.

In Europe we only know that great war in America which gave to the world a free people. We are unaware that blood flowed for the miserable interests of a few fur merchants. The Hudson's Bay Company sold, in 1811, to Lord Selkirk[145] a vast territory on the edge of the Red River; the establishment was made in 1812. The Northwest Company, or Canada Company, took offense. The two companies, allied with different Indian tribes and encouraged by the *bois-brûlés*, fell to blows. This little domestic war, which was horrible, took place in the icy wastes of Hudson Bay. The colony of Lord Selkirk was destroyed in June 1815, precisely at the moment at which the battle of Waterloo was taking place. In these two theaters, so different by their brilliance and obscurity, the misfortunes of the human race were the same. The two companies, exhausted, felt that it was better to unite than to rend one another. Today they push together their operations to the west as far as the Columbia,[146] to the north as far as the rivers that flow into the Polar Sea.

In short, the proudest nations of North America have kept only the language and the dress of their race; even this is altered; they have learned a bit how to cultivate the earth and raise flocks. Instead of the famous warrior that he was, the savage of Canada has become an obscure shepherd, a kind of extraordinary herdsman driving his mares with a tomahawk and his sheep with arrows. Philip, successor of Alexander, died

183

a petty official in Rome; an Iroquois sings and dances for a few coins in Paris:[147] one should not look on the aftermath of glory.

In tracing this tableau of a savage world, speaking endlessly of Canada and Louisiana, seeing on the old maps the extent of the former French colonies in America, I was pursued by a painful idea: I wondered how the government of my country had allowed these colonies to perish, colonies that would be for us today an endless source of prosperity.

From Acadia and Canada to Louisiana, from the mouth of the Saint Lawrence to that of the Mississippi, the territory of New France surrounded what initially formed the confederation of the 13 original United States. The other 11 states, the District of Columbia, the Territories of Michigan, the Northwest, Missouri, Oregon, and Arkansas belonged to us or would belong to us as they belong today to the United States by cession from the English and the Spanish, our first heirs in Canada and Louisiana.

Take your starting point between the 43rd and 44th degree of north latitude on the Atlantic at Cape Sable of Nova Scotia, formerly Acadia; from this point draw a line that will pass behind the first United States, Maine, Vernon,[148] New York, Pennsylvania, Virginia, Carolina, and Georgia; let this line pass by the Tennessee to join the Mississippi and New Orleans, let it go then as far as the 29th degree (latitude of the mouths of the Mississippi), and go back up through the territory of Arkansas to the Oregon Territory; let it cross the Rocky Mountains and end at Point Saint George on the Pacific coast around the 42nd degree of north latitude: the immense territory contained inside this line, the Atlantic on the northeast, the Polar Sea on the north, the Pacific Ocean and the Russian possessions on the northwest, the Mexican Gulf on the south—that is, more than two thirds of North America—all that would recognize the laws of France.

What would have happened if such colonies had still been in our hands at the time of the emancipation of the United States? Would this emancipation have taken place? Would our presence on the American soil have hastened it or retarded it? Would New France itself have become free? Why not? What misfortune would there be for the mother country in seeing flourish an immense empire that had sprung from her breast, an empire that would spread the glory of our name and our language in another hemisphere?

We possessed beyond the seas vast countries that could offer asylum to the excess of our population, a considerable market for our commerce, supplies for our navy; today we find ourselves forced to shut up in our prisons the guilty condemned by the court, for lack of a corner of land on which to deposit these unfortunates. We are excluded from the new universe where mankind begins anew. The English and Spanish languages serve in Africa, in Asia, in the islands of the South Seas, and on the continent of the two Americas to interpret the thoughts of several million men; and we, disinherited of the conquests of our courage and our genius, scarcely do we hear spoken, except in a few villages of Louisiana and Canada under foreign domination, the language of Racine, of Colbert, and of Louis XIV; it remains there only as a witness to the reversals of our fortune and the mistakes of our politics.

Thus France has disappeared from North America like those Indian tribes with which she sympathized and of which I glimpsed a few remains. What has happened in that North America since the time when I traveled there? That is what must now be said. To console the readers, I shall in the conclusion of this work fix their view on a miraculous picture: they will learn what liberty is capable of for the happiness and dignity of man when it is not separated from religious ideas and when it is both intelligent and holy.

The United States Today

If I were to see the United States again today, I would no longer recognize it: there where I left forests, I would find plowed fields; there where I cleared a trail for myself through the brush, I would travel on highways. The Mississippi, the Missouri, and the Ohio no longer flow in solitude; great three-masted vessels sail up them and more than 200 steamships animate their shores. At Natchez, instead of Céluta's[149] hut, there rises a charming city of about 5,000 inhabitants. Today Chactas could be a member of Congress,[150] and travel to Atala's country[151] along two different routes, one of which leads to St. Stephen[152] on the Tombigbee, and the other to Natchitoches;[153] a road book would place the number of relays at eleven: Washington,[154] Franklin,[155] Homochitt,[156] etc.

Alabama and Tennessee are divided, the first into 33 counties containing 21 cities and the second into 51 counties containing 48 cities. Some of these cities, such as Cahawba, capital of Alabama, preserve their savage names; but they are surrounded by other cities differently named—there are in Muskogee, Seminole, Cherokee, and Chickasaw country cities called Athens, Marathon, Carthage, Memphis, Sparta, Florence, and Hampden, and counties of Columbia and Marengo: the glory of all the countries has placed names in this same wilderness where I met Father Aubry[157] and the humble Atala.

Kentucky boasts a Versailles; a county called Bourbon has Paris as its capital. All the exiles who have withdrawn to America have taken with them the memory of their homeland.

> Falsi Simoentis ad undam
> Libabat cineri Andromache.[158]

The United States offers then in its breast, under the protection of liberty, an image and a remembrance of most of the famous places of ancient and modern Europe, just as in the garden in the Roman countryside Hadrian had caused the different monuments of his empire to be represented.

It is to be noted that there are almost no counties that do not have a city, a village, or a hamlet of Washington, touching unanimity of a people's thanks.

The Ohio now waters four states: Kentucky, Ohio itself, Indiana, and Illinois. Thirty representatives and eight senators are sent to Congress by these four states. Virginia and Tennessee touch the Ohio at two points; it numbers along its banks 191 counties and 208 cities. A canal that is being dug at the portage around its rapids and that will be finished in three years, will make the river navigable for large vessels as far as Pittsburgh.

Thirty-three highways leave Washington, as once the Roman roads started from Rome, and separate to reach the four corners of the United States. Thus you can go from Washington to Dover, in Delaware; from Washington to Providence, in Rhode Island; from Washington to Robbinstown, in the territory of Maine, frontier of the British states to the north; from Washington to Concord; from Washington to Montpelier, in Connecticut [sic]; from Washington to Albany, and from there to Montreal and Quebec; from Washington to Havre de Sackets, on Lake Ontario; from Washington to the falls and fort of Niagara; from Washington, by Pittsburgh, to the straights and Michilimackinac, on Lake Erie [sic]; from Washington, by Saint Louis on the Mississippi, to Council Bluffs on the Missouri; from Washington to New Orleans and the mouth of the Mississippi; from Washington to Natchez; from Washington to Charlestown, to Savannah and Saint Augustine, forming in all an internal road system of 25,747 miles.

One can see by the places these roads link that they pass through places, which although formerly wild are now cultivated and inhabited. On a great number of these roads the post houses are established; public conveyances take you from one place to another at moderate prices. You take the diligence for Ohio or for Niagara Falls, as in my time you took a guide or an Indian interpreter. Byways branch off from the principal highways and are likewise provided with means of transportation. These means are almost always double, for since there are lakes and rivers everywhere, you can also travel by rowboat, sailboat, or steamboat.

Vessels of this latter type make regular trips from Boston and New York to New Orleans; they are likewise established on the Canadian lakes—Ontario, Erie, Michigan, and Champlain—those lakes where 30 years ago there were scarcely to be seen a few Indian canoes, and where now battleships contend with one another.[159]

Steamboats in the United States serve not only the needs of commerce and travelers, but they are also used for the defense of the country. Some of them, of enormous size, placed at the mouths of rivers and armed with cannons and boiling water, resemble at once modern citadels and fortresses of the middle ages.

To the 25,747 miles of main roads must be added the extent of 419 local roads, and 58,137 miles of water routes. Canals augment the number of these latter routes: the Middlesex canal joins the port of Boston with the Merrimack river; the Champlain canal causes that lake to communicate with the Canadian seas; the famous Erie or New York canal now unites Lake Erie with the Atlantic;[160] the Santee, Chesapeake, and Albemarle canals are due to the states of Carolina and Virginia; and since long rivers, flowing in different directions have sources close to one another, nothing is simpler than to join them to one another. Five roads are already known to go to the Pacific Ocean; only one of these roads passes through Spanish Territory.

A law of Congress of the session of 1821 to 1825 orders the establishment of a military post in Oregon. The Americans, who have a settlement on the Columbia, thus penetrate to the great Ocean between English, Russian, and Spanish America by a zone of land about six degrees wide.

There is however a natural boundary to colonization. The timberline stops at the west and north of the Missouri, at the edge of immense steppes which do not afford a single tree and which seem to refuse cultivation, although grass grows there abundantly. This green Arabia serves as a passage for the settlers who go in wagons to the Rocky Mountains and New Mexico; it separates the United States of the Atlantic from the

United States of the Southern Sea, as those deserts in the Old World separate fertile regions. An American has proposed to open at his own expense a great railroad from Saint Louis on the Mississippi to the mouth of the Columbia for a concession of land ten miles wide to be given him by Congress on both sides of the railroad; this gigantic bargain was not accepted.

In the year 1789 there were only 75 post houses in the United States; now there are more than 5,000.

From 1790 to 1795 these houses were increased from 75 to 453; in 1800 there were 903; in 1805 they rose to 1,558; in 1810, 2,300; in 1815, 3,000; in 1817, 3,459; in 1820, 4,030; in 1825, about 5,500.

Letters and dispatches are transported by post wagons, which do about 150 miles a day, and by foot and horse couriers.

A great postal route extends from Anson in the state of Maine, by Washington, to Nashville in the state of Tennessee: distance, 1,448 miles. Another line joins Highgate in the state of Vermont, with St. Mary in Georgia: distance, 1,369 miles. Post relays are established from Washington to Pittsburgh: distance, 226 miles; they will soon be established as far as Saint Louis on the Mississippi, by way of Vincennes, and to Nashville, by way of Lexington, Kentucky. The inns are good and clean, and sometimes excellent.

Offices for the sale of public lands are open in the states of Ohio and Indiana, in the Michigan, Missouri, and Arkansas territories, in the states of Louisiana, Mississippi, and Alabama. It is believed that there remain more than 150 million acres of land suitable for cultivation, without counting the land of the great forests. These 150 million acres are valued at about 1,500 million dollars, if one evaluates them at a flat 10 dollars per acre rate and calculates the dollar at only 3 francs —an extremely conservative calculation in all ways.

There are in the northern states 25 military posts, and 22 in the southern states.

In 1790, the population of the United States was 3,929,326; in 1800, it was 5,305,666; in 1810, 7,239,903; in 1820, 9,609,827. Included in this population must be counted 1,531,436 slaves.

In 1790, Ohio, Indiana, Illinois, Alabama, Mississippi, and Missouri did not have enough settlers to be counted. Kentucky alone in 1800 had 73,677, and Tennessee 33,691. Ohio, without inhabitants in 1790, numbered 45,365 in 1800; 230,760 in 1810, and 581,434 in 1820; Alabama, from 1810 to 1820, rose from 10,000 inhabitants to 127,901.

Thus the population of the United States has grown from decade to decade, from 1790 to 1820, in the proportion of 35 individuals per 100. Six years have already passed of the ten that will be completed in 1830, time at which it is assumed that the population of the United States will be about 12,875,000;[161] Ohio's part will be 850,000 inhabitants, and Kentucky's 750,000.

If the population continues to double every 25 years, in 1855 the United States will have a population of 25,750,000; and 25 years later, that is in 1880, this population will rise to more than 50,000,000.

In 1821, the exports of local and foreign products from the United States rose to the sum of $64,974,382; public revenue in the same year rose to $14,264,000; the excess of receipts over expenses was $3,334,826. In the same year, the national debt was reduced to $89,204,236.

The army at times has been increased to 100,000 men; 11 battleships, 9 frigates, 50 warships of different sizes make up the navy of the United States.

It is unnecessary to speak of the constitutions of the different states; it suffices to know that they are all free.

There is no dominant religion; but each citizen is obliged to practice a Christian denomination; the Catholic religion is making considerable progress in the western states.

Supposing, as I believe is the case, that the statistical résumés published in the United States are exaggerated by national pride, even so the general prosperity would still be worthy of all our admiration.

To complete this surprising tableau, one must picture cities such as Boston, New York, Philadelphia, Baltimore, Savannah, and New Orleans illuminated at night, filled with horses and carriages, offering all the enjoyment of luxury which thousands of vessels introduce into their ports; one must picture those

Canadian lakes, once so solitary, now covered with frigates, corvettes, cutters, barks, and steamships, which pass the canoes and boats of the Indians as the great ships and the galleys do the pinks, sloops, and caïques in the waters of the Bosphorus. Churches and houses embellished with Greek columns rise in the midst of the forests, on the edge of these rivers which were the ancient ornament of the wilderness. Add to that vast colleges, observatories established for science in the domain of savage ignorance, all religions, all opinions living in peace, working in concert to improve mankind and to develop mankind's intelligence: such are the prodigious feats of liberty.

The Abbé Raynal[162] had proposed a prize for the solution to this question: "What will be the influence of the discovery of the New World on the Old World?"

The writers lost themselves in calculations relative to the exportation and importation of metals, the depopulation of Spain, the growth of commerce, the perfecting of navies: no one, as far as I know, sought the influence of the discovery of America on Europe in the establishment of the American republics. They still saw only the old monarchies just about as they were, society stationary, human spirit neither advancing nor retreating; they had not the least idea of the revolution which in the space of forty years took place in men's minds.

The most precious of the treasures that America held in her breast was liberty; each people is called upon to draw from this inexhaustable mine. The discovery of the representative republic in the United States is one of the greatest political events in the world. That event has proved, as I have said elsewhere, that there are two types of practical liberty. One belongs to the infancy of nations; it is the daughter of manners and virtue—it is that of the first Greeks, the first Romans, and that of the savages of America. The other is born out of the old age of nations; it is the daughter of enlightenment and reason—it is this liberty of the United States which replaces the liberty of the Indian. Happy land which in the space of less than three centuries has passed from the one liberty to the other almost without effort, and that by a battle lasting no more than eight years!

Will America preserve her second kind of liberty? Will not

the United States divide? Can we not see already the seeds of that division? Has not a representative of Virginia already defended the thesis of the old Greek and Roman liberty with the system of slavery, against a representative of Massachusetts who defended the cause of modern liberty without slaves, such as Christianity has made it?

The western states, extending more and more, too far away from the Atlantic states, will they not want a separate government?

Finally, are Americans perfect men? Do they not have their vices as do other men? Are they morally superior to the English from whom they draw their origin? This foreign immigration that constantly flows into their population from all parts of Europe, will it not at length destroy the homogeneity of their race? Will not the mercantile spirit dominate them? Will not self-interest begin to be the dominant national fault?

Once again it must be sadly said that the establishment of the republics of Mexico, Colombia, Peru, Chile, and Buenos Aires is a danger for the United States. When it had before it only the colonies of a transatlantic kingdom, no war was probable. Now will not rivalries rise up among the old republics of North America and the new republics of Spanish America? Will not the latter forbid alliances with European powers? If on both sides they had recourse to arms, if the military spirit took hold of the United States, a great captain could arise. Glory loves a crown; soldiers are only brilliant makers of chains, and liberty is not certain to preserve her patrimony under the guidance of victory.

Whatever the future, liberty will never entirely disappear from America; and it is here that we must point out one of the great advantages of liberty, daughter of enlightenment, over liberty, daughter of manners.

Liberty, daughter of manners, disappears where her principle is altered, and it is of the nature of manners to deteriorate with time. Liberty, daughter of manners, begins before despotism in the days of obscurity and poverty; she finally is lost in the centuries of brilliance and luxury. Liberty, daughter of enlightenment, shines after the ages of oppression and corruption; she walks with the principle that preserves and renews her; the enlightenment of which she is the effect, far from weakening with time, as do the manners that give birth to the first liberty, the enlightenment, I say, fortifies itself rather with time; thus it does not abandon the liberty it has produced; always in the company of that liberty, it is at the same time the generative virtue and the inexhaustible source of liberty.

Finally, the United States has another safeguard: its population occupies only an eighteenth of its territory. America still inhabits solitude; for a long time yet her wilderness will be her manners, and her enlightenment will be her liberty.

I would like to be able to say as much for the Spanish Republics of America. They enjoy independence; they are separated from Europe: it is an accomplished fact, an immense fact no doubt in its results, but a fact that does not immediately and necessarily lead to liberty.

The Spanish Republics

When English America rose up against Great Britain, its position was much different from the position in which Spanish America finds itself. The colonies that formed the United States had been peopled at different times by Englishmen who were discontented in their native land and who left in order to enjoy civil and religious liberty. Those who established themselves principally in New England belonged to that republican sect famous under the second of the Stuarts.

The hatred of the monarchy was preserved in the rigorous climate of Massachusetts, New Hampshire, and Maine; when the revolution exploded at Boston, one could say it was not a new revolution but rather the revolution of 1649 which reappeared after a hiatus of a little more than a century, and which the descendants of Cromwell's Puritans were going to carry out. If Cromwell himself, who had embarked for New England and whom an order of Charles I forced to disembark, if Cromwell had gone over to America, he would have remained obscure, but his sons would have enjoyed that republican liberty which he sought in a crime and which only gave him a throne.

Some royalist soldiers made prisoner on the battlefield, sold as slaves by the parliamentary faction, and not recalled by Charles II, also left in North America children who were indifferent to the cause of kings.

As Englishmen, the colonists of the United States were already accustomed to a public discussion of the interests of the people, the rights of the citizen, the language and form of constitutional government. They were learned in the arts, letters, and sciences; they shared all the enlightenment of their mother country. They enjoyed the institution of the jury; they had moreover in each of their establishments charters by virtue of which they administered and governed themselves. Those charters were based on principles so generous that they still serve today as the individual constitutions of the several United States. The result was that the United States did not actually change their existence at the moment of their revolution; an American congress was substituted for an English parliament, a president for a king, the chain of the vassal was replaced by the bond of the federalist, and by chance there appeared a great man to tighten that bond.

The heirs of Pizarro and Hernando Cortez, did they resemble the children of Penn's "brothers" and the sons of the independents? In old Spain were they educated in the school of liberty? Did they find in their former nation the institutions, teachings, examples, and enlightenment that form a people for constitutional government? Did they have charters in those colonies placed under military authority, where poverty in tatters was seated on mines of gold? Did Spain not carry to the New World its religion, its manners, its customs, its ideas, its principles, and even its prejudices? A Catholic population, subject to a large, rich, and powerful clergy, a mixed population of 2,937,000 whites, 5,518,000 Negroes and mulattos either free or slaves, 7,530,000 Indians; a population divided into noble and common classes; a population dispersed throughout immense forests, in an infinite variety of climates, in two Americas and along the coasts of two oceans; a population almost without national bonds and without common interests—is such a population as appropriate to the democratic institutions as the homogeneous population, without class distinctions and seven-eighths Protestant, of the 10,000,000 citizens of the United States? In the United States education is universal; in the Spanish republics almost the entire population is unable even to read. The priest is the scholar of the villages; these villages are rare, and to go from a given city to another, it takes no less than three or four months. Cities and villages have been devastated by war; there are no roads, no canals; the immense rivers that one day will carry civilization to the most secret parts of these countries as yet water only the wilderness.

From the Negroes, Indians, and Europeans has come a mixed population, lethargic in that very gentle slavery which the Spanish manners establish wherever they reign. In Colombia there exists a race born of the African and the Indian,

195

which has no other instinct than to live and serve. The principle of the liberty of the slaves has been proclaimed, and all the slaves have wanted to remain with their masters. In some of these colonies, forgotten even by Spain and oppressed by little despots called governors, a great corruption of manners had been introduced; nothing was more common than to meet with ecclesiastics surrounded by families whose origin they did not hide. There was one inhabitant who speculated on his commerce with Negresses, enriching himself by selling the children he had by the slaves.

The democratic forms were so unknown, the very name of a republic was so foreign in those countries, that without a volume of the history of Rollin,[163] they would not have known in Paraguay what was meant by dictator, consuls, and senate. In Guatemala, two or three young foreigners drew up the constitution. Nations whose political education is so little advanced always leave us with fears for liberty.

The superior classes in Mexico are educated and distinguished; but as Mexico is lacking in ports, the general population has not been in contact with the enlightenment of Europe.

In contrast, Colombia has by the happy disposition of its coasts more communication with foreign countries, and a remarkable man has risen up from its breast.[164] But is it certain that a generous soldier may manage to impose liberty as easily as he could establish slavery? Force does not replace time when the first elements of political education are lacking to a people; this education can only be the work of years. Thus liberty would rise up with difficulty when sheltered by dictatorship, and it would always be feared that a prolonged dictatorship might give to him who exercised it a taste for perpetual despotism. It becomes a vicious circle. Civil war exists in the republic of Central America.

The Bolivian republic and that of Chile have been tormented by revolutions. Placed on the Pacific Ocean, they seem excluded from the most civilized part of the world.[165]

Buenos Aires has the drawback of its latitude. It is only too true that the temperature of a given region can be an obstacle to the play and action of popular government. A land where the physical forces of man are beaten down by the heat of the sun, where it is necessary to hide during the day and remain almost motionless stretched out on a mat, a country of that nature does not favor the deliberations of the forum. No doubt we must not exaggerate the influence of climate;[166] in the temperate zones we have seen first free peoples and then enslaved peoples in the same place, but in the arctic and torrid zones there are undeniable demands of climate which must produce permanent effects. The Negroes, by this necessity alone, will always be powerful, if they do not become the masters in South America.

The United States rose up of their own accord, tiring of the yoke and loving independence; when they had broken their chains, they found within themselves sufficient enlightenment to guide themselves. A very advanced civilization, longstanding political education, and developed industry took them to the degree of prosperity where we see them today, without their having to resort to foreign money and intelligence.

In the Spanish republics the facts are of a quite different nature. Although miserably administered by the mother country, these colonies moved first rather by the effect of a foreign stimulus than by the instinct of liberty. The war of the French revolution produced it. The English, who since the reign of Queen Elizabeth had never ceased turning their gaze toward the Spanish Americas, in 1804 directed an expedition against Buenos Aires, an expedition foiled by the bravery of a single Frenchman, Captain Liniers.

The question for the Spanish colonies was then to know if they would follow the policies of the Spanish cabinet, then allied with Buonaparte, or if, looking upon that alliance as a forced one and against nature, they would detach themselves from the Spanish government to remain faithful to the king of Spain.

Already in 1790, Miranda[167] had begun negotiating with England over the emancipation question. The negotiations were resumed in 1797, 1801, 1804, and 1807, at which time a great expedition was being prepared at Cork for the Terra-Firma. Finally in 1809 Miranda was thrust into the Spanish colonies; the expedition was not fortunate for him, but the Venezuela insurrection took form and Bolivar extended it.

The question had changed for the colonies and for England;

Spain had risen up against Buonaparte; the constitutional regime had begun at Cadiz under the direction of the Cortes; these ideas of liberty were necessarily carried back to America by the authority of the Cortes itself.

England, on its side, could no longer openly attack the Spanish colonies, since the king of Spain, a prisoner in France, had become their ally; thus England published bills to prevent the subjects of His Britannic Majesty from giving aid to the Americans; but at the same time 6,000 or 7,000 men, enrolled in spite of the diplomatic bills, went to reinforce the insurrection in Colombia.

When Spain returned to the former government after the restoration of Ferdinand, it committed grave errors. The constitutional government, reestablished by the insurrection of the troops of Leon, showed itself no more adroit; the Cortes was even less favorable to the emancipation of the Spanish colonies than had been the absolute government. Bolivar, by his activity and victories, finally broke the bonds the colonies had not at first sought to break. The English, who were everywhere, in Mexico, Colombia, Peru, and Chile, with Lord Cochrane, finally recognized publicly what was in large measure their secret work.

It can be seen therefore that the Spanish colonies were not, as were the United States, driven to emancipation by a powerful principle of liberty; the principle did not have, at the beginning of the troubles, that vitality and force which announce the firm will of nations. A stimulus from without, political interests, and extremely complicated events—that is what is to be seen at first glance. The colonies detached themselves from Spain because Spain was invaded; then they gave themselves constitutions as the Cortes gave one to the mother country; finally no reasonable propositions were made to them, and they did not want to resume the yoke. That is not all; foreign money and speculation tended to deprive them of what might remain of their liberty which was native and national.

From 1822 to 1826 ten loans were made in England for the Spanish colonies, amounting to 20,978,000 pounds sterling. Those loans, on the average, were contracted at 75 percent. Then two years' interest at 6 percent was discounted on them, and then 7,000,000 pounds sterling was withheld for supplies. In all, England disbursed an actual sum of 7,000,000 pounds sterling, or 175,000,000 francs; but the Spanish republics nevertheless were liable for a debt of 20,978,000 pounds sterling.

To these already excessive loans were joined that multitude of associations or companies destined to exploit the mines, fish for the pearls, dig the canals, open the roads, and clear the land of this new world which seemed newly discovered. These companies rose to the number of 29, and their nominal capital was 14,767,500 pounds sterling. The subscribers furnished only about a quarter of that sum; so 3,000,000 pounds sterling (or 75,000,000 francs) must be added to the 7,000,000 pounds sterling (or 175,000,000 francs) of the loans: in all 250,000,-000 francs advanced by England to the Spanish colonies, for which it is owed the nominal sum of 35,745,500 pounds sterling by the governments and by individuals.

England has vice consuls in the smallest bays, consuls in the ports of some importance, consuls general and ministers plenipotentiary in Colombia and Mexico. The whole country is covered by English commercial houses, English traveling salesmen, agents of English companies for exploitation of mines, English mineralogists, English soldiers, English suppliers, English colonists to whom land was sold at three shillings an acre, which cost the stockholders 12½ sous. The English standard floats over all the coasts of the Atlantic and the South Sea; ships go up and down the navigable rivers, loaded with the products of British manufacture or the goods exchanged for these products; packetboats, furnished by the admiralty, regularly leave Great Britain every month for the different points of the Spanish colonies.

Numerous failures have been the result of these immoderate enterprises; the people in several places have broken the machines for the exploitation of the mines; the mines sold to exploiters have not been found; lawsuits have begun between the Spanish-American and the English businessmen, and disputes have arisen among the governments relating to the loans.

As a result the former colonies of Spain at the moment of their emancipation have become in a manner English colonies. The new masters are not beloved, for one does not love masters; in general the British pride humiliates the very ones it protects; but it is nonetheless true that this kind of foreign supremacy represses in the Spanish republics the movement of national genius.

The independence of the United States was not bound up with so many diverse interests: England had not undergone, as had Spain, an invasion and a political revolution while its colonies were detaching themselves. The United States was supported militarily by France who treated it as an ally; it did not, by a host of loans, speculations, and intrigues, become a debtor and a foreign market.

Finally, the independence of the Spanish colonies is not yet recognized by the mother country. This passive resistance of the Madrid cabinet has much more strength and inconvenience than one might think; right is a power which outweighs the fact for a long time, even when the events are not in favor of right: our restoration proved it. If England, without having made war in the United States, had been content not to recognize its independence, would the United States be what it is today?

The more obstacles the Spanish republics meet with in their new career, the more merit they will have in surmounting them. They contain within their vast limits all the elements for prosperity: variety of climate and soil, forests for the navy, ports for the ships, a double ocean which opens to them the commerce of the world. Nature has been prodigal in everything with these republics; everything is rich on and under the land that supports them; the rivers fecundate the surface of the land and gold fertilizes its breast. Spanish America has therefore before it a propitious future; but telling these countries they can achieve it without effort would be deceiving them, lulling them into false security: the flatterers of peoples are as dangerous as the flatterers of kings. When a man is creating utopias, he considers neither the past, nor history, nor facts, nor manners, nor character, nor prejudice, nor passions. Enchanted by his own dreams, he does not forearm himself against events, and he spoils the fairest of destinies.

I have indicated frankly the difficulties that may impede

liberty in the Spanish Republics; I must also indicate the guarantees of their independence.

First, the influence of the climate and the lack of roads and cultivation would make unfruitful any efforts one might make to conquer those republics. The coast could be occupied for a time, but it would be impossible to advance into the interior.

Strictly speaking, Colombia no longer has any Spaniards on its territory; they were called Goths; they have perished or have been driven out. In Mexico, they have recently taken measures against the natives of the former mother country.

All the clergy in Colombia is American; many priests, by a sinful infraction of the Church discipline, are family men, like the other citizens; they do not even wear the habit of their order. Manners suffer from this state of affairs no doubt; but also there is another result: the clergy, in spite of being Catholic, fears more intimate relations with the court of Rome and is therefore favorable to emancipation. The monks have mixed in the troubles, soldiers rather than clerics. Twenty years of revolution have created rights, property, and places which could not easily be destroyed; and the new generation, born during the revolution of the colonies, is full of ardor for independence. Spain once boasted that the sun never set on its territory: let us hope that liberty will never more cease enlightening man.

But could this liberty be established in Spanish America in an easier and surer way than the one that was used, in a way which, put into practice at the proper time when events had not yet decided anything, would have done away with a host of obstacles? I think so.

In my opinion, the Spanish Colonies would have gained much by setting themselves up as constitutional monarchies. Representative monarchy is in my estimation a government far superior to the republican government because it destroys individual pretension to the executive power and unites order and liberty.

It also seems to me that representative monarchy would have been more appropriate to the Spanish genius and the actual state of persons and affairs in a land where great landed property dominates, where the number of Europeans is small and that of the Negroes and Indians considerable, where slavery is customary, where the state religion is the Catholic religion, and especially where education is completely lacking in the popular classes.

The Spanish Colonies, independent of the mother country and formed into great representative monarchies, would have perfected their political education sheltered from the storms that can overthrow newborn republics. A people suddenly emerging from slavery, rushing into liberty, can fall into anarchy, and anarchy almost always gives birth to despotism.

But if there existed a system capable of forestalling these divisions, you will no doubt tell me: "You were in a position of power. Were you content to wish for peace, happiness, and liberty in Spanish America? Did you limit yourself to sterile wishes?"

Here I shall anticipate my *Memoirs*, and I shall make a confession.

When Ferdinand was delivered in Cadiz,[168] and when Louis XVIII had written to the Spanish monarch to encourage him to give a free government to his peoples, my mission seemed finished. I had the idea of handing back to the king the portfolio of foreign affairs and begging His Majesty to return it to the virtuous Duke of Montmorency.[169] How many troubles I would have saved myself! How much division would I perhaps have spared public opinion! Friendship and power would not have given a sad example. Crowned with success, I would have left the ministry in the most brilliant manner possible, to dedicate the rest of my life to repose.

It was the interests of the Spanish Colonies, of which my subject has led me to speak, which caused the last rebound of my capricious fortune. I am able to say that I sacrificed myself in the hope of assuring repose and independence for a great people.

When I thought of retirement, important negotiations had been carried on to a great extent; I had directed and was directing them; I had formed a plan that I thought was useful to the two Worlds; I flattered myself that I had established a basis on which would repose both rights of nations and the interests of my own and other countries. I cannot explain the details of that plan; it is fairly clear why not.

In diplomacy, a plan conceived is not a plan executed. Governments have their routine and their pace; patience is a requisite; foreign cabinets cannot be assaulted as the Dauphin captured cities; politics does not proceed as rapidly as glory at the head of our soldiers. I unfortunately resisted my first inspiration, and I remained in office to finish my work. I imagined that since I had prepared it, I would understand it better than my successor; I also feared that the portfolio might not be given back to M. de Montmorency and that another minister might adopt some outdated system for the Spanish possessions. I allowed myself to be persuaded by the idea of attaching my name to the liberty of the second America, without compromising that liberty in the freed colonies, and without exposing to danger the European states' principle of monarchy.

Assured of the good will of the several cabinets of the continent, with one exception, I did not despair of overcoming the resistance that the statesman who has just died[170] showed me in England, a resistance that was due less to him than to the unenlightened mercantilism of his nation. The future will perhaps know the personal correspondence that was exchanged between me and my illustrious friend on that great subject. As everything is bound up in the destiny of man, it is possible that Mr. Canning, by associating himself with plans which moreover were little different from his own, had found more repose and had avoided political worries that wearied his last days. Talented people are rapidly disappearing; a tiny Europe is being arranged patterned on mediocrity; to reach the new generations, it will be necessary to traverse a desert.

At any rate, I thought that the administration of which I was a member would allow me to complete an edifice that could only do honor to it; I was naïve enough to believe that the affairs of my ministry, being external, would not throw me across anyone's path; like the astrologer, I was looking at the sky and fell into a well. England applauded my fall. It is still true that we had a garrison in Cadiz under the white flag of the Bourbons and that the royal emancipation of the Spanish Colonies, through the generous influence of the elder son of the Bourbons, would have raised France to the highest degree of prosperity and glory.

Such was the last dream of my mature age. I thought I was in America, and I woke up in Europe. I have yet to say how I returned long ago from that very America, after having seen in just the same way the first dream of my youth disappear.

The End of the Trip

Wandering from forest to forest, I had approached an American clearing. One evening I located on the bank of a stream a farmhouse built of logs. I asked for hospitality; it was offered me.

Night came. The dwelling was lit only by the flame of the hearth. I sat on the edge of the fireplace. While my hostess was preparing supper, I amused myself reading by the firelight, lowering my head, an English newspaper which had fallen on the floor. I saw, printed in large type, these words: FLIGHT OF THE KING. It was the description of the escape of Louis XVI and the arrest of the unfortunate monarch at Varennes. The newspaper also told of the progress of the emigration and the gathering of almost all the army officers under the flag of the French Princes. I seemed to hear the voice of honor, and I abandoned my plans.

I returned to Philadelphia and embarked. A storm drove me in 19 days to the coast of France, where I was half-shipwrecked between the islands of Guernsey and Origny. I landed at Le Havre. In July 1792 I emigrated with my brother. The Army of the Princes was already in the field, and, without the intercession of my unfortunate cousin Armand de Chateaubriand,[171] I would not have been received. It served me little to say I had just arrived from Niagara Falls for that express purpose; they would hear nothing of it, and I was on the point of fighting to obtain the honor of carrying a haversack. My comrades, the officers of the Navarre regiment, formed one company at the camp of the Princes, but I entered one of the Breton companies. What became of me can be seen in the new preface to my *Historical Essay*.

Thus what I conceived as a duty upset my first plans and brought on the first of those crises that have marked my career.

No doubt the Bourbons had no need for a Breton younger son to return from abroad to offer them his obscure devotion, no more than they had need of his services afterward when he had emerged from his obscurity. If, continuing my trip, I had lit my hostess's lamp with the newspaper that changed my life, no one would have noticed my absence, for no one knew I existed. A simple argument between me and my conscience brought me back to the theater of the world. I could have done what I wanted, since I was the only witness of the dispute; but, of all the witnesses, that is the one in whose eyes I would most fear blushing.

Why do the solitudes of Lake Erie and Lake Ontario present themselves to me today with more charm than the brilliant spectacle of the Bosphorus? It is that at the time of my trip to the United States, I was full of illusions; France's troubles were beginning at the same time as my life was beginning; nothing was finished in me or my country. Those days are sweet to recall because they reproduce in my memory only the innocence of the feelings inspired by the family and by the pleasure of youth.

Fifteen or 16 years later, after my second trip, the revolution had already run its course; I no longer flattered myself with illusions; my memories, which then flowed from society, had lost their candor. Misled in my two pilgrimages, I had not discovered the Northwest Passage; I had not carried glory away from the midst of the forests where I had gone to seek it, and I had left it behind sitting on the ruins of Athens.

I left to be a traveler in America; I returned to be a soldier in Europe. I did not fully carry out either of these careers; an evil genius snatched away the staff and the sword, and thrust a pen into my hand. In Sparta, contemplating the sky during the night,[172] I remembered lands that had already witnessed my peaceful or troubled sleep. I had, on the roads of Germany, amidst the heather of England, in the fields of Italy, in the center of the oceans, and in the Canadian forests, greeted the same stars that I saw shining over the land of Helen and Menelaus. But of what use was it to complain to the stars, motionless witnesses of my vagabond destiny? One day their gaze will no longer tire in following me; it will stop on my grave. As for now, indifferent as I am to my own destiny, I shall not ask those unfriendly stars to shape that destiny with a milder hand, nor to give me back what the traveler leaves of his life in the places through which he passes.

Bibliography

I. WORKS OF CHATEAUBRIAND

Correspondance générale. Paris: Champion, 1912. 5 vols.
Mémoires d'Outre-Tombe. Paris: Flammarion, 1948. 4 vols.
Œuvres complètes. Paris: Garnier, n.d. 12 vols.
Œuvres complètes. Paris: Ladvocat, 1826–1831.
Travels in America. London: Colburn, 1828. 2 vols.
Voyage en Amérique. Critical edition by Richard Switzer.
   Paris: Didier, 1964. 2 vols.

II. WORKS REFERRED TO BY CHATEAUBRIAND

Atala (1801).
Essai historique sur les révolutions (1797).
Etudes historiques (1827).
Génie du Christianisme (1802).
Itinéraire de Paris à Jérusalem (1811).
Mémoires d'Outre-Tombe (1848–1850).
Natchez, les (1826).

III. CHATEAUBRIAND'S SOURCES

Bartram, William. *Travels* (1791). Edited by Francis Harper.
   New Haven: Yale, 1958.
Bonnet, J. E. *Les Etats-Unis de l'Amérique à la fin du XVIIIᵉ*
   siècle. Paris: Maradan, n.d. 2 vols.
Carver, Jonathan. *Travels to the Interior Parts of America.*
   London, 1778.

Charlevoix, François-Xavier de. *Histoire et description générale de la Nouvelle France.* . . . Paris: Rollin, 1744. 6 vols.

Imlay, G. *Topographic Description of the Western Territory of North America.* London, 1792.

Lahontan, Louis-Armand, baron de. *Dialogues curieux entre l'auteur et un Sauvage de bon sens . . . et Mémoires de l'Amérique septentrionale* (1703). Baltimore: Johns Hopkins, 1931.

Le Page du Pratz, Antoine. *Histoire de la Louisiane.* . . . Paris: De Bure, 1758. 3 vols.

Lettres édifiantes et curieuses écrites des missions étrangères des jésuites. Paris: Merigot, 1781. Vol. VI.

Mackenzie, Alexander. *History of the Fur Trade.* London, 1801.

Notes

[1] The details of this controversy can be found in the 1964 French edition of the text of the *Voyage en Amérique* (see Bibliography).

[2] The French edition reproduces *in extenso* these source materials.

[3] A well-known journalist who had served in Spain as a soldier.

[4] I have eliminated three paragraphs of the Notice dealing with the other *Travels* published with the *Travels in America* in the 1827 edition. In addition, the preface has not been included in this translation. It is merely a vast retelling of the major voyages of man and has nothing to do with the present text.

[5] *Historical Essay*, part II, ch. 23. [C's note.] Here and elsewhere when C. refers to his own works, he is directing us to the Ladvocat ed. of his complete works. See also the Garnier ed., I, 540–44. (See Bibliography.)

[6] This intrepid sailor had set out again for Spitzbergen with the intention of going all the way to the pole by sled. He stayed on the ice 61 days without managing to go beyond 82° 45′ N. latitude. [C's note.]

[7] Chateaubriand was 59 in 1827.

[8] That is, they, as many other regiments, refused to serve the Republic.

[9] Coblentz saw the grouping of the royalists in an antirevolutionary army, the "Army of the Princes."

[10] The Indian hero of the epic.

[11] *Itinerary from Paris to Jerusalem.*

[12] "And the child, like the sailor whom the furious waves cast upon the shore." Lucretius, *De Rerum Natura*, V, 222–23.

[13] Mlle de Rosambeau, granddaughter of M. de Malesherbes, executed with her husband and her mother the same day as her illustrious grandfather. [C's note.]

[14] Part II, ch. 54. Garnier ed., I, 603–609.

[15] Tulloch (or Tullow), one of the seminarians.

[16] Garnier ed., I, 605.

[17] Philadelphia was the capital of Pennsylvania until 1799, and the capital of the United States from 1790 to 1800.

[18] Part I, ch. 33. Garnier ed., I, 363.

[19] That is, Europeans who had fled Haïti during the revolution which had just begun in 1791.

[20] Washington was ill, not absent. According to Washington's reply to the Marquis de la Rouerie, this visit between Washington and Chateaubriand did not take place: "Being indisposed on the day when Monsieur de Combourg [Chateaubriand] called to

deliver your letter I did not see him, and I understand that he set off for Niagara the next day." Letter of Sept. 5, 1791. George Washington, *Writings* (Washington: Government Printing Office, 1939), XXXI, 355. There is still, of course, the possibility that Chateaubriand saw Washington at the end of his trip, after September 5 and before November 26 when he appears to have embarked.

[21] Roman hero and dictator (born *c.* 519 B.C.).

[22] Contemporary engravings show the house to be essentially as Chateaubriand describes it.

[23] This key seems to be an authentic detail. In 1840 Martha Washington showed the key to the French ambassador, saying it was a gift from Lafayette.

[24] The Catholic church of Saint Denis contains the tombs and monuments of the kings of France.

[25] Chateaubriand invariably spells Buonaparte, to emphasize the non-French origins of the emperor.

[26] The reference is to Napoleon's Egyptian campaign.

[27] Triumph of Alexander the Great over Darius (331 B.C.) and of Caesar over Pompey (48 B.C.), respectively.

[28] That is, the classic position of the conqueror toward the conquered.

[29] Corneille, *Attila*, I, i.

[30] Lafayette's two trips to America were 1777–1781 and 1824–1825.

[31] *Historical Essay*, I, 213. [C's note.] Garnier ed., I, 540.

[32] M. de Fontanes. In Praise of Washington. [C's note.]

[33] The Erie Canal had just been completed (1825).

[34] *Historical Essay*, II, 417. [C's note.] Garnier ed., I, 622.

[35] Chateaubriand is obviously following the Mohawk Trail.

[36] This episode seems almost certainly imaginary. No trace of an authentic "M. Violet" has ever been found.

[37] A popular air of the period.

[38] *Itinerary*, III, 103. [C's note.] Garnier ed., V, 422–23.

[39] Hut. Chateaubriand's spelling alternates between *ajouppa* and *ajoupa*.

[40] According to Morris Bishop, the arrival of the first piano west of the Hudson dates from after Chateaubriand's trip.

[41] Chateaubriand appears to be the only traveler ever to write of such a bed in this region.

[42] *Genius of Christianity*. [C's note.] Part I, book 3, ch. 2. Garnier ed., II, 63.

[43] Part II, ch. 57. Garnier ed., I, 622–27.

[44] Part I, book 5, ch. 12. Garnier ed., II, 112–15.

[45] *Itinerary*. [C's note.]

[46] Obviously this is either a description of another part of the country or something other than the true cotton plant.

[47] Chateaubriand will explain *infra* how the Indians use necklaces for recording events.

[48] A cooked mixture of grain and meat.

[49] Part II, ch. 23. Garnier ed., I, 543–44.

[50] In the *Historical Essay* Cha-

teaubriand says his arm was broken *below* the elbow.

[51] *Historical Essay*, II, 237. [C's note.]

[52] This section has been largely adapted from Carver, Charlevoix, and Mackenzie.

[53] The source of this word and its meaning are unclear.

[54] Chateaubriand misread his source (Charlevoix) here; 100 leagues is the length of the lake.

[55] The name is coined by Chateaubriand.

[56] A mistake for Astikamegue (Charlevoix).

[57] A misreading of Manitoualin (Charlevoix); correctly, Manitoulin Island.

[58] Chateaubriand seems to be transposing what he read about Spanish moss into a winter scene.

[59] That was the erroneous geography of the time: it is no longer so today. [C's note.] This erroneous geography appears to have come from Carver. The River of the West is the Columbia.

[60] I leave as they are these expressions of youth: the reader will kindly excuse them. [C's note.]

[61] Since the time when I wrote that Dissertation, scholars of the American archaeological societies have published *Memoirs on the Ohio Ruins*. [C's note.]

[62] These ruins are attributed today to the Adena and Hopewell Indians. Carbon-14 dating has indicated them as being built from 1000 to 900 B.C.

[63] This is a variation of the Icelandic tradition and the poetic sagas. [C's note.]

[64] Today the sources of the Missouri are known: only savages have been found in this area. It is likewise necessary to relegate to legend the story of a temple where a Bible was supposed to be found. This Bible could not be read by the *white* Indians, who owned the temple, and who had lost the art of writing. Moreover, the Russian colonies in the northwest of America could well have given birth to these rumors of a white people established around the sources of the Missouri. [C's note.]

[65] Chateaubriand's text reads *below*, a simple misreading. The Chanon is the French Broad.

[66] A mistake for *whet-saw*.

[67] Lewis Evans (1700–1756), geographer and cartographer.

[68] James Macbride.

[69] John Finley.

[70] Daniel Boone.

[71] Abraham Wood (1748–1823) or Samuel Wood (1752–1836), both were American ministers.

[72] Simon Kenton (1755–1836), American pioneer.

[73] Steamships have eliminated the difficulty of upstream navigation. [C's note.]

[74] An unidentified fish.

[75] According to Charlevoix: "it firms the flesh and gives it a very sweet smell" (IV, 360–61).

[76] According to modern usage, *canneberge* means "cranberry," but it is not certain this is the plant referred to by Chateaubriand.

[77] All these passages are mine; but I owe it to historical truth to say that if I saw these Indian ruins of Alabama today, I would

not consider them so old. [C's note.] Despite his protestations, Chateaubriand almost certainly never visited Alabama.

[78] This comparison is confusing at first glance. It is a recurring image with Chateaubriand, however, so its meaning can be clarified. He means the fruit in its arrangement around the stem resembles the way prisms hang around a candelabrum.

[79] Again although *canneberge* today means "cranberry"; here Chateaubriand appears to be speaking of another plant.

[80] Chateaubriand does not distinguish between crocodiles and alligators.

[81] I have seen them since. [C's note.] In all probability this was written not during the actual trip but long after, when he had seen Athens. Thus the need for the "I have heard" and the note.

[82] There are obviously many inaccuracies in this account.

[83] Beavers have been found between the Missouri and the Mississippi; they are extremely numerous beyond the Rocky Mountains, on the branches of the Columbia; but since the Europeans have penetrated into these regions, the beavers will soon be exterminated. Already last year (1826) at Saint Louis on the Mississippi there were sold 100 bales of beaver pelts, each bale weighing 100 pounds, and each pound of this precious merchandise fetching the price of five gourdes. [C's note.] The *gourde*, still the monetary unit of Haïti, varied in value, but approximated 10 francs.

[84] The famous minister of Louis XIV, Colbert, undertook extensive canal-building projects in France.

[85] La Fontaine, "The Heron," *Fables*, VII, iv. "He followed a strict diet and ate on schedule."

[86] The exact reference is questionable here. Chateaubriand may be remembering imperfectly La Fontaine's "The Fox and the Guinea Hens" (*Fables*, XII, xviii).

[87] This hobby of establishing exotic gardens in Europe was a widespread practice. Chateaubriand himself attempted to plant magnolia trees around his home.

[88] A not entirely exact reference to Ode XII of Sidonius Apollinaris.

[89] Ceremonial rattles.

[90] See *The Natchez*, II, 30. [C's note.]

[91] *Atala, The Genius of Christianity, The Natchez*, etc. [C's note.]

[92] On the education of children, see the letter quoted above. [C's note.] The reference is to the letter (p. 31) where C. describes the children at their games.

[93] *Atala.* [C's note.]

[94] Hickory nuts ground in water.

[95] Opossum.

[96] *The Natchez.* [C's note.]

[97] This section is essentially drawn from Bonnet.

[98] Virgil, *Eclogue* VI, 11. 27–28. "Then indeed you might see Fauns and fierce beasts sport in measured time."

[99] Chateaubriand is writing during the Greek revolution against Turkey.

[100] Tobacco.

[101] Beltrami. [C's note.]

[102] Chateaubriand is no doubt thinking here of the Indian method of cooking. For the sweat baths, water was thrown on the hot stones; putting hot stones in water would not produce steam.

[103] One of the eighteenth-century Jesuit missionaries.

[104] Chateaubriand said in the first edition "seven cònsonants" but only listed six. Later editors changed to the version "six consonants." However there were in fact seven consonants in the language, and Chateaubriand omitted one by error. I have therefore added this seventh consonant (*g*).

[105] I found most of the curious information I have just given on the Huron language in a little manuscript of Iroquois grammar sent me by M. Marcoux, missionary at St. Louis Falls, in Lower Canada. Moreover the Jesuits have done considerable work on the savage languages of Canada. Fr. Chaumont, who had spent 50 years among the Hurons, wrote a grammar of their language. Precious documents are due to Fr. Rasle, ten years a prisoner in an Abnaki village. A French-Iroquois dictionary is completed—a new treasure for the philologists. There is also the manuscript of an Iroquois-English dictionary; unfortunately the first volume, from A to L, has been lost. [C's note.] Joseph Marcoux (1791–1855). Fr. Denis Chaumont (1752–1819). Fr. Sebastien Râle (1657[?]–1724). All three spent their lives as missionaries in America.

[106] Chateaubriand is obviously mistaken on the width of the snow-shoes. If only 8 inches wide they would not be as awkward as he describes. Chateaubriand's source, Charlevoix, says they are 16 inches wide.

[107] Another name for gopher.

[108] In Europe.

[109] It is really a question of the chief's *bag* rather than his *mat*. Charlevoix uses here the French word *natte* which does normally mean *mat*, but Charlevoix indicates clearly that it is a *bag* (no doubt made of a sewn-up mat).

[110] See *The Natchez*. [C's note.]

[111] This return is described in the twelfth book of *The Natchez*. [C's note.]

[112] Chateaubriand is referring to the hieroglyphic cartouches regularly engraved on the arms of the Egyptian colossi.

[113] The reader can see in *The Natchez* the description of a savage council held on the Rock of the Lake: the details of it are rigorously historical. [C's note.]

[114] This had a slightly narcotic effect.

[115] These traditions of Indian migrations are obscure and contradictory. A few learned men regard the tribes of the Floridas as a remnant of the great nation of the Alleghewis, who inhabited the valleys of the Mississippi and the Ohio and who were driven out, around the twelfth and thirteenth centuries, by the Lenni-Lenapes (the Iroquois and the Delaware Savages), a nomadic and bellicose horde, which had come from the north and the west, that is, from the coast near Bering Straits. [C's note.]

[116] As is often the case with

Chateaubriand, this is not an authentic "song." It is based on an event described by Bartram (p. 71).

[117] Brandy. [C's note.]

[118] Courtesan. [C's note.] The Indian word comes from the glossary of Indian terms which Lahontan included in his book.

[119] Brandy. [C's note.]

[120] This curious reference to the papaya as a hard fruit indicates probably that the actual fruit was unfamiliar to Chateaubriand.

[121] Six, according to the division made by the English. [C's note.]

[122] Other traditions, as has been seen, make of the Iroquois a column of the great migration of the Lenni-Lenapes, who had come from the shores of the Pacific Ocean. This column of Iroquois and Hurons is supposed to have driven out the peoples of North Canada, among whom were the Algonquians, while the Delaware Indians, more to the south, are supposed to have continued to the Atlantic, dispersing the primitive tribes established both to the east and the west of the Alleghenies. [C's note.]

[123] Most of these names are more or less deformed by Chateaubriand.

[124] Most of these tribes belonged to the great nation of the Lenni-Lenapes, of which the two principal branches were the Iroquois and the Hurons in the north and the Delaware Indians in the south. [C's note.]

[125] The reader can consult with profit, as to Florida, a work called: *View of Western Florida . . .* Philadelphia, 1817. [C's note.]

[126] Chateaubriand's information is distorted here. General Jackson is the future president Andrew Jackson. Ferdinand Claiborne, brother of the governor of the Orleans territory, distinguished himself in the battles against the Creeks. John Floyd was the commander of the Georgia troops in the expeditions against the Creeks. General White is known especially for the incident in which he was sent to attack the Hillabees at the very moment Jackson was negotiating peace with these Indians. The towns Chateaubriand mentions are the sites of American victories over the Indians and the English during the last months of 1812. They are all in a small region of Alabama, then the Mississippi territory. The correct names are Talladega, the Hillabee towns, Auttose, Econonchaca, and Enotochopco River.

[127] Chief of the Shawnees.

[128] The future president William Henry Harrison.

[129] Henry A. Proctor (1765–1859), later a general.

[130] On the Maumee River, near Lake Erie.

[131] This is probably a mistake for the town of Malder, near Detroit, in Canadian territory.

[132] Battle of the Thames, War of 1812.

[133] The Minnesota River, which flows into the Mississippi at Mendota, Minnesota.

[134] Chateaubriand's error. The Red River flows into Lake Winnipeg.

[135] "The Great Mountain," Indian name for the French governor of Canada. [C's note.]

[136] Fr. Daniel was a Canadian missionary.

[137] Jean de Bréboeuf (1593–1649) was a Jesuit missionary massacred by the Iroquois.

[138] Beltrami's *Travels*, 1823. [C's note.]

[139] Fr. Isaac Jogues (1607–1646), a missionary in Michigan.

[140] Fr. Louis Lallemant (1578–1635), Jesuit missionary.

[141] "Woodsmen, frontiersmen."

[142] Genesis, 3:16.

[143] Literally, "burnt wood."

[144] Another confusion of names. Chateaubriand jumbles together the American Fur Company, the Columbia Fur Company, and the Missouri Fur Company.

[145] Thomas Douglas, Earl of Selkirk (1771–1820), the well-known colonist of the Red River concession in Canada.

[146] The North West Territory.

[147] Ever since the discovery of America, Indians had been paraded through Europe as curiosities.

[148] Obviously a mistake for Vermont.

[149] Céluta is one of Chateaubriand's heroines (*The Natchez*).

[150] The *Globe* had published in Paris an article (Oct. 8, 1824) about Indian representatives walking about Washington almost nude. Chateaubriand may well have been recalling that article here.

[151] That is, from the Natchez country (along the Mississippi) to the Creek country (southeast United States).

[152] No doubt Fort Stephens on the Tombigbee.

[153] Louisiana, west of Natchez.

[154] Which particular Washington that Chateaubriand had in mind is not clear.

[155] Tennessee.

[156] Homochitto, Mississippi (south of Natchez).

[157] The missionary of *Atala*.

[158] *Aeneid*, III, 302–303. "By the waves of a foreign Simois Andromache was offering her yearly feast and gifts of mourning."

[159] Chateaubriand is referring to the naval battles of Admiral Perry during the War of 1812.

[160] The Erie Canal had just been finished in 1825.

[161] Chateaubriand's guess was accurate. The population in 1830 was 12,866,020.

[162] French historian and philosopher (1713–1796).

[163] French humanist and historian (1661–1741). *Ancient History. Roman History.*

[164] Simón Bolívar, born in Caracas. (In Chateaubriand's time, Venezuala was still part of Grand Colombia.)

[165] As I write, the public papers of all opinions announce the troubles, divisions, and bankruptcies of these various republics. [C's note.]

[166] The theory of the influence of climate on man was still being hotly debated.

[167] Francisco Miranda (1752–1816), Venezuelan revolutionary general.

[168] When the French had interceded in the abortive revolution of 1822 to deliver the King from captivity.

169 The Duke de Montmorency (1767–1826) was foreign minister from 1821 to 1822.

170 George Canning (1770–1827), Foreign Secretary (1807–1809, 1822–1827) and Prime Minister (1827) of England.

171 C's cousin Armand was to be executed by the Revolutionaries.

172 *Itinerary*. [C's note.]

Index

Abnakis, 153, 174, 175
Acadia, 175, 184
Adena Indians, 213 n. 62
Adirondack Indians, 169
Agannonsioni, the Five Nations of the Iroquois, 169
Ajoues, 177
Akouessan (Abnaki warrior), 153
Alabama, 175, 176, 186, 189
Albany, 16, 20, 21, 22, 187
Albemarle Canal, 188
Algonquians, 152, 169, 174, 175, 177, 216 n. 122; departure ceremony of, 135; language of, 113, 114–15
Allegheny Mountains, 53, 216 n. 122
Allegheny River, 50
Alleghewis, 215 n. 115
Alligator, 66
Allouez (guards of the Sun), 158–62
American Fur Company, 183
Amikouès, 175
Amilao (beloved of Hondioun), 153
André, Major, 21
Anson, Me., 189
Apalachicola (village), 68, 166
Appalachians, 47, 50
Areskoui (god of war), 134, 150
Arkansas River, 57
Arkansas Territory, 184, 189
Armand, Colonel. See La Rouerie
Army of the Princes, 205
Assiniboins, 175, 177
Astikamegue, 213 n. 56
Atabou (Illinois chief), 145
Atala. See Chateaubriand, Works
Athaënsic, 101, 151, 152, 153

Athens, 68, 206, 214 n. 81
Atlantis, 49
Attikamègues, 175
Aubry, Fr. (C's character), 186
Autossees, 176
Azores, 10

Baltimore, xviii, 8, 13, 14, 190
Bartram, William, xviii, 216 n. 116
Bastille, 17
Bayogoulas, 176
Bear, 74
Bear hunt, 125–26
Beaver, 70–74
Beaver hunt, 123–24
Becanachaca, 176
Bédier, Joseph, xviii
Bees, 80
Beltrami, J. C., xviii, 179–80, 214 n. 101
Bering Straits, 6, 215 n. 115
Bersiamites, 174–75
Big Bone Lick, 52–53
Biloxis, 176
Birds, 78
Bishop, Morris, xvii, 212 n. 40
Bison, 75–76
Bison hunt, 127–28
Black Bayou, 58
Blue Mountains, 50, 53
Bolívar, Simón, 197, 198
Bolivia, 196
Bonnet, J. E., xviii, 214 n. 97
Boone, Daniel, 53
Boston, 15, 20, 188, 190, 194
Bourbon monarchs in S. A., 201–202
Bréboeuf, Fr., 179, 180
Bristol, Gulf of, 7

Brookfield, Mass., 175
Buenos Aires, 196

Cadiz, 198
Cahawba, Ala., 186
California, 6, 178
Canada Company, 183
Canning, George, 203
Canoes, 135
Carolinas, 175, 184
Carthaginians, 48
Cartier, Jacques, 169, 174
Carver, Jonathan, xviii, 213 n. 52, 213 n. 59
Celebrations, Indian, 93–97
Céluta (C's character), 186
Chactas (C's character), 8, 10, 186
Champlain, Samuel, 169, 174
Champlain, Lake, 188
Champlain Canal, 188
Chanon River, 51
Charles II, 194
Charlestown, S.C., 187
Charlevoix, Fr. Xavier, xviii, 53, 213 n. 52, 213 n. 54, 213 n. 57, 213 n. 75, 215 n. 106, 215 n. 109
Chateaubriand: biography, xi–xii; itinerary in America evaluated, xvi–xx; literary career, xiv–xvi; political posts, xiv
—Works: *Atala*, 5, 35, 59, 91, 148, 186, 214 n. 91, 214 n. 93; *Essay on English Literature*, xx; *Genius of Christianity*, 8, 10, 11, 31, 48, 212 n. 42, 214 n. 91; *Historical Essay on Revolutions*, 5, 6, 7, 8, 10, 15, 20–21, 22, 31, 35, 205, 211 n. 5, 212 n. 31, 212 n. 34, 212 n. 50, 213 n. 51; *Itinerary from Paris to Jerusalem*, 4, 8, 211 n. 11, 212 n. 38, 212 n. 45, 218 n. 172; *Memoirs*, xix, 3, 8, 9, 202; *Natchez*, xix, 3, 8, 15, 59, 91, 148, 214 n. 90, 214 n. 91, 214 n. 96, 215 n. 110, 215 n. 111, 215 n. 113
Chateaubriand, Armand de, 205

Chateaubriand, Mme de (C's mother), 7
Chattahoochee River, 68
Chaumont, Fr., 215 n. 105
Cherokee [Tennessee] River, 55
Cherokees, 53, 56, 175, 176
Chesapeake Bay, 12
Chesapeake Canal, 188
Chicago, 177
Chickasaw River, 57
Chickasaws, 49, 50, 57, 93, 145, 158, 175, 176; language of, 113, 114
Children, 88–90
Chile, 196
Chinard, Gilbert, xviii
Chippewa months, 106
Chippewas, 177
Chocktaws, 57
Chugachimint Indians, 7
Cincinnatus, 16
Circular bed, 30
Clayborne, General, 176
Cochrane, Lord, 198
Colburn (publisher), xx
Colombia, S. A., 195–96, 198, 200
Columbia, District of, 184
Columbia River, 7, 183, 188, 189, 213 n. 59
Columbian Fur Company, 183
Columbus, Christopher, 12
Combourg (C's home), 9
Concord, Mass., 187
Congress of the U.S., 176, 187, 188, 189
Congress of Verona, 6
Connecticut, 175
Cook, Gulf of, 7
Corette (Huron village), 175
Corneille, 212 n. 29
Cortes of Spain, 198
Cortez, 195
Council Bluffs, Iowa, 187
Coweta (Muskogee town), 166
Creeks, 67–69, 113, 162–68, 175, 176
Crees, 175
Cristinaux, 175
Crocodile. *See* Alligator

Cromwell, Oliver, 194
Cumberland River, 55
Cuscowilla (Seminole village), 68

Dances, Indian, 28–29, 75, 101–102, 138
Daniel, Fr., 179
Deer, 74–75
Delaware, 175
Delaware River, 14
Delawares, 53, 215 n. 115
Del Vilde (?), 179
De Soto, Hernando, 48, 158, 175
Dovecote, reef, 10
Dover, Del., 187
Dreams of the Indians, 143–44, 150
Duquesne, Fort, 50, 53
"Dutchman" (C's guide), 22, 23, 30, 31, 32, 37

Econonchaca, 216 n. 125
Egypt, 12, 18
Egyptians, 49
Endless Mountains. See Allegheny Mountains
Enotochopco River, 216 n. 126
Entonopeka, 176
Erie, Lake, 37, 38, 50, 55, 152, 188, 206
Erie Canal, 188
Esmenard, Chevalier d', 3
Essay on English Literature. See Chateaubriand, Works
Etchemins, 174
Evans, Lewis, 53

Feasts, Indian, 93–97, 125, 126, 130
Ferdinand of Spain, 202
Fish, 78
Fishing, 99–101
Five Nations. See Iroquois
Flint River, 166
Floods (of the Mississippi), 58
Floridas [i.e. S. E. United States], 59–69, 175
Flour chief of the Natchez, 159
Floyd, General, 176

Fontanes, M. de, 212 n. 32
Fox, 76–77
Fox Indians, 177
Franklin, Captain (explorer), 5, 7
Franklin, Tenn., 186
French Broad River, 213 n. 65
Funerals, Indian, 90–92

Games, Indian, 101–105
Genesee concessions, 29
Genesee River, 30, 153
Genesis, 217 n. 142
Genius of Christianity. See Chateaubriand, Works
Georgia, 175, 176, 184
Gopher, 215 n. 107
Gordon (commander at Niagara), xvii, 31
Government: of the Hurons, 168–73; of the Iroquois, 168–73; of the Muskogees, 162–68; of the Natchez, 155–62
Graciosa (Azores), 10
Great Beaver, 38, 151
Great Bend (of the Tennessee), 55
Great Britain, 194
Great Hare, 150, 152, 154
Great Spirit, 50, 151, 152
Great Spirit Island, 39
Great tiger cat, 150
Guatemala, 196

Hadley, Mass., 175
Haïti, 211 n. 19
Harrison, General, 176, 177
Harvests, 92–93, 97, 98–99
Hearne River, 5
Highgate, Vt., 189
Hillabee towns, 176
Historical Essay on Revolutions. See Chateaubriand, Works
Hochelaga River. See Saint Lawrence River
Homochitto, Miss., 186
Hondioun (Iroquois chief), 153
Hopewell Indians, 213 n. 62
Hudson Bay, 6, 39, 74, 177
Hudson River, 20

Hudson's Bay Company, 21, 182, 183
Hunting, 120–30
Huron, Lake, 38, 151, 169
Hurons, 142–43, 144, 153, 168–73, 174, 175, 216 n. 122; language of, 113, 115–20

Icelandic tradition and sagas, 213 n. 63
Illinois (state), 187
Illinois Indians, 53, 142, 145, 177
Indian tribes. *See names of specific tribes*
Indian woman (with the cow), 24–27
Indiana, 187, 189
Iroquois, 22, 53, 153, 168–73, 174, 175, 178, 216 n. 122
Itinerary from Paris to Jerusalem. See Chateaubriand, Works

Jackson, General, 176
Jogues, Fr., 180
Jones, Finlay, 53
Jouskeka, squaw-chief of good Manitous, 151

Kalapaoian, 176
Kanawha River, 51
Kansas Indians, 177
Kappas, 176
Kaskaskias, 53
Kenton, Simon, 53
Kentucky, 49, 187
Kentucky River, 53
Keweenaw, Point, 39
Kittatinny Mountains. *See* Allegheny Mountains

Labrador, 6
Lafayette, Marquis de, 212 n. 22, 212 n. 30
La Fontaine, 76, 214 n. 85, 214 n. 86
Lahontan, Baron, xviii, 175, 216 n. 118
Lake of the Two Mountains (Iroquois settlement), 175

Lallemant, Fr., 180
Land offices, 189
Languages, Indian, 113–20
La Rouerie [Rouairie], Marquis de, 7–8, 16–17
Lenni-Lenapes, 215 n. 115, 216 n. 122
Le Page du Pratz, Antoine, xviii
Lexington, Ky., 189
Lexington, Mass., 20
Liberty, concepts of, 190–93
Lick River, 52
Licks, 52
Liniers, Captain, 197
Loans, made by English, 198–99
Louis XIV, xviii
Louis XVI, 7
Louis XVIII, 202
Louisiana, 184, 189
Lynx, 77

MacBride, James, 53
Mackenzie, 5, 213 n. 52
"Madelon Friquet" (air), 22
Madoc, of Wales, 50
Maine, 175, 184
Malder (town), 216 n. 131
Malesherbes, M. de, 211 n. 13
Mammoth, 52
Manhattan, 169
Manitoulin Island, 213 n. 57
Maple sugar making, 97–98
Marcoux, Fr., 215 n. 105
Margette (hills and river), 57
Marriage, Indian, 82–88
Maryland, 11, 175
Matimoulin [Manitoulin] Island, 38
Maumee River, 216 n. 130
Maurepas Island, 39
Medicine, Indian, 108–13
Meigs, Fort, 177
Memoirs. See Chateaubriand, Works
Menominees, 177
Merrimack River, 188
Messou (Indian god), 151
Mexico, 186
Mexico, Gulf of, 184
Miami, Big Miami River, 49

Miami of the Lake River, 55
Miamis, 53, 175
Michabou (god of waters), 150, 152
Michigan, Lake, 38, 151, 188
Michigan Territory, 184, 189
Michillimackinac, 187
Michipicoten River, 39
Mico of the Creeks, 162–68, 176
Middlesex Canal, 188
Milden, Fort, 177
Minabeaujou, Cape, 39
Minnesota River, 216 n. 133
Minong Island, 39
Miranda, General, 197
Missionaries in Canada, 179–80
Mississippi River, xviii, 42, 47, 48, 50, 56–59, 176, 177, 178, 184, 186, 189
Mississippi Territory, 175, 176, 189, 216 n. 125
Missouri Fur Company, 183
Missouri River, 50, 56, 176, 177, 186, 213 n. 64
Missouri Territory, 184, 189
Mohawk River, 22
Mohawk Trail, 212 n. 35
Molly (ship), xviii
Monongahela River, 50
Montagais, 175
Months, Indian names of, 106
Montmorencey, Duke, 202–203
Montpelier, Vt., 187
Montreal, 187
Moose, 75
Moose hunt, 127
Mortemart, Marquis de, 7
Murder, 173
Muskingum River, 49, 178
Muskogee villages, 165–66
Muskogees, 65, 67–69, 162–68, 176
Muskrat, 77

Nagot, Abbé (superior of the seminarians), 8
Nakotas, 177
Napoleon, 17–20, 21, 197, 198
Nashville, Tenn., 189

Natchez. See Chateaubriand, Works
Natchez (village), 58, 186, 187
Natchez country, 58
Natchez Indians, 57, 93–97, 155–62, 176; language of, 113–14
Natchitoches, La., 186
Navarre regiment, 7
New Brunswick, 175
New Cornwall, 7
Newfoundland, 11
New Hampshire, 175
New Jersey, 175
New Mexico, 177, 188
New Orleans, 58, 184, 187, 188, 190
New York (city), xvii, 15, 20, 169, 188, 190
New York (state), 175, 184
New York Canal, 22
Niagara, xvii, xviii, 21, 31, 35–36, 37, 153, 187, 205
Nile, 12, 58, 71
Nipigon River, 39, 41
Nipissing, Lake, 151
Nipissings, 175
Nipmucks, 175
Nokais, 175
Nontouka (ocean), 42
Northwest Company, 183
Northwest Passage, 206
Northwest Territory, 184
Nova Scotia, 175, 184

Octotatas, 177
Ogan, Prince of Wales, 50
Ohio (state), 187, 189
Ohio Indian mounds, 48–50, 213 n. 61, 213 n. 62
Ohio River, xviii, 7, 21, 47, 48, 49, 50–56, 176, 178, 186, 187; rapids of, 54
Ojibways, 142
Onondagas, 23–30
Ontario, Lake, 37, 50, 153, 154, 187, 188, 206
Opossum, 214 n. 95
Oregon Territory, 184
Osages, 177

223

Osoukatchies, 175
Otasses (Muskogee village), 166
Otchagras, 175
Ottawa River, 42, 151
Ottawas, 38, 145

Pacific Ocean, 6, 184
Papinachois, 175
Paraguay, 196
Paris, Ky., 186
Paroustis, 175
Parry (explorer), 5
Pawnees, 177
Penn, William, 12
Pennsylvania, 175, 184
Pequots, 175
Perry, Admiral, 217 n. 159
Philadelphia, xvii, xviii, 14–15, 16, 20, 190, 205
Philip of Macedonia, 183–84
Phoenecians, 48
Piankashaws, 53
Pico (Azores), 10
Piscataways, 175
Pitt, Fort, 50, 53
Pittsburgh, xvii, 21, 50, 53, 187, 189, 197
Pizarro, 195
Plants, 79–80
Plato, 49, 66
Polar Sea, 183, 184
Pontchartrain Island, 39
Population statistics, 189–90
Post houses, 189
Potawatomis, 142, 175
Powhatan, 175
Proctor, Colonel, 177
Providence, R.I., 187

Quakers, 15–16
Quebec, 29, 74, 170, 187

Railroads, 189
Rasle, Fr., 215 n. 105
Raynal, Abbé, 191
Red River, 177, 183, 216 n. 134
Religion in U.S., 190
Religion of the Indians, 149–54
Roads, 186, 189
Robbinstown, Me., 187

Rochambeau, General (M. Violet's commander), 23
Rock of the Lake, 215 n. 113
Rocky Mountains, 177, 184, 188
Rollin (historian), 196
Rosambeau, Mlle de, 211 n. 13

Sable, Cape, 184
Sachem of the Onondagas, 27–28
Saint Anthony Falls, 151, 177
Saint Augustine, Fla., 187
Saint Francis River, 57
Saint François (Abnaki village), 175
Saint George, Point, 184
Saint Lawrence River, 42, 169, 184
Saint Louis, Mo., 187, 189
Saint-Malo, 7, 10
Saint Mary, Ga., 189
Saint Peter's River, 177
Saint Pierre (island), 10, 11
Saint-Pierre (ship), xii
Saint Stephen (city), 186
Saint-Sulpice (seminary), 8
Sainte Marie, Strait, 40, 151
Saketchak (Indian god), 151
Santee Canal, 188
Santo-Domingo [Haïti], 16
Saukes River, 177
Savanna language, 166
Savannah, Ga., 187, 190
Savantica language, 166
Scalping, 147
Schuylkill River, 14
Scioto River, 49
Selkirk, Lord, 183
Seminarians of Saint-Sulpice, 8, 13
Seminoles, 49, 67–69, 93, 162–68, 176
Shanawon [Cumberland] River, 55
Shawnees, 53, 216 n. 127
Shelikof's Strait, 7
Silver Creek, 54
Sioux, 177; language of, 114
Sioux months, 106
Skunk, 76
Slave Lake, 76

224

Snake charmer, 30–31
Snakes, 78–79
"Song of the Paleface" (Indian ode), 167–68
Sotouis, 176
Souls, Island of the, 39
Souriquois, 174
Spanish moss, 213 n. 58
Spanish Republics, 3, 193, 194–204
Spirit of the Iroquois, 153
Spitzbergen, 211 n. 6
Squaw chief, 159–62
Standingrock, Cape, 39
Stephens, Fort, 217 n. 152
Stony River, 58
Sun of the Natchez, 158–62
Superior, Lake, 38–42, 52
Swift (trader at Albany), 21, 22
Swimming accident (of C), 11

Talladega, Ala., 176
Tansas, 176
Tecumseh, 176, 177
Temiscamings, 175
Tennessee (state), 175, 176, 186, 187
Tennessee River, 49, 55, 178, 184
Thames (battle), 177
Thunder, Cape, 39
Tibeïma (Indian girl), 167–68
Tippecanoe River, 176
Tomb Creek, 49
Tomb River, 41
Tombigbee River, 178, 186
Torimas, 176
Traders, 181–83
Traps, hunting, 120–23
Trees, 79–80
T[ulloch] (one of the seminarians), 10

Uche (Muskogee village), 166

Vancouver, 6
Venezuela, 197
Vermont, 184
Versailles, Ky., 186
Vincennes, Ind., 189
Violet (dancing master), 22–23
Viper [Rattlesnake] Islands, 38
Virginia, 11, 175, 184, 187
Vodilla (?), 179

Wabash River, 55, 176
Wakon-Teebe (cavern), 151–52
Wampanoags, 175
War, 129–49
Washington (an unidentified city), 186
Washington, D.C., 187, 189
Washington, George, xvii, 7, 16–20, 29
Waterloo, 183
Wayaoes, 53
Wells, Captain, 177
Welsh Indians, 49–50
West, River of the, 42
White, General, 176
White Indians, 49–50, 213 n. 64
Wildcat, 77–78
Winnebagos, 177
Winnepeg, Lake, 177
Wolf, 77, 129
Wolfe, General, 29
Wood, Doctor, 53

Yamasees, 163–65
Yazoo River, 57–58
Yazoos, 57–58, 176
Year, divisions of, 105–107
Yellow Banks, 55, 56